A BAND OF BROTHERS

Jack
The marines transformed my
life.
I'm proud of your accomplishments.
Keep up the good work. Happy
16th Birthday.

Love
Poppy.

Cover: Gun Crew from India Battery, 3rd Battalion, 12th Marines firing a 105-mm howitzer. Picture taken by 2nd Lieutenant John Booth.

Photo on preceding page: India Battery, 3rd Battalion, 12th Marines, prior to re-embarking for Vietnam. I was with India for seven months and this unit was home in every sense that the word "home" means. Picture taken in March of 1966 at Camp Hanson, Okinawa. I am standing directly behind the kneeling Marine holding the flag and to the left of the Naval officer with the black tie, Bob Franklin.

Author's Note

Any depictions of events in this book other than what is clearly stated in the formally classified Command Chronologies, which are referenced in the Government Publications section of the bibliography, are my personal recollection of events, which I have stated to the best of my knowledge. Some identities have been changed.

Revision August 14, 2018

This book is dedicated to all those Marines who did not return from Vietnam

And whose names are both in this memoir

And on the Vietnam Wall today.

CONTENTS

PART 4   FIND THE NORTH VIETNAMESE ARMY AND PICK A FIGHT   133
              April 11 1966 – July 16, 1966

FORWARD

I am not a professional writer!

I started writing of my war experiences almost two decades ago when I was president of The India Battery Association and we needed material for our newsletter. At the same time I discovered my Mother had kept all my letters from Vietnam in her cedar chest, where she preserved memories near and dear to her heart. Later I learned the Marine Corps had released classified war records to the public through the National Archives.

All this heightened my interest and I discovered I have a passion for research, am able to sweep away the cobwebs and emotions of the past and view events in which I participated with remarkable clarity. I took writing classes, joined two writer's critique groups, and began my memoirs of the war.

My primary audience is my children and grandchildren, and since civilians will have difficulty understanding the abbreviations and shorthand of military language, I have purposefully stripped out all such references except where necessary for my secondary audience, the Marine Corps. The Archives and Special Collection Branch of the Library of the Marine Corps, located on the Marine Base in Quantico, Virginia, has graciously opened a collection of my writings entered into the records as the John R. Booth Memoir Account 2009-574 / Collection 4848.

I fought in two wars!

The first was a counterinsurgency war against Viet Cong guerrillas that my fellow citizens today still do not understand. We fought for the allegiance of the South Vietnamese people with a strategy of winning their hearts and minds. That strategy was successful.

The second was a conventional war against the North Vietnamese Army that used a strategy of firepower and attrition. The idea was that we would kill more of them than they killed of us. We did. That strategy was not successful.

I served in Southeast Asia thirteen months, from June 1965 through July 1966, and my memoirs are divided into four parts.

PART 1 JOURNEY INTO WAR: Details my arrival on Okinawa and subsequent landing in Vietnam.

PART 2 INDIA BATTERY AND THE 3RD BATTALION 4TH MARINES: Covers my initiation into a counterinsurgency war in the upland foothills and mountains west of the airstrip and village hamlets of Phu Bai, ten miles south of the old imperial capital city of Hue.

PART 3 HILL 41: Continues my counterinsurgency war when my rifle company is transferred fifty miles south to a combat outpost, Hill 41, south of the city of Da Nang.

PART 4 FIND THE NORTH VIETNAMESE ARMY AND PICK A FIGHT: I am promoted and transferred to the 1st Battalion 4th Marines where we fight a conventional war and attempt to bring elusive North Vietnamese Army units to bay, and we use every weapon in the Marine Corps arsenal. We will fight northwest of Hue City, south of the Demilitarized Zone and North Vietnam and in the foothills of the Annamese Mountains.

Our unit leaves Vietnam temporarily on the USS Valley Forge on December 24, 1965, and we return to Okinawa for replacements and re-supply. We return to Vietnam on the USS Paul Revere and land on March 21, 1966. I have not written about this time period, and hopefully it will be a 2nd edition of this work. I have been at this for so long that I feel a sense of urgency to turn these yarns into something more permanent. Part 4 begins on April 11.

This narrative is a collection of stories I have written and revised over twenty years. I have unexpectedly found this process cathartic and therapeutic for me, and hopefully both informative and entertaining for you. I have tried to stir your emotions so that you, Dear Reader, will want to turn the page.

John R. Booth, Colonel USMC (Ret) August 14, 2018.

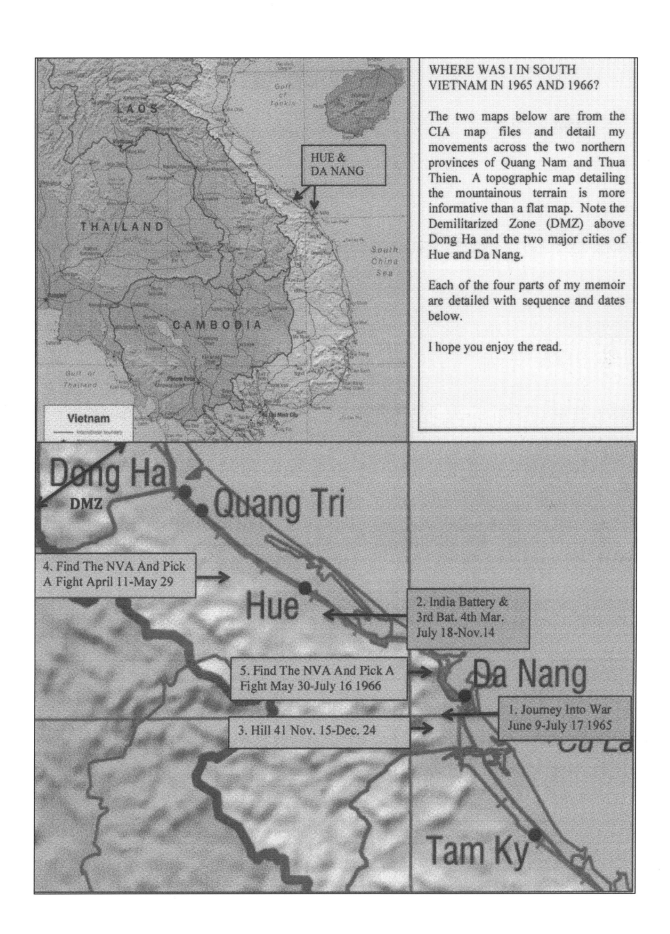

WHERE WAS I IN SOUTH VIETNAM IN 1965 AND 1966?

The two maps below are from the CIA map files and detail my movements across the two northern provinces of Quang Nam and Thua Thien. A topographic map detailing the mountainous terrain is more informative than a flat map. Note the Demilitarized Zone (DMZ) above Dong Ha and the two major cities of Hue and Da Nang.

Each of the four parts of my memoir are detailed with sequence and dates below.

I hope you enjoy the read.

HUE & DA NANG

Vietnam

Dong Ha
DMZ
Quang Tri

Hue

4. Find The NVA And Pick A Fight April 11-May 29

2. India Battery & 3rd Bat. 4th Mar. July 18-Nov.14

5. Find The NVA And Pick A Fight May 30-July 16 1966

Da Nang

1. Journey Into War June 9-July 17 1965

3. Hill 41 Nov. 15-Dec. 24

Tam Ky

IX

PART ONE JOURNEY INTO WAR

AKA 96 USS MATTHEWS
OKINAWA JUNE 9 1965 THROUGH DA NANG VIETNAM JULY 17 1965

RIKKI-TIKKI-TAVI

"Hey, Marines, come see habu-mongoose fight to death."

It's a hot, humid, tropical night. My buddy Dick and I are wandering through an Okinawan fair, and a greasy-looking dark-skinned huckster with a filthy turban and scraggly beard is haranguing us to enter a tent and view his show. We are dressed in civilian attire, but there is no mistaking us as anything but young Marine lieutenants with our short haircuts and youthful faces. To paraphrase Samuel Johnson we are "towering in the confidence of twenty-three."

We look at one another, and say "Why not." We will see a spectacle worthy of the Roman gladiators, a fight to the death between a venomous serpent and a furry squirrel- like mammal.

On June 9 1965 I arrived on Okinawa to join the rear elements of the 3rd Marine Division in transit to Vietnam. The island was the site of the last major battle of the Pacific campaign of WWII. In a bloody eighty-two day battle from April through June of 1945 in which over 12,000 Americans were killed and 50,000 wounded, the island was seized from Japan. We still occupied it twenty years later, and the island became the home of the 3rd Marine Division, and an unsinkable aircraft carrier in the Western Pacific in the ongoing conflict of the Cold War.

The detritus of war was still there twenty years later, and the rugged terrain still held unexploded ordnance from the conflict, and if one probed deep enough into the caves one could still find Japanese skeletons. As part of my orientation I was warned that if I chose to explore the terrain of the battlefield to be wary of unexploded munitions and then, as if by afterthought,

"By the way Lieutenant Booth, look out for the habu. They are all over the place and that's one snake you want to steer clear of."

Here are some interesting facts about one of the contenders in the mongoose-habu match. The habu is a venomous pit viper endemic to Okinawa. It's been known to grow to eight feet in length, and is much more dangerous than any snake in North America. It has relatively long hinged fangs that permit deep penetration. During a strike, which is very fast, the mouth can open 180 degrees and the venom causes death by collapse in blood pressure. It can strike anywhere in a 360 degree circle, can reach two-thirds of its body length, and can deliver a number of bites in a short time. Due to the location of the venom glands it has a triangle shaped head distinct from the neck. The paired pit organs provide the habu thermal rangefinder capabilities, in effect a sixth sense to help it find and judge the size of its prey.

Oddly enough, the snake is a key ingredient in something called Habushu, otherwise known as Habu Sake or Okinawan Snake Wine. It's a rice- based liqueur made in Okinawa. The wine is mixed with herbs and honey giving the liquid a yellow hue, and then the habu is inserted into the wine and stored until it is consumed. Some brands come with the snake still inside the bottle.

There are two methods for inserting the snake into the bottle. The maker may choose to submerge the snake in the alcohol and seal the bottle, thus drowning the snake. Alternately the snake may be put on ice until it passes out, at which point it is gutted, bled and sewn up. Oddly enough the habu still clings to a spark of life, and when the viper is thawed and awakens, it quickly dies in an aggressive striking manner, which is what producers look for. The manufacture's will then put the habu in an ethanol bath to preserve it, and then process it further in alcohol before putting it into the wine.

Appreciated since ancient times, Habushu is believed by some to have medicinal properties. A habu can go without eating for as long as a year and still have immense energy. Another desired trait that is thought to be passed on is the positive effect on the male libido. A habu snake can mate for as long as twenty-six hours, which causes some to believe that a drink of Habushu may help sexual dysfunction in men. A common superstition is that these strengths are passed on to those who drink Habushu.

The habu's opponent, the small Asian mongoose, was introduced to Okinawa in 1910 in an attempt to control the population of venomous habu snakes. It didn't work, and the mongoose became a pest in itself, hunting birds, bird's eggs and many other island species. The body of the mongoose is slender and the head is elongated with a pointed snout. The length of the head and body is thirteen to seventeen inches. The ears are short, and they have five toed feet with long claws.

The mongoose is very bold and inquisitive but wary. It is a skillful hunter, which actively searches for prey by using its strong senses of smell and sight. It kills its prey while both are running by delivering a bite to the neck or head. It eats snakes including the venomous cobra, and, of course, the habu.

Rudyard Kipling immortalized the mongoose with what some have said is the best short story ever with the publication of *Rikki-Tikki-Tavi* in *The Jungle Book* in 1894. A young mongoose named Rikki-Tikki-Tavi is adopted into a British Army family residing in India as a pet as well as a guard against venomous cobra snakes. Rikki becomes friends with many creatures inhabiting the garden where he is warned about two cobras, Nag and Nagaina, that plan to attack the family. Rikki ultimately kills the cobras and continues to protect the family by keeping the garden free from any further intrusion by snakes.

Rikki is on the side of righteousness, and Nag and Nagaina are on the side of evil.

In my high school years I had read much of Kipling, enjoyed his yarns immensely and fell in love with his poetry, especially tales of the British Army in India. All this adds to my sense of adventure as a young Marine lieutenant newly arrived in the exotic and alluring lands of Rudyard Kipling's Asia.

Dick and I enter the tent.

On our right are cages filled with creatures, and on our left are bleachers filled with locals. We stand out like sore thumbs, but no matter, we take our seats high up so we will have a good view of the fight.

Trash is everywhere, and there is a smell of unwashed bodies and animal feces. If back in the United States the health authorities for sure would shut the show down, and this sort of thing would be prohibited to begin with.

On the stage in front and below us is a glass-enclosed cage, and at the bottom of the glass, not moving and minding its own business is a habu.

Our friend, the greasy-looking dark-skinned huckster with the turban and scraggly beard struts onto the stage and lectures the audience in Japanese. We understand nothing, but sense something momentous is about to happen. He then approaches a pen, lifts out a squirming furry mongoose, and deposits the poor creature into the same glass-enclosed cage as the "I could care less" habu.

Nothing happens!

We wait, and wait, and still nothing happens. The habu lies still, patiently minding its own business. The mongoose moving around sniffing the cracks in the cage could care less about the habu.

This is plainly unsatisfactory! Our friend, the greasy huckster, picks up a prod and proceeds to poke both the habu and mongoose.

And still nothing happens!

We hear explosive language in Japanese, which we assume is profanity, and our friend then proceeds to beat both the mongoose and the habu until at last there is action.

There is a quick jump by Rikki-Tikki-Tavi as he clamps down on the habu's mouth. The snake squirms a bit and then turns over and lies belly up. It's all over in one second. More words in Japanese and then the locals leave the tent. We hang around a bit to investigate the murder scene and gather evidence.

Upon close examination it appears the mongoose has ripped out the fangs of the habu. We are told later the mongoose likes the taste of salty blood, and this is typical of what happens in the fight. Our habu moreover is not dead and is still squirming, whereupon our friend, the greasy huckster removes the snake and places him in the Habu Hospice cage where there is plenty of company with dying, squirming snakes, all with bloody mouths, flopping around the bottom.

Rikki is placed back into the living mongoose cage, and for his reward gets to fight yet again another day.

But wait, there is yet another cage. The habu is not always so passive, and occasionally will land a glancing strike where a fang penetrates mongoose flesh. That's all it takes. The venom works slowly, and this last cage is full of dying, suffering mongooses dragging themselves around by their two front paws and flopping around the bottom.

Looks like no one wins in this game, for the odds are against you. Sooner or later Rikki's number will come up, and he too will proceed to mongoose heaven.

I will learn in Vietnam that combat is like that. The odds are against you, and sooner or later, if you hang around long enough, your number too will come up.

Welcome to Rudyard Kipling's Asia, Lieutenant Booth.

Notes:

This story is entirely from my memory. It's all true and I remember that night at the fair as if it were yesterday. I did research on the Internet for information on the habu, the small Asian mongoose, and Rudyard Kipling. His poetry can still stir my emotions. You can also view mongoose-habu and mongoose-cobra fights on the Internet.

THE USS NEVER SAIL

"Mount out for Vietnam." We'd been waiting for that command ever since I joined my unit on June 15, 1965, in Camp Sukiran, Okinawa. The words convey a sense of urgency. We are needed in Vietnam immediately.

As a young 2nd Lieutenant I stood in front of my Regimental Commander as he warmly welcomed me to the 12th Marines. The tall, grey-haired, distinguished combat veteran of three wars, Colonel William Pala, explained that most of the regiment was already in Vietnam, and that we would join them soon. We exchanged small talk, and then he shook my hand and wished me the best. His staff assigned me to a mortar outfit, otherwise known as Whiskey Battery of the 2nd Battalion 12th Marine Regiment.

My battery was actually called a howtar battery, the word *howtar* being a cross between the words *how*itzer and mor*tar*. The battery was air-mobile, could be completely heli-lifted by the Marine CH-34 helicopter, and was an evolution in amphibious doctrine that incorporated the third dimension of vertical envelopment in an amphibious assault. Landing craft would attack the beaches while troops and howtars were heli-lifted ashore.

Whiskey Battery was the artillery equivalent of a rifle company and was composed of six mortars, ten trucks, jeep-like vehicles called mighty-mites, various assorted equipment, sixty-four Marines and one Navy corpsman, commanded by three officers, which now included me. All this would now be precisely loaded onto a US Navy warship in a mathematically calculated method with not a cubic foot of wasted space.

The Marines are the world's experts in amphibious operations, and over the next thirteen months in Asia I would embark on three US Navy amphibious warships, and come ashore twice on two different types of landing craft.

The Marines and the Navy have been joined at the hip since the Revolutionary War when Marines served as ship's guards, on landing parties, on gun crews, and as snipers in the rigging when boarding enemy ships. We use Navy terminology in our language, walls become bulkheads and latrines become heads. Our emblem is the Eagle, Globe and Anchor, and the word Marine means Soldier of the Sea.

In the late 1800's when the Navy underwent the transformation from sail to steam the Marines became more important as a landing force, because now the Navy was permanently bound to land-based coaling stations, and there needed to be a professionally trained landing force to seize these stations if held by the enemy. This evolution in naval warfare would result in the Marines undertaking the formal study of the doctrine, tactics and equipment necessary in amphibious landings against a hostile shore.

The Marines would prove their mettle as a fighting force and become famous in World War I. In 1920 a brilliant, but eccentric and alcoholic Marine officer, Lieutenant Colonel Pete Ellis, would produce a Top Secret prophetic document that forecast the events of World War II two decades later.

He predicted the surprise attack on Pearl Harbor and the subsequent island-hopping campaigns in the central Pacific. His report revised United States strategy regarding possible hostilities with Japan and formalized the Marine Corps role in the study of amphibious operations. Except for a few far-seeing thinkers Ellis was regarded as a ridiculous crackpot. Lieutenant Colonel Ellis died under mysterious circumstances on the Japanese-held island of Palau in the Carolina Islands on May 12, 1923.

Over the next two decades the formalization of the study of amphibious warfare led to the development of specific warships necessary for the US Navy amphibious fleet, otherwise known as the "Gator Navy," Gator being shorthand for alligator, the amphibious creature that when it comes ashore, people vacate the scene quickly! And this led to the design and building of the ship that would become my home for the next two weeks.

The USS Matthews, designated AKA-96, was an attack cargo ship designed specifically to carry troops, heavy equipment and supplies in support of amphibious assaults, and to provide naval gunfire support during these assaults. A total of 108 of these ships were built between 1943 and 1945, which worked out to an average of one ship every eight days and was a testament to the industrial capacity of the United States that helped win World War II.

The USS Matthews was commissioned on March 15, 1945, and participated in the last two months of World War II in the Pacific theater. She participated in the Korean War, the Cuban Missile Crisis, and was one of the few remaining attack cargo ships still in active service at the start of the Vietnam War. In other words she was like an old war-horse still going strong.

She was 459 feet long, 63 feet broad, had a 40-foot depth with a 25-foot draft, and a speed of 15.5 knots. Her five holds were configured to optimize combat loading where the items needed first ashore such as ammunition, medical supplies, and water, were readily available. She had a crew of 223 enlisted sailors and 24 officers, which included a Marine officer specifically designated as the Combat Cargo Officer. His role was to know the location of every cubic foot of cargo space, and how best to load the ship to her capacity of 4,900 tons and 440,000 cubic feet. She also carried 24 landing craft of three types with which to attack the beach.

All these types of landing craft were known collectively as Higgins boats. Over 20,000 had been built for World War II, and they ferried troops, artillery and tanks ashore in every amphibious operation from North Africa and Normandy, to Iwo Jima and Okinawa, and General Dwight Eisenhower credits them with winning the war.

The boats had two key design components: a flat bottom with a propeller housed in a protective half-tunnel shaped like an inverted V, and a drop-bow ramp. The boat would run hard aground with the operator holding the engine at full throttle to keep the bow firmly anchored on the beach. The bow ramp would drop, and troops and vehicles would swiftly exit. The engine at full throttle enabled the propeller to keep churning to blast away sand at the stern so the boat could withdraw quickly, all this within three minutes.

The protective propeller design was the brainchild of Andrew Jackson Higgins, an eccentric, entrepreneurial, small boat builder in New Orleans. Legend has it he sold his small, fast, rugged swamp boats to the coast guard to chase rumrunners. He then sold yet faster boats to the rumrunners, and then followed with selling again yet faster boats to the coast guard.

Then 1st Lieutenant Victor Krulak, who was serving with the Marines in Shanghai, China, stole the drop-bow ramp design from the Japanese in 1937. He borrowed a U.S. Navy tug, and inserted himself, an Admiral's aide and a Navy photographer in the middle of a Japanese landing on the Yangtze River. Japan and the United States were not yet at war, so with the Japanese firing and with the U.S. flag flying, he proceeded to photograph and document the amphibious landing. He noticed the flat bows of the landing craft, and how powerful, seaworthy and stable they were, and realized the Japanese were years ahead of the United States in landing craft design. All this was documented in a thirteen-page report of close-up photographs, engineering drawings and sketches, and sent to the U. S. Navy with the full support of his superiors.

In 1939 Krulak, then assigned to Quantico, Virginia, and working on amphibious doctrine, went looking for his report and discovered it in the back of a Navy file cabinet with a note, "Prepared by some nut out in China."

To say that Higgins and Krulak would form an unlikely partnership that resulted in the design and building of the Higgins boats in spite of the U.S. Navy, is not far from the truth. Higgins lost all patience and said while he would build boats for the Navy, he would deal only with Marines. Harry Truman, senator and future president, would write a letter to the Secretary of the Navy saying that Bureau of Ships navy officers were guilty of negligence and willful misconduct, and that only the ability and energy of Higgins had kept the Navy from causing irreparable injury to the war effort.

From such stories as these are legends made, and Higgins and Krulak are legends.

The Marines know the meaning of the word "NOW." When something needs to happen immediately the Marines make it happen yesterday. Not for nothing is our reputation "The First to Fight." Actually my father taught me the meaning of that word, but the Marines imparted an additional graduate-school education sense of urgency to the meaning.

In World War II my father, Howard R. Booth, was an engineer working in the Pentagon on the development and manufacturing of the bazooka, a new anti-tank weapon to destroy the German Panzer tanks, against which we had no effective defense. General George Marshall had seen a demonstration of the effectiveness of this weapon at the Aberdeen Proving Grounds in Maryland and immediately scrawled an urgent production order of so many to be delivered by a certain date. This order quickly reached my father's supervisor who instructed Dad:

"Howard, I need you to accompany me to the General Electric Plant in Connecticut. They are converting a sewing machine factory to the manufacturing of the bazooka."

Dad assumed the trip would transpire the next day, and that he would go home, pack an overnight bag, and prepare for a normal business trip, but he quickly surmised he was to leave now, immediately. On his way out the door as he grabbed his coat he asked one of his associates:

"Call Ellen (my Mother) and tell her I don't know when I'll be home," and asked another co-worker to lend him some money.

On arriving at the Anacostia airfield he was the junior of several government officials, and the Army Air Corps pilot summoned to fly their single propeller aircraft was obviously unfamiliar with the airplane as Dad observed his fumbling with the controls. Be that as it may they soon arrived at a Connecticut airfield where a General Electric vice-president met them, and personally drove them to the facility where sewing machines were even then being removed from the factory floor. That night Dad slept on a couch in the factory conference room. He would make many trips to the factory in the coming weeks and would later receive an award for his efforts.

When I was a young lad, Dad told me that story and others, and he conveyed the sense of urgency and immediacy that united the entire country in the war effort. Dad lived his personal life the same way and provided a shining example to his son.

Back in our battery area, pre-constructed wooden containers suddenly appeared on the streets and sidewalks. Painted green with yellow numbers and letters, they told what was inside each box and the exact cubic footage. These were our mount-out boxes, and each piece of equipment that was to be embarked was duly placed in its appropriate container and the results tabulated.

To the uninitiated 2nd lieutenant that was me, it suddenly seemed our battery area had been turned upside down, and we all were running around like chickens with our heads cut off. Orders were rampant.

"Do this - No - do that."

Actually there was a method to this organized chaos for very quickly we had the total cubic footage necessary to embark our battery. There were quick conferences comparing numbers with those of our Marine Combat Cargo Officer, and soon we proceeded to load our battery aboard the USS Mathews.

I have a memory of standing in the ship's innards hearing engines roar, smelling exhaust fumes, forklifts driving around me, all intermingled with the shouts of Marines and sailors in the background and observing the ship's cranes lowering pallets of our mount-out boxes into the vast empty darkness of the ship's hold.

We spend our first night aboard ship. I'm bunking with my buddy Dick in officers' country above deck on the second level. Unfortunately, our cubbyhole abuts the main combustion stacks, and our room temperature exceeds 100 degrees. Water from the spigots in our room is too hot to drink. No way can we sleep in here so we blow up air mattresses and sleep on deck under the stars.

We expect immediate orders to sail for Vietnam.

Wed June 30

Dear Mom and Dad

Doing fine. I am on a ship, cargo-troop type. I've nicknamed her the USS Never Sail. We've been at anchor about 1 week, and will probably be at anchor another.... Going to Vietnam but place we're going to is pretty safe, don't worry...Ship is so hot that I've been sleeping on deck.... This part of the Pacific Ocean is very blue and pretty; however, we can't go swimming due to sea snakes....

love

John

Notes:

1. The USS Matthews was decommissioned on October 31, 1968 in San Diego California. She was sold for scrap in 1969.

2. Colonel William Pala, veteran of three wars, who made such a favorable impression on me as a young officer with his warm welcome, retired in 1967, and then taught high school math. He passed away at age 84 on December 13, 2000, in Arlington, Virginia.

3. The details on the evolution of the U.S. Marine Corps amphibious doctrine and Lieutenant Colonel Pete Ellis are from my own knowledge of Marine Corps history backed up by research on the Internet.

4. Details on the Higgins boats are from *Brute, The Life of Victor Krulak, U.S. Marine* by Robert Coram, Back Bay Books, 2010, chapters 3,4 and 5, as well as research on the Internet and my own knowledge of Marine Corps history.

5. In 1965 former 1st Lieutenant Victor Krulak was a Lieutenant General. He was the backbone of the Marines counterinsurgency strategy, and would visit our rifle company in late 1965. He passed away on January 4, 2009, and his obituary in the New York Times states: *Victor H. Krulak, Marine Behind the U.S. Landing Craft, Dies at 95.*

LEFT BEHIND

Blinding light shines in my eyes. Rough hands shake my shoulders. A loud voice, a sense of urgency, penetrate my consciousness.

"Are you Lieutenant Booth?"

" Yes," I answer groggily.

"Sir, your ship has sailed. A fast mover has been left behind to pick up stragglers. You are to report back to White Beach immediately."

It's 3:00 a.m. I'm asleep fully clothed on a bunk in a barracks on a Marine base in Okinawa. My boots are off. I have on my person the cash payroll for sixty-five Marines. I'm armed and my 45-caliber pistol is stuck in my boots close by. My unit is thirty miles away, embarked on a ship, the USS Matthews, part of a larger convoy in White Beach Harbor awaiting orders to sail for Vietnam. As the junior 2nd Lieutenant I have been sent ashore as pay officer.

The Marine Corps has done unusual things when our nation has called it to duty.

On November 7, 1921, two bandits sneaked aboard a train and brought it to a halt at gunpoint. The robbers then used the engineer to trick the mail clerks into opening the mail car, but when the mail clerks saw a robbery was in progress, they pulled the engineer inside and relocked the door. The robbers then set off explosives under the car breaking it open and then absconding with the registered mail, leaving behind wounded postal employees.

Other mail robberies took place, and between 1919 and 1921 about six million dollars were stolen. Mail robbery was a lucrative business, and the situation became so bad by the end of 1921 that President Harding ordered United States Marines to guard United States Mail. Within a few days 2,200 Marines and 53 officers were spread around the country working in small detachments of two or three Marines.

The Secretary of the Navy, a former Marine himself, sent a message to the Marine Corps, which read in part:

You must, when on guard, keep your weapons in hand and, if attacked, shoot and shoot to kill. There is no compromise in this battle with the bandits. If two Marines guarding a mail car, for example, are suddenly covered by a robber, neither must hold up his hands, but both must begin shooting at once. One may be killed, but the other will get the robber and save the mail. When our Marine Corps men go as guards over the mail, that mail must be delivered, or there must be a dead Marine at the post of duty.

The Marines were provided a training manual in a 105 question-and-answer format, which gave the information they needed to fulfill their duties. Here is a sample.

Q. Suppose the robber is using a gun or making threats with a gun trying to escape?

A. Shoot him.

Q. Is there a general plan for meeting a robbery?
A. Yes; start shooting and meet developments as they arise thereafter.

Q. Is it possible to make a successful robbery?
A. Only over a dead Marine.

Mail robberies came to a screeching halt, and until the Marines were withdrawn on March 15, 1922, not a single attempted mail robbery took place.

Mail robberies commenced again in April of 1923, and by 1926 things were again at a crisis point with the shooting of a driver and the heist of $150,000. President Coolidge yet again ordered in the Marines. The bandits had increased their firepower by use of automatic weapons and machine guns, and the Marines responded by adding Thompson submachine guns in addition to pistols and shotguns.

This time there was gunfire. A Marine found a stranger on his mail car platform. Despite the train traveling 25 miles per hour, he ordered the man off the train. When he refused, the Marine shot over the bandit's head. Needing no further persuasion, the rascal leaped out the door onto the passing cinders, while an additional round was fired over his head for emphasis. Once again mail robberies ceased abruptly.

Writing these words resurrects a memory from five decades ago.

I'm in a column of Marines lined up on a company street outside a World War II metal Quonset hut. On the sidewalk in front of the hut sits a small table covered with a green cloth. Behind the table sits a 2nd lieutenant with the company roster and a black pen. On the tablecloth are neatly stacked piles of five, ten and twenty dollar bills, and on the cloth next to the bills, rests a loaded 45-caliber pistol. We are to receive our pay, and I still remember the instructions.

"You will sign your payroll signature, which is your first name, middle initial and last name in black ink." Everything is signed in black ink, signing in blue ink is a sin.

Now I wasn't guarding the United States mail, but I was guarding a United States payroll, and all Marines, officer and enlisted, had been inoculated with tales of Marines guarding the mail. The pay officer version was, if this payroll is stolen there better be a dead 2nd Lieutenant.

What should I do with the payroll?

I'm not at all confident I will reach the fast mover in time, and then what happens? I'm stranded on a foreign shore with all this cash, and who knows how long before I can catch up to my unit?

The decision is easy. Return the payroll to disbursing and then scramble to reach White Beach in time.

Groggy no more, I awake as adrenalin takes over. I say a hurried thank you to the Marine who brought me the message. Finding me must have involved extreme persistence and just plain luck. I could have been sleeping any number of places. I yank on my boots, grab pack and pistol and rush to find the 3rd Marine Division disbursing office somewhere in the surrounding darkness.

The office appears. I pound on the door and shout, "Wake up, wake up, wake up". There is a stirring within, a panel opens, and I see a shotgun and hear an inquiry. I explain. The door opens. There is a quick accounting of currency, I turn over the payroll and scrawl a signature on a paper.

"All accounted for, Lieutenant," and as I leave, the words "Good Luck" follow me as I hurry back into the darkness.

I leave Camp Sukiran through the main gate and enter the town. This is a military town on a foreign shore, full of bars and the like, and everything stays open legally and illegally to odd hours in the early dawn. Taxi drivers are used to seeing strange phantoms in the middle of the night, and carrying drunken Marines back to base. I flag down a "skosh cab" or in modern day parlance, a taxi and in pidgin Japanese that Marines learn say "White Beach, Hiako, Hiako" which in polite terms means, "Get there quickly." I offer him extra cash.

My next memory is like a beautiful photograph bathed in light with warm fuzzy edges. I'm walking toward the pier at White Beach. The sun is peeking over the Pacific, and outlined against the horizon are silhouettes of sailors and, most joyful of all, a landing craft bobbing in the waves. I've made it, but just barely. As the sky brightens this becomes a Rudyard Kipling moment as I recall his poetic words, "And dawn comes up like thunder outer China 'crost the bay."

We have a brief respite to await more stragglers but none show. I'm the last. We pile aboard and cast off for the ship left behind to pick us up. She's a fast mover, sleek and gray, floating in the harbor. I'm reminded of a greyhound straining at its leash. We pull alongside, scramble up cargo nets and almost immediately the landing craft is hoisted up, bells ring, whistles blow, commands sound and the ship is underway at top speed if I'm any judge by the wind and spray on my face. I leisurely go below to find the officers wardroom and have breakfast. I wonder how I will get back on board my ship.

At mid-day we catch up with the convoy, and start to pull alongside the USS Mathews. Soon the distance between us is less than fifty feet, and crew on both vessels line the rails. It's a beautiful day with the sun shining, wind in our faces and white-capped waves sparkling all around in a deep blue ocean. The two ships are like galloping horses, rising and falling in the waves, and the speed and closeness force up the ocean between us so that it becomes a foaming cauldron with spray reaching us standing at the rails. It's difficult to hear.

I look astern, see all white capped waves and think if there is a man overboard at this speed he'll be five miles astern before a ship can turn around to come back after him. With all the whitecaps and the vastness of the ocean I wonder how one would ever be found.

A shotgun blasts into the air and a line arches toward the USS Matthews. Sailors grab the line, hold and pull. Soon more ropes appear, and a highline with a boson's chair is rigged between the ships. A few packages are sent across, and then it's my turn.

I'm the only Marine standing in a group of sailors and grizzled chiefs who are old enough to be my father. It occurs to me this is probably their third war. I receive good-natured kidding in that I'm a Marine and also a young officer.

"Ever been high-lined before, Lieutenant?"

"No, Chief, this is my first time."

"Well, don't worry, sir; I don't think we'll drown you."

I slip on a life jacket, get strapped in, and am pulled across to the Matthews. Imagine being pulled over Niagara Falls, spray in your face and the roar in your ears. It was quite a ride!

I report to my Commanding Officer and thank him for getting off a message about my being ashore, and also tell him I turned the payroll back in. My 2nd Lieutenant buddy, Dick, comments,

"Where you been, John, goofing off on liberty?"

I give him an answer I don't want to print here.

It feels good to be home. I've been away a little over twenty-four hours. It felt like twenty-four days.

Life on board soon settles into a routine. Because the officer's room I'm assigned to with my buddy Dick is, as I've stated before, hotter than hell, we blow up air mattresses and sleep outside on the deck each night with an ocean wind on our faces, surrounded by darkness, and a heaven so beautiful and covered with stars you cannot see the sky. The hand of God seems to reach down and touch us. Sunrise over the Pacific awakens us in the early dawn, and a light layer of ash from the boilers gently covers us.

It dawns on me, "I'm going to war!" I spread a blanket on the deck and for several days practice disassembling and assembling my 45-caliber pistol until I can do it with my eyes shut.

The 45, formally designated as the *Pistol, Caliber.45, automatic, M1911A1*, was the mainstay sidearm of the United States military through World War I and II, Korea and Vietnam. The M1911 pistol originated in the late 1890s as the result of a search for a suitable self-loading or semi-automatic pistol to replace the variety of revolvers then in service.

The search was given a sense of urgency during the Philippine Insurrection in the early 1900s. Fanatical Moro natives, who had a culture of warfare, were also using drugs to inhibit the sensation of pain, and consequently were not stopped when hit by a slug of the 38-caliber revolver then in use. The heavier 45-caliber round was found to knock a man down if hit anywhere on his body.

The design is simple and rugged and in 1910 testing, over 6000 rounds were fired from a single pistol over two days. When the gun began to grow hot, it was simply immersed in cold water to cool it. There were no malfunctions.

The M1911 was designed by John Browning and was officially adopted by the United States Navy and Marine Corps in 1913. Minor changes were made as a result of experiences during World War I, and in 1924 the pistol received a modified classification as the M1911A1.

The 45 receives many unfavorable comments because it kicks like a mule, which makes it difficult to hold on target, but not for me. I'm a crack shot and earned Expert in marksmanship training.

The whole time I was in Vietnam that three-pound weight of the 45 on my right hip was a source of constant comfort and became as much a part of my body as my right arm. It would fire even when dropped in rice paddy mud. I would draw it from my holster twice to defend myself.

The ocean and sky remain a breathtaking deep blue. Sparkling whitecaps dance on the sea. I look over the side and observe sea snakes swimming in the water. I'm told they're poisonous.

An order. Officers are to inspect the men's living quarters to make sure they're clean... or something like that. I go below decks feeling slightly awkward. I'm still green and feeling my way in command of Marines, a few of whom are much older than me. A staff sergeant politely shows me around, and gently chides either the order or me.

"You don't need to be down here. Sir. This is my job to keep the place clean."

The Navy lives a good life! In the officers' wardroom we dine on white tablecloths with silverware and the like. There are even stewards to wait on us, and we don't start eating until the *Matthews* Captain arrives. All this is an alien culture to Marines.

Dick and I become good friends, and have lots of philosophical discussions about the Marine Corps and the war. We read. We wait.

Notes:

1. The history of the Marines guarding the mail was taken from an article published by the Marine Corps Association October 1993 and research on the Internet.

2. The history of the M1911A1 45-caliber pistol is taken from the Internet.

Tue July 6

Mom & Dad

Everything O.K. — doing fine. I'm writing this at sea — ship finally sailed. However I was 30 miles away when the convoy left. One ship was left behind to pick up stragglers, I made that one. Later, at sea I was transferred 'back to my ship by "highlining"

MY SHIP

ME

BOTH SHIPS MOVING AT 15-20 KNOTS

WAVES - LOTS OF SPRAY

Most interesting experience. We're due to offload at Da Nang Tomorrow. However that might be changed — as orders have been changed 6 times already.

John

17

A GOAT ROPING

We sense the presence of land before we see it. The water is not quite so blue, vegetative debris floating, and strange birds circling overhead. Finally, late in the afternoon, way off in the distance a faint smudge appears which soon develops into mountains and jungle: Da Nang Harbor in central Vietnam.

Our convoy of six ships and 1500 Marines, the rear of the 3rd Marine Division, continues to plow forward as we enter the harbor and discover we are in a large traffic jam of ships, all waiting to be unloaded. The forward division elements landed in April of 1965, it's now July, and all division supplies, ammunition, C-rations, vehicles, barb-wire and all the multitudinous minutiae needed to equip 10,000 Marines in the conduct of a war continue to be unloaded via landing craft across a 200 yard narrow beachhead, called Red Beach II, twenty-four hours a day. The Matthews gets in line and we wait.

The next picture is etched in my brain. It's the middle of the night and I'm lying on top of a truck in a landing craft inching forward. Floodlights bathe the beach, forklifts silhouetted in black scurry like ants, and heat, humidity, insects, smells and sounds flood my senses. We get our battery ashore, line up our trucks in convoy and drive forward until we encounter darkness and relative quiet away from the beach. Ammunition and hand grenades have been issued. We are armed and apprehensive, for we are now in a war zone. We post guards, and in what's left of the night, lie down and attempt to sleep.

Dawn awakens us with a shout. "We're under attack!" Another shout, "Hold on, it's only monkeys throwing coconuts." Good Morning, Vietnam.

That first day "in-country" is a blur with crushing heat and humidity. Our convoy snakes through the narrow streets of Da Nang with children begging for candy and cigarettes. Hot dry wind throws dust in our faces, which soon permeates every open orifice. Filth and garbage abound and remind me of a cesspool. There is evidence of French architecture, but everything is decayed and run down.

We meet a Marine rifle company in column slogging in from somewhere in the afternoon heat beneath a blue sky. They look bronzed, lean, and professional. With mountains in the background and dust rising from the road, I think of Stonewall Jackson and his foot soldiers slogging through the Shenandoah Valley in the Civil War.

Division hasn't decided what to do with us. Our battery is not even assigned a short-term mission so we have not prepared our mortars to fire. We will spend the next few days with a counter-mortar radar unit on our left, and a rifle company on our right. We are interspersed in groves of trees with light vegetation. Cows graze nearby on small rolling hills as we are in the piedmont between the rice paddies and mountains.

Marines have a common base in that everyone is trained initially as a rifleman and every officer as an infantry leader. However, there is a wide difference between a green, inexperienced, counter-mortar radar unit, and a combat-experienced rifle company. Dick and I think our battery is somewhere in between on that spectrum.

It's late afternoon and we are all busy, especially the officers and sergeants, with the myriad details of putting in a defensive perimeter, such as the proper placement of individual firing positions, where we should place our automatic weapons, and assessing whether our positions are mutually supporting.

We have a large 50-caliber machine gun, which we put in our center because we don't know where else to emplace it. It is heavy, difficult to move, will penetrate vehicles with its large shell and is deadly at long range, but is worthless in the counterinsurgency and guerrilla warfare we will encounter. We would have much preferred two more of the lighter caliber M-60 machine guns. Several of our sergeants are Korean War veterans, and their experience helps. Dick and I laugh and joke about the counter-mortar radar unit on our left, what with all their shouts and commands. We compare them to clowns and a herd of undisciplined goats.

I haven't seen the infantry company on our right and am beginning to wonder if they will show up. Suddenly, as if by magic, apparitions suddenly appear within the trees, mingled together with the leaves by the late afternoon sun and a faint breeze. I blink my eyes to make sure they're real. They weren't there a second ago. The phantoms suddenly have uniforms, they're Marines! Silent, stealthy, they instinctively move into position. A rain poncho suddenly appears, and beneath it the company command post. I haven't heard a single sound, and I think of the legendary Roger's Rangers in our French and Indian War in the 1700s. They remind me ever so much of a pack of lean hungry wolves. I am in awe.

This is early in the war and our mission ashore is only to guard the airfield, and we are not, repeat not, to engage in offensive operations against the enemy. We have rules of engagement.

> *Rounds will not be inserted in the chamber of individual weapons unless an encounter with the enemy is obvious, and in the judgment of the senior Marine present, this measure must be taken to preserve the lives of USMC personnel.*

> *Magazines will not be inserted in weapons in a camp area during daylight hours unless under attack.*

Not long after, as twilight gathers, one of our Marines approaches me.

"Mr. Booth, there is a hole in our lines with the infantry company. No one is on our right."

I think, "How can this be? There must be some mistake."

Being a conscientious young officer I respond,

"Follow me," and we set out to investigate.

Sure enough, no one is there, and we continue to walk and further explore.

19

Now Da Nang is sixteen degrees north of the equator, which means there isn't much twilight. One minute it's light and the next minute it's dark. Night comes quickly with no warning and darkness falls with a thud. A faint breeze is blowing causing moonlit shadows to move and shuffle, so you're never really sure what you see. It occurs to me that we could be in front of our lines, and if we are, we're in deep trouble.

If this had been anywhere else, it would have been a lovely evening what with the mild breeze blowing, and the moonlight playing with the shadows. As I write these words I'm reminded of the academy award-winning film *From Here to Eternity*, and the scene with Frank Sinatra, right before a nervous sentry in the dancing darkness kills him.

In my camping and canoeing adventures in scouting as a teenager, I learned if you want to see an individual at night, do not look directly at them, but slightly to the side. Adrenalin kicks in and all my senses go into overdrive. I gesture to my companion to follow, and we start walking slowly back whence we came. I am listening, looking, and sensing with everything I have. Suddenly I hear a sound so faint as to be almost inaudible... a single click.

That sound to me is as identifiable as hearing a beer can roll down the pavement. If you have heard that sound once, you know it forever after. A Marine has clicked off the safety on his rifle, has it pointed directly at my chest, and is a nano-second from squeezing the trigger. How I respond will determine whether I live or die.

Without thinking I instinctively react by stepping quickly into full moonlight, throw both arms in the air, and say loudly,

"Don't shoot, don't shoot, don't shoot."

Silence follows. A long pause. Suddenly, a quiet voice from somewhere in front commands,

"Advance and be recognized."

I quickly identify myself and say there is another Marine behind me. The phantom instructs us to come in quickly, and as we pass I am still unable to determine exactly where he is. We reenter our perimeter.

That Marine sentry either came into position after we passed by or we didn't see him the first time, but it makes no difference. I screwed up. I am so embarrassed by this incident that I will not tell another Marine about it until years later. My first days in Vietnam, and I'm almost killed by a stupid mistake. I think if I had dropped to the ground he would have pulled the trigger.

But wait Dear Reader. This night ain't over yet, and this yarn gets better.

The goat herd (the inexperienced counter-mortar-radar unit) on our left lives up to our expectations as shouts, lights and occasional rifle shots permeate the evening. The wolves (the experienced rifle company) on our right are graveyard silent, and give nary a peep or show a light.

And so we put everyone on fifty percent alert and decide among the three officers how to split the watch. Dick and I argue that the staff sergeants should stand watch with us, but we are over-ruled by our commanding officer. Officers only will man the command post, and so I take my turn and then stretch out on my air mattress, boots on, pistol at my fingertips.

The chug-chug-chug of our 50-caliber machine gun blasts me awake in the still of the night. A garden-hose stream of shells is sweeping the terrain in front with every fifth round a tracer. Our entire battery is scrambling to arms, and I can hear bolts slamming home in rifles and shouts of "What's going on?" The goat herd on our left has erupted into a pyrotechnic display worthy of the 4th of July with rifles and machine guns firing. Tracers race through the night air. Grenades explode. It's quite beautiful, actually. The wolves on our right remain silent-nothing.

A sane voice from somewhere within our battery screams out, "Cease fire, Cease fire." Officers and sergeants take command, and quickly all firing stops except for an occasional round from the goat herd on our left. Still nothing from the wolves on our right. Officers pounce on the poor Marine manning the 50- caliber.

"What are you firing at?" accompanied by oaths and curses worthy of the devil himself.

"Did someone shoot at you?"

"Lieutenant, I saw someone running by the bushes over there."

The Marine sticks to his story, and whether he did or didn't see someone lurking we don't know. He's instructed,

"Next time throw a hand grenade, do not give your position away, and only fire this monster of a machine gun if we're about to be overrun."

No one heard any incoming rounds and we opine that he was shooting at shadows. We're greener than we thought. We settle back in for the remainder of the night except the goats never really quiet down and random shots continue until the dawn. The wolves keep their fire discipline with not a shot fired, nor a sound heard. We are lucky no one was killed or wounded. Thus begins my education on developing a sixth sense and surviving in a war.

Dick and I would agree: this night was a real goat roping, and we were the goats!

Notes: Details on the landing of the USS Matthews and the subsequent location of our command posts are contained in the 9th Marine Regiment Command Chronology, July 1965, pages 4,11, 15. I cannot determine the exact date of the goat-roping incident. My unit, Whiskey Battery, 2nd Battalion, 12th Marines landed on July 8. See pages 152-153 for Rules of Engagement. See 4th Battalion, 12th Marine Regiment Command chronology July 1965, page 3, for date we are airlifted to Phu Bai July 17, 1965.

JOHN FIORENTIN

"Mr. Fiorentin, please share with the class why you joined the Marines."

It's a bright cheerful day with sunshine streaming through the windows of our classroom, bathing us in a warm glow. It's the early months of 1965, and I'm a student at The Officer Basic School in Quantico, Virginia, which all new 2nd Lieutenants attend after graduating from college and commissioning as a Marine officer. It makes no difference whether you were commissioned via the Naval Academy in Annapolis, Maryland, or Elks Breath University in northern Nebraska. You will attend The Basic School, receive a six-month graduate-school education on becoming a Marine officer, and upon graduating no one can discern from whence you were commissioned. The rigorous academic, physical and leadership training, the camaraderie of the Marine Corps, and the probability of fighting in Southeast Asia created a strong bonding experience among us all.

My buddy, 2nd Lieutenant John V. Fiorentin, was a fellow student, and he and I had dated the young ladies at Mary Washington Women's College close by in Fredericksburg, Virginia. I have fond memories of John and me swapping stories while waiting for our dates in the college parlor. We had affectionately nicknamed John "Frog," because he was Italian, and yes I know that Frog is a pejorative term for someone of French descent, and no I can't explain it five decades later.

John has related a moving story to the instructor on his motivation for joining the Marines and was asked to share with the rest of the class.

"I was born in Italy in 1941, and as a child I was engulfed in World War II behind German lines. One day, German soldiers in coalscuttle helmets came into our village, and as a young boy I was lifted aboard a truck to join my fellow Italians on a journey to who knows where. Older adults protested, a discussion ensued, a loaf of bread was given to the Germans, and I was lifted back off the truck and rejoined my family. My life was exchanged for a loaf of bread!

At war's end I vividly remember liberation by black American soldiers in tanks with a white star on their side, and realized I was free. I felt I should give something back to America which gave me my freedom."

On November 23, 1965, in the early morning hours, 2nd Lieutenant John Fiorentin, only four days in Vietnam, was inspecting his platoon's position with two other Marines. He was in front of his lines when a Marine mistakenly fired and shot him in the neck.

He was the beloved only son of Emila and Silvio Fiorentin who owned a restaurant in Anaheim California. John is laid to rest alongside his parents in Holy Sepulcher Cemetery, Orange California. He is memorialized on the Vietnam Wall, Panel 03E, line 110.

John was not as lucky as I was.

Notes: For details on 2nd Lieutenant John V. Fiorentin, see 3rd Marine Regiment Command Chronology, November 1965, page 73.

ACCIDENTS AND OTHER YARNS

Most Americans know that over 58,000 servicemen and women were killed during the Vietnam War. What most do not realize is almost 11,000 of them or 19% died of non-hostile causes.

"How can that be?" you ask.

My friend, let me count the number of ways you can die by accident.

You can be shot by carelessness, other's and your own. Like me for instance, I was almost killed my first week in country. I tried to do the right thing the wrong way. My Basic School buddy, 2nd Lieutenant John Fiorentin as I have shown, was not so lucky. By November, I am a seasoned combat veteran but in spite of that while cleaning my pistol out pops a round. I forgot to unload it and could have blown my head off.

Our rifle company institutes a procedure where an officer or non-commissioned officer would insert their finger into the chamber of every rifle of every Marine returning from patrol and entering a safe area, to insure the weapon was empty. Safe Area was a relative term.

Marines on patrol develop the unsafe habit of carrying their weapon via sling over their shoulder with the safety off, and accidently shoot the Marine to their front. A Marine on an ambush slithers to the rear to relieve himself and upon return accidentally wanders into the killing zone. What was left of his body was hamburger meat. Accidental shootings become so prevalent that the 3rd Marine Division issues an order threatening courts-martial for any Marine involved in one.

You can drown. A rope snaps on a river crossing and a Marine draped with ammunition plunges fifteen feet to the bottom. This I witnessed. Another Basic School buddy, 1st Lieutenant Phil Rath was unlucky enough to have his boat overturn while on a fast-flowing river, and his body washes ashore a day later. You can be swept off rocks into the sea. This happened to a battalion staff officer.

You can be crushed or mangled. A two-ton truck overturns on a muddy road partially washed away by monsoon rains, and three Marines in the back are crushed when the vehicle rolls on top of them. One is killed, but two survive. A Marine becomes entangled in the launch catapult at the Chu-Lai airfield. His body is torn apart into several pieces.

At the more esoteric end you can be attacked by a tiger, of which there are documented instances. One happened while I was there, and I read the incident in The Stars and Stripes. The tiger must not have been hungry though, because the Marine survived to fight another day.

A serpent can sink his fangs into your body. A Marine, hiding in tall grass by a jungle trail, discovers a snake occupying the same real estate. The snake doesn't like it. As I made my living for several months doing the same thing, I could well understand the Marine's discomfort and surprise. I hear his screams over the radio, and in the strange convoluted way that only another combat Marine can understand, I laugh! He lived, and I still find it hilarious over five decades later.

The list goes on, and suffice to say over the next thirteen months I develop survival instincts.

We continue our sojourn in Da Nang as the 3rd Marine Division still struggles to place us with a parent unit and mission.

I finally complete my assignment as pay officer. I grab a jeep, a driver, a rifle, some hand grenades, and we inch our way through the grimy, smelly, crowded streets of Da Nang to the 3rd Marine Division Headquarters and Disbursing Office. Even within the division compound this place looks and acts like Fort Knox, what with triple concertina barbed wire and multiple armed guards. Inside the building I observe shotguns casually leaning against wooden field desks, and think, "This place is the wild west." I discover why all the precautions because everywhere are stacks of United States negotiable greenback dollars. I sign for the battery payroll, and am issued a wad of cash. We insure our weapons are loaded, have our hand grenades within easy reach, and have an uneventful return trip to our unit.

Before the end of September, all United States dollars are exchanged for military payment currency, and all Marines must turn in their cash. There is too much temptation for black market United States dollars, and if you want a quick trip to Leavenworth military prison take a few greenbacks, and go out on the Vietnamese economy.

Another collateral duty I have is motor transport officer.

"Mr. Booth, should I remove some tools from the truck tool kit, or play it straight and give 'em a full box." I'm talking to our battery mechanic, a Marine private and wonder why he is a private, and not a private first class. I will find out why the next day!

It's becoming quickly apparent the Marine Corps supply system isn't working, and I'm starting to think about the "art of the cumshaw," or borrowing equipment from the Army and the Navy, and more specifically "borrowing" equipment from other Marine units and using it ourselves. That's not really stealing, is it?

I think about it for a moment, "No, play it straight," I say. Six months later when we return to Okinawa I will evolve into a master thief and perhaps have missed my calling for a lifetime career.

We are to exchange a truck with our goat herd friends, the counter-mortar radar unit on our left. Who has decided and why they decided to exchange a truck, I do not remember for it sounds against regulations and probably is but we make the trade anyway.

The next morning the exchanged truck and private are missing, AWOL in a war zone. Where could he go? Months later I hear this story. A lone Marine private is seen driving a truck up north close to the Demilitarized Zone. An alert Army warrant officer thinks, "That's odd." He stops the truck, asks a few questions, discovers all is not right, and turns the Marine over to the Military

Police. The timing is about right, and the storyteller and I think it's our guy, but we never really know.

Do not ask me what goes through the mind of a nineteen-year old Marine private.

Still awaiting a decision on our destination, stories and rumors abound, and life goes on.

I bathe and shave out of my helmet, sleep on the ground beneath the stars, fully clothed, always with pistol close at hand. No tents for us. We eat C-rations which if you have the time and inclination you can improve their taste, which I would soon learn to do. I did not want to worry my parents so I make a conscious decision about what not to write in letters home.

A Marine artillery unit is laying in their night defensive fires and somehow in the process machine gun fire accidentally kills a twelve-year-old Vietnamese young lady. General Walt, the division commander, relieves the commanding officer. A Marine patrol meets a Viet Cong unit led by two Caucasian males who are Russian advisors. The Viet Cong unit escapes, so no one really knows whether the story is true or not.

Black Bart, a North African deserter from the French Foreign Legion, leads a Viet Cong battalion operating around Da Nang. Ebony magazine is coming to do a story on Black Bart. Did this really happen? No one knows.

Viet Cong prisoners wrapped in barbed wire are thrown from helicopters onto the Da Nang airfield. I would hear some variation of this story the entire time I was in Vietnam, but when I would ask, "Did you see it?" the answer was always no.

Fortunately, I only had to deal personally with a minor infraction of misbehavior, but in the coming months I would hear and witness enough to learn the Marine Corps will not tolerate anything close to this. Even in a war there are things you do not do. Mistreatment of prisoners and brutality will spread quicker than the common cold and metastasize worse than cancer. Are we a disciplined fighting force or a bunch of Nazi goons?

Decades later I am talking to a friend who is a retired CIA officer, but in Vietnam was a young Army sergeant assigned to the South Korean Army. He was a witness to some basis for the story. He is in a helicopter with a South Korean officer, who says,

"The problem with you Americans is you're not mean enough," and promptly throws a Viet Cong prisoner out the door. My buddy is horrified, promptly reports this to his superiors, but since the Korean officer is not under the legal jurisdiction of the United States Code of Military Justice, there is nothing we can do except expel him from Vietnam.

"We're going to Pleiku in the South Vietnam highlands."

"Pleiku, at least it's cool up there."

"Naw, we're going to India."

"India, where did that come from? I don't want to go to India, too many snakes."

At last we have resolution on our destination. We are attached to the 4th Battalion of the 12th Marine Regiment, and are to be flown to an airfield fifty miles north of Da Nang, close to the villages of Phu Bai and only five miles south from the city of Hue, the old imperial capital of Vietnam. We are to support the 3rd Battalion of the 4th Marine Infantry Regiment already ensconced in the area.

As the curtain falls on this chapter of my journey in the war, my last memory is of a hot food mess line underneath canvas awnings next to the airstrip where we are deafened by the roar of aircraft. It's blinding sunshine, stifling heat, smothering humidity, no breeze and no shade.

We file down a line of garbage cans filled with boiling soapy water in which we immerse and clean our metal mess gear. We are to eat B-rations, which are heated up "stuff" out of large cans for group meals. As we move down the mess line Marines in filthy white aprons on the other side of the table ladle out the hot mush and dump it into our mess tins. The meal has a foul taste, and the fact that I remember this over five decades later is testimony to its unsavoriness. The meal will haunt me in the coming week. Stay tuned.

We landed in Da Nang on July 8, and are leaving on July 17. As we board the cargo plane we check to insure our equipment is tied down in the dark cavernous cargo hole. We sit scrunched along the sides with weapons in hand, strap ourselves in, observe the rear hatch close, and listen to the engines roar as we ascend into the wild blue yonder for the next phase of our war.

We were in the Da Nang enclave from July 8 until July 17.
This is the only letter I wrote home.

July 16

Dear Mom & Dad:

Everything o.k.- doing fine.
I'm now in a sector outside of
Da Nang Air Base. We're due to
fly out soon to another area in
Viet Nam, will write when I get
here.

Mom- went one week without
a shower. However, did manage to
bath out of my helmet - I didn't
smell- too much.

Lately its been cloudy, but
when the sun is out heat is
unbelievable. The humidity is also
very high.

Vietnamese kids are everywhere-
all begging for cigarettes and candy.
Cows are grazing around our tents.

Our battery 1st Sgt reminds
me of Uncle Roy and Mr. Owen-
quite an interesting character.
Will write again

John

P.S. New change in address.
It is now
3RD MARINE DIVISION FORWARD -
this will save about 4 days on
mail

27

PART 2 INDIA BATTERY AND THE 3rd BATTALION 4th MARINES

PHU BAI JULY 18, 1965, THROUGH NOVEMBER 14, 1965

Picture: Forward Observer 2nd Lieutenant John Booth standing in front of a 155 Self Propelled 155mm Howitzer. The howitzer would throw 95-pound high explosive shells about 9 miles. When I called them in they sounded like a freight train going over my head. Picture taken in the Marine enclave next to the Phu Bai airfield in September 1965.

EASY LIVING

"Gee, Lieutenant, you must feel pretty rotten." A Navy Corpsman speaks the words as he removes the thermometer crammed into my mouth. That's an understatement and I want to reach up and strangle him.

I'm lying on an ammunition box floor and wood splinters are poking me in the cheek, but actually it feels good just to lie here. I'm a battle casualty, but no enemy bullet has laid me low. Instead, a scourge as old as mankind: dysentery. It was that meal at the airstrip before we boarded the plane.

A voice grates in the background: "I heard there was one more out there, guess he finally gave up and came on in for medical help. Marines are knuckleheads!"

As I was an officer and felt I had to set the example, I guess I had been a bit stubborn and tardy in holding out to the end. Finally, misery overcame me, and I asked a fellow Marine to drive me to the aid station whereupon I staggered into the medical tent, and promptly collapsed onto the floor. If wounded, expect tender loving care, but if merely sick, expect no sympathy.

Prominent people have died of dysentery.

The infamous King John of England died of dysentery in 1216 while attempting to crush the Magna Carta, as did Vice Admiral Sir Francis Drake who died in 1596 while attacking El Morro Castle in San Juan, Puerto Rico.

Many of mankind's medical discoveries have been made within the context of warfare. The Roman Emperor, Caesar Augustus, recognized that the empire was built upon the success of its legions and its superior military organization, and identified the importance of health and hygiene to cut down on losses. He developed a medical corps and implemented procedures such as always obtaining drinking water upstream of latrines. The legions even developed a treatment for dysentery.

"Yolks of eggs are taken for dysentery with the ash of their shells, poppy juice and wine."

Well, no yokes of eggs with poppy juice and wine for me, but

"Warm pineapple juice, no food, and confinement to the medical tent."

Fluid is running out of me like poop through a goose, and I see why early pioneers died of dysentery, otherwise known as the "bloody flux." "Stay hydrated, Lieutenant," a chirping corpsman instructs me as I slurp warm pineapple juice straight from the can.

I wear a trail to the outside privy, which is the exclusive club of us six Marines who shared "The Last Lunch" before boarding the plane. After a day or so we hear shouts of "Fire in the Hole," which signifies low ranking enlisted Marines are pouring gasoline into the privy hole followed by a match, and a brief "woof" of an explosion. The contents are burned and a fresh privy hole and shack are constructed at a different location.

On this particular move a nest of poisonous vipers is discovered inches beneath the old privy seat. Wouldn't that be a hoot if one of us had been bitten! Embarrassing to say the least.

We are confined to a tent built over a wood frame with cots and screened rolled up sides. It's stifling hot with no air movement, and next to us is an air- conditioned tent with an operating room for the wounded. We're glad we don't rate the air conditioning. We read. We talk. We wait.

I cannot remember how long I was confined to the aid station. My medical records have disappeared, but I find on a 1967 insurance policy that I have listed five days, but that sounds too long. Dysentery will plague me in some form my entire tour in Vietnam, during which the veneer of civilized living will be slowly stripped away, and my assignments will move me steadily down the food chain.

I return to my battery where a staff sergeant remarks, "Mr. Booth, you've lost some weight."

"Yeah, Staff Sergeant, I've discovered the Marine Corps weight-loss program: dysentery, no food and warm pineapple juice!"

Well, Dear Reader, after this unpleasant tale one might ask, "How did you urinate? Do Marines wander around like feral dogs sniffing truck tires and bushes until they smell the right spot? Some people, depending on their opinion of Marines, would answer yes, but that's still a good question for over one thousand Marines will be living in base camp in close proximity, and all must practice good hygiene.

The medical invention of the ubiquitous "Piss Tube," is an under-appreciated contributor to clean living. A four-inch diameter plastic tube is inserted several feet into the ground at a 70-degree angle, the open end is covered with a tight mesh screen to keep flies out, and when one needs to pass water, use the tube. They are strategically placed and are out in the open for there is no modesty in combat. Like latrines they are moved at a set frequency set by the medical corps. As you might imagine, burning out body waste associated with privy holes and piss tubes is not the most sought after chore by junior enlisted Marines.

We actually live a fairly plush life in this base camp at Phu Bai. We live in tents and sleep on cots. We eat a combination of hot food and C-rations and have makeshift showers. A good analogy would be advanced camping. An under-appreciated success of the United States military is how we were able to move tens of thousands of young men to the other side of the world and for the most part keep them hale and hearty!

Base Camp at Phu Bai in 1965 is easy living!

FIRE DIRECTION OFFICER

Night has fallen, and in the Fire Direction Center tent sides are down to hide the light. My pistol is low on my hip and rifles lean against desks and charts. A large map hangs on one side, field telephones sit on several desks, and in the background one hears the hiss of propane lanterns and the crackle of static. A radio operator's voice breaks the static,

"Primrose radio check. If you hear me, key your handset twice."

On the other end a forward observer hides in the weeds on an ambush deep in Indian Country. He maintains strict radio silence and keys the handset twice to acknowledge the message. In the tent we hear two breaks in the static and know that Primrose is alive and well. There are several patrols out tonight, and it is the radio operator's duty to check each one on the hour to insure they are still alive and still awake.

What with the heat given off by the gas lanterns and the bodies of Marines dripping sweat, it's a relief to step outside into the steamy night. The voices of other Marines softly intermingle as they carry out their duties. Overseeing all is the watch officer. Silent and listening, he occasionally says one word, "check," signifying he agrees with the mathematical calculations. One four-digit number and one three-digit number are then relayed to the howitzers and seconds later shells roar into the night.

This is my first time as watch officer in our battalion fire direction center, commanding eighteen howitzers and mortars and over one hundred Marines. At my command three different caliber batteries will unleash enough firepower to blow up a city block. Responsibility of this magnitude is normally given to a seasoned 1st Lieutenant or Captain, and here I am, a green 2nd Lieutenant, not long out of gunnery school and new to combat.

I've prevailed upon 1st Lieutenant Don Rosenberg, the experienced outgoing watch officer, to stick around, and help guide me through the long night. He obliges, goes over to a corner, lies down, and promptly goes to sleep. All through the night as our howitzers roar and fire shells into the blackness, I go over, wake Don, and ask my question. He wakes up, cheerfully answers, and goes back to sleep. Don must have a sleep switch in his brain. One night with Don is all it takes to snap me in, and then I'm on my own.

In my thirteen months in Southeast Asia I would have three assignments. This is my first and is at the top of the food chain. Of course "top" is a relative statement, given that this is the Marine Corps, and all are trained as infantry. It was the most intellectually demanding, and had the best living conditions. I slept on a cot in a tent, and had access to cold showers and hot food.

I was a graduate civil engineer and had all the requisite training to intuitively understand the Science of Gunnery. All maps and all calculations are on the metric system. Just keep the zeros and decimals straight and I could almost do the math in my head.

Second lieutenants normally start at the bottom of the Marine hierarchy as forward observers with a rifle company. Sleep on the ground, in the rain, no bathing, and cold C-rations. Plus various and sundry people try to kill you. So things were a bit upside down. Well, all this will be corrected in one month and things will be right side up so to speak. I just don't know it yet.

My last assignment would be as a Fire Support Coordinator on an infantry battalion staff. It was supposed to be somewhere in between, but it was the toughest of all. But I'm getting ahead of myself, back to the story.

It's a hot afternoon in the battalion fire direction center. The sides of the tent are up and a faint breeze is attempting to stir the air, but not making much progress. Not much is going on, and we're collapsed in varying degrees of slothfulness from writing letters home to reading. Faint static from several radios buzz in the background. I'm playing chess with Corporal Bill Henry. I don't know who's ahead in wins, me or him, but he's a worthy opponent, and I'm engrossed in planning a move that I hope will devastate him.

Corporal Henry is bald, wears glasses, like me, and reminds one of a college professor. He has a fierce intellect, like most Marines who gravitate to working in the mathematics of gunnery. You can tell that by the books they read, and interest in pastimes like chess. He's part of the India Battery fire direction team led by Staff Sergeant Hoskins, a most capable non-commissioned officer. I spend little time worrying about mistakes when I command this crew.

Other Marines can misinterpret this intellectual cerebral bent, as I remember a certain peevishness exhibited by the top enlisted Marine in the battery, Gunnery Sergeant Carl Satterfield, as he commented in formation one day:

"You fire direction Marines think you're better than anyone else but you need to carry your share of the load."

He was in the process of handing out less desirable work assignments necessary for keeping living conditions in the field clean and sanitary, burning out latrines, for example. I stayed out of Satterfield's relations with the troops because no one wanted to get on the bad side of Gunnery Sergeant Satterfield, not even 2nd Lieutenants.

Suddenly the static breaks and the radio crackles: "Bearmat, this is Bird Dog, Fire Mission, Victor Charlie in open, over." We respond "Bird Dog, send your mission, over."

Bird Dog is the air observer who has been flitting over the whole area in a single engine spotter plane. We would occasionally hear the faint engine drone in the distance. The target is one Viet Cong soldier casually walking in the open. I cannot imagine what's going through his mind and why he would be so stupid! The air observer wants to blow him apart with artillery.

Now, Dear Reader, you may object and say, "Isn't this grossly unfair, brutal, and all out of proportion, to kill this one individual with all this artillery?"

That's the wrong question to ask. First: In a war there is no such thing as a fair fight and if you find yourself in one, there's something wrong with you. Second: There is no such thing as a proportionate response. "Hit 'em hard and make it hurt." Third: "War is brutal and there is no way you can refine it." That's a quote from Civil War General Tecumseh Sherman as he laid waste to Georgia in 1865.

A better question to ask is:

"Is it worth the expenditure of shells to get this one bad guy?"

Based on the amount of ammunition we have thrown into the air on Harassing and Interdiction Fires, Preparation Fires and what all, the answer is yes. I have the authority to refuse the mission if the answer is no.

In addition, this is not as unfair as it seems. Artillery is an area weapon, it takes time to adjust and unless we get lucky on the first salvo, Mr. Charles, otherwise known as the Viet Cong, stands a good chance of escaping if he can run fast and get to cover.

Two shells speed into the sky on the first adjustment rounds, and as expected they are off. Mr. Charles is now aware he is being observed, and starts to run. Bird Dog adjusts with "Drop 400" and two howitzers roar again. We play this cat and mouse game of run, shoot and adjust for several minutes until Mr. Charles makes a fatal mistake – or so we think. He runs into a small structure on top of a hill and makes himself stationary.

Why he would run into a hut I have not the slightest idea, except that in the Battle of Starlite earlier this month, grass huts were discovered to have concrete bunkers inside, and Marines subsequently reverted to World War II tactics used against the Japanese to root out the Viet Cong. Maybe there is a concrete bunker inside.

We narrow the shell adjustments to as small as our calculations and instruments permit, and surprisingly the shells either explode just below the crest of the hill or fly harmlessly over the top and explode way beyond. The problem is that in low angle fire, below 45 degrees, and at this range, the shell trajectory is almost horizontal. The howitzer cannot make the minute adjustments necessary, and if we did hit the hut, the shell would pass through and continue on. Mr. Charles may have lucked out after all.

I think for a moment. Suddenly, this becomes a math problem. I think of a garden hose and what happens when you elevate the nozzle to an angle greater than 45 degrees. The stream comes down almost vertical.

I call for high angle fire so the shells will come down vertical like a mortar, and the command goes to the guns. Artillerymen hate high angle fire. The gun crews must dig high angle pits, as the recoil of the barrel will slam into the ground unless there is a hole. They must then crank the barrel down to horizontal, cram powder and shell into the breech, and then crank the barrel back up to above 45 degrees. The gun crews pride themselves on speed and often will race to see who can shoot the fastest. This slows things down dramatically and works the gun crew hard.

However, it works. With a few adjustments we hit the structure, Bird Dog says the magic words "Fire for Effect." I unleash the entire battery, the hut is smothered in high explosives and disappears. I don't know for sure, but in all probability, I just killed another human being. Did it bother me? In one word, no. I ate well and slept well that night as always. It was also clean, antiseptic, and impersonal. That helps. Later that would not be the case.

Later, an old grizzled Master Gunnery Sergeant laughingly comments, "I haven't seen high angle fire since Korea, Lieutenant, when we fired at the Chinese. The gun crews should have had their high angle pits dug and they didn't. You worked 'em to death."

On another hot drowsy afternoon, I have almost the identical situation. "Bearmat this is Bird Dog, Fire Mission, Victor Charlie in open." Yet again, a single Viet Cong is in the open, only this time he appears either drunk or on drugs, as he is staggering and behaving erratically. I think,

"Well, nice to know the Viet Cong have stupid privates also, but this one is going to be a dead one."

The observer adjusts with two shells, Mr. Charles runs and we briefly play cat and mouse as before, only this time he escapes to the safety of a large grove of trees and underbrush where he cannot be observed. However the woods have a discrete boundary, and Bird Dog hovering above can observe if he breaks cover.

Bird Dog and I discuss the situation, and in what is a lapse of judgment on my part, decide to pursue him. I calculate how many grid squares the woods occupy, and decide to work each grid square over with the two batteries of artillery each firing three volleys, or thirty-six high explosive shells into 1000 square meters, or two-thirds of a square mile. If high explosives don't kill him, falling trees will. There are many grid squares and this will require many shells.

I give the commands, and the batteries jump into action. The continuing roar of the guns signal to the Battalion Operations Officer, Major Hawkins, that something really significant is underway. Perhaps a unit is being overrun somewhere. I am already thinking,

"I screwed up, this isn't worth it, and I should call this off." Major Hawkins walks in.

"What's up, Lieutenant Booth?" he asks. I sheepishly explain, and he suggests that this is perhaps overkill and for me to shut things down.

"Yes Sir," I reply and give commands to cease-fire.

Later I conclude he and Major Brosnan, the battalion commander, must have a lot of confidence in me for I never hear another word about this incident.

Strangely, in writing these words decades later, I hope Mr. Charles got away and is sitting somewhere telling his grandchildren about the crazy Marines who tried to kill him but couldn't.

Notes:

1. In the early 1970's I cross paths with Major Brosnan in the Marine Corps Reserves where he is a Colonel and my Regimental Commander. He remembers me very well from Vietnam, and positively I might add.

2. In 2005 I run into Corporal Bill Henry at a reunion. He looks exactly the same, and has retired as a successful banker in Albany, New York.

3. In 2007 I run into 1st Lieutenant Don Rosenberg at a reunion, and thank him for that evening he watched over me in the Fire Direction Center. He retired as a Lieutenant Colonel after twenty plus years in the Marine Corps, and he and his wife live in Florida.

TRANSFER TO INDIA BATTERY

On September 7, 1965, the upside-down-top-of-the-food-chain-life of 2nd Lieutenants John Booth and Dick Cavagnol abruptly ends for we are both transferred to India Battery as forward observers and immediately go to the bottom of the food chain where we should have been all along. 1st Lieutenants Sam Turner and Larry Walker replace us in Whiskey Battery as fire direction officer and executive officer, respectively.

In civilian terms we will serve as artillery spotters for the rifle companies, and when we observe the enemy we will call in fire. Of course the enemy, will also observe us, which will lead to some interesting situations. Actually, both Dick and I welcome the change. Most people won't understand that, but then most people don't volunteer for the Marines.

I dash off a quick letter to Mom and Dad, *"my new job is forward observer –I'm attached to K Co – so consequently where they go so do I. "* and I say nothing more about what my new assignment entails!

In Vietnam I was assigned to three artillery batteries and worked with three infantry battalions. India Battery was the unit that became home with all the connotations that the word home means. The battery was part of the 1st Marine Brigade, had landed in Vietnam in April of 1965, and the officers and men had served together for several years and had formed a tight-knit bond. I would be with India Battery for the next seven months, and it was where I was fully transformed into an Officer of Marines.

The commanding officer was Captain Donnie Newt Harmon. He had served in Korea as an enlisted Marine, had later been commissioned as an officer, and was a real character. He kept a journal, which 1st Lieutenant Steve Soechtig, our Naval Gunfire Spotter, typed into a readable format. Soechtig had a literary streak and a dry wit, and the journal became a rich and humorous chronological narrative of our adventures and covered the gamut from the funny to the tragic. For example:

2 Sep. The men were paid in MPC (military payment dollars) today. The legal rate of exchange for piasters (Vietnamese currency) is 118 per MPC dollar. The rate of exchange for greenbacks is about 10 years.

4 Sep. LtCol. Taylor advised Capt. Harmon to allow cows to graze in the ravine by his tent between 0800 and 1600. There is a young cow herder named Bao who the Capt has semi-adopted. He has given the boy a toothbrush.

We also have goats mating in the area.

14 Sep. Capt. Harmon has rounded up two goats for Capt Bao. One is for stud service and the other is for fattening up.

Oh for the life of a goat, the first goat anyway!

Rumor had it the Captain envisioned writing a book later in life. Captain Harmon was transferred to the battalion staff as the logistics officer on October 15, and regrettably the battery journal stopped. First Lieutenant Bill Schaeffer becomes our commanding officer.

Dick and I move into a large tent where all the junior officer forward observers and naval gunfire spotters are billeted. There are six of us, Dick Cavagnol, Rob Kelly, Wayne Hawkins, John Booth, Steve Soechtig and Bob Franklin. We all become fast friends and in recent years have re-connected at reunions where we lie a lot, and talk about how brave we were.

My first patrol becomes eventful for what it was not. A reconnaissance platoon needs a forward observer for a night ambush and I volunteer. It's not a deep patrol and we arrive in position on the edge of a gravel road after a short hike. I lie on my stomach on a bed of gravel the entire night. Nothing happens and I return in the morning, bored, sleep-deprived, and sore from lying on a bed of rocks.

Now, Dear Reader, think about this for a moment, and if you wish to duplicate this experience go out into your front yard at dusk, take a broomstick, pretend it's a rifle, lie on your stomach all night, and pretend to shoot anyone who ventures down the street. In the morning you are allowed to come in for a cold shower and a hot meal. Repeat the following night.

I will serve as a forward observer in Phu Bai for Kilo Company of the 3rd Battalion 4th Marine Regiment from September 7 until November 14, when I will be assigned to a new rifle company and we will be ordered to a combat outpost south of Da Nang. During this time our battalion will sustain five killed in action and thirty-six wounded.

With the South Vietnamese Army

It's the usual hot steamy afternoon on September 9. Steve Soechtig and I, along with our forward observation teams, are crowded into the back of a two and one-half ton truck traveling into Hue City. Route One is packed as we pass a steady stream of Vietnamese humanity, women in white flowing dresses, farmers in rice paddies with water buffalo, and lots of laughing children. The wind in our faces is a welcome relief.

A joint operation is to be held with the Vietnamese Army to sweep the villages of Viet Cong in the Nam Hoa subsector on both sides of the Ta Trach River. The operation is within range of our artillery, and Steve and I volunteered to be the forward observers with a rifle company of the South Vietnamese Army. We are to meet two advisors, Captain Furman of the United States Army and Warrant Officer Doan of the Australian Army, at the Military Assistance Advisory Compound in Hue City.

We enter the compound and suddenly find ourselves in a different world. Since July our living conditions had come under the category of advanced camping, but not this place. The sudden blast of cold air as we open the door is a surprise and welcome relief, air conditioning! Next, we are instructed to hang our weapons on wall pegs, which we reluctantly do, and suddenly feel naked. The wall is covered with an assortment of hanging weaponry from tommy guns, carbines, rifles, pistols, and I don't know what all, and reminds one of a gangsters' convention.

Then we walk into the dining room where, surprise, surprise, we see tables covered with tablecloths, china, silverware, napkins, and ice tinkling in cold drinks! We sit down for a regular meal with pretty young waitresses and food cooked in a kitchen with real chefs. The patrons in this surreal scene are all Marine and Army advisors. We meet Captain Furman and Warrant Officer Doan, get acquainted and have a sumptuous feast.

My reaction? Furman and Doan are advisors with the South Vietnamese Army and spend most of their time in the rice paddies and jungle and deserve every bit of luxury they can get. During the Tet Offensive in January of 1968, the North Vietnamese Army will seize Hue City, and this advisors' compound will become a lone holdout and the scene of heavy fighting.

It's dark when we scramble back aboard the trucks and continue on our journey, which takes us through back streets and sections of Hue we didn't know existed. Hue is the old imperial capital of Vietnam when it was part of French Indochina, and we see French influence everywhere, houses, paved streets, sidewalks, street lights, shade trees, all delight our eyes, and for a moment I'm back home on Stanhope Avenue in Richmond, Virginia, on a cool summer evening.

We soon leave the bright lights of civilization and abruptly enter the dark world of the jungle. Pavement ceases, the road narrows, the truck slows, branches scrape the sides and we duck our heads and keep on going. The word ambush enters my mind, but our advisors continue on with seemingly not a care, so I quit worrying.

We enter a Vietnamese Army compound in darkness. This is my first encounter with Vietnamese troops and dogs, cats, chickens, wives and children surround us. There are two howitzers inside the wire, and I observe that the howitzer trails, which absorb the recoil when the cannons are fired, are embedded in concrete. This restricts the howitzers to only firing within an arc of 50 degrees.

Not good, this place can be overrun pretty easily! If the Viet Cong attack outside the arc of 50 degrees the howitzer cannot be moved to change the direction of fire. Our battery has perfected a technique where we can fire a complete circle of 360 degrees.

I tell myself, "Oh well, nothing I can do about this now. Get a good night's sleep, Booth."

We're shown a patch of ground where we bed down. Now my insides had never completely recovered from the bout of dysentery I had in late July. We live and work in a world of dirt and filth so we all suffer to some degree with intestinal discomfort. Well, this intestinal discomfort suddenly hits me and I have to go, quickly. There is a privy close by, but the stench flowing through the yawning opening is unbearable, and the huge blackness inside means I could fall in the hole. I don't have a flashlight and we are in complete black out with no lights, so I decide the privy where I cannot see is not an option. Like a cat, I scramble on my hands and knees to find some bushes, scrape a hole, do my business and then do my best to cover the mess. I crawl back to where my team is stretched out and go to sleep.

The next day the operation begins bright and early, and I have two memories from that day.

We're straggling along a road in no particular formation. It's mid-morning beneath a deep blue sky, and the sun is hot and getting hotter. Our forward observation team is spaced out and we are as tactically sound as we can make ourselves. Vietnamese soldiers are in front of us, behind us, talking, ambling, holding hands (it's a part of their culture), and generally not paying attention to anything.

Shots suddenly ring out and rounds start zipping and cracking overhead. Then they stop. Nothing much changes with the Vietnamese, and they don't seem to care. It occurs to me,

"These guys are about as tactical as peanut butter, and   if we get into a fight, we're in trouble."

We never do find out who was shooting at us.

The next memory is of ancient ruins, massive columns and structures overrun with vines, and hulking trees pushing aside stone slabs. Sunlight filters through heavy canopy and dappled shadows dance on steps covered with leaves.   No movement or sound except the Vietnamese and us. The map shows royal tombs in the area. Maybe so, but this place is eerie, which leads to the expectation of an ambush on us. Nothing happens and we are back in base camp by nightfall.

There are three levels to the Vietnamese Army:

The Army of the Republic of Vietnam, (ARVN) or the Regular Army.

The Regional Forces, (RF's) roughly equivalent to our National Guard.

The Popular Forces, (PF's) roughly equivalent to our Colonial Militia.

These troops are Regional Forces. In defense of the Army, they have been fighting communist insurgents, known originally as the Viet Minh and now the Viet Cong, for close to twenty years and appear worn out.

I would work with and fight with the Vietnamese Army during parts of my tour in Vietnam. I know they had units that fought well, because I had friends who were advisors either to the Vietnamese Army or Marine Corps. From my personal experience though, the words "worn out" are as good as any to describe how I felt. In 1969 when President Nixon announced the policy to turn the ground fighting over to the South Vietnamese Army, I never felt warm and fuzzy that the plan would work.

As I write these words a scene tumbles into my mind's eye. I'm perched on an observation post on a high hill at night. We're surrounded by triple concertina barbwire, and the slope is so steep a mountain goat would have difficulties. We are gathered around what passes for a small fire, well hidden, where we are sharing smoky air, C-rations and a Vietnamese dish that sounds like its called "muc-nong.

Through an interpreter I ask one old wrinkled veteran,

"How long have you been fighting communists?"

"Forty years," he answers.

"Tell me more," I say.

"I fight with Chiang Kai-shek, and when he go Taiwan I go south to Burma."

Somehow this old buzzard wound up in the South Vietnamese Army.

"Why do you still fight?"

"I hate Communists."

I'm getting a lesson in the geopolitics of Southeast Asia.

Which leads to the question, what did I believe at age twenty-three as a young Marine Officer?

I believed that communism was evil, and that the United States had a strategy of containment, which to me meant we fought communism wherever it tried to expand. I believed that South Vietnam was our ally and would fall to communism if we didn't help. I believed we held the moral high ground, and that South Vietnam would be a better nation if we prevailed, and whether one believed that or not, the alternative of communism was far worse.

President Kennedy's Inaugural Address inspired me:

Let every nation know, whether it wishes us well or ill, that we shall pay any price, bear any burden, meet any hardship, support any friend, oppose any foe to assure the survival and the success of liberty.

And so my fellow Americans, ask not what your country can do for you, ask what you can do for your country.

I believed President Lyndon Johnson when he described the Gulf of Tonkin incident as an unprovoked attack by North Vietnam on two American warships on the high seas, plainly an Act of War. I believed our civilian and military leaders knew how to fight a war, and I still believe all the above, except this last paragraph.

The Gulf of Tonkin Incident was not "unprovoked". Only one warship was attacked and that was probably aggravated by a gross communication failure on our part. President Lyndon Johnson, Secretary of Defense Robert McNamara, and General William Westmoreland did not know how to fight the war!

THE KILLING ZONE

War is about killing people, and sometimes you kill the wrong people. Tonight I will learn that lesson in spades, and will also learn we fight another enemy in addition to the Viet Cong. Anyone who thinks war is rational and organized is crazy. War is confusion and mistakes.

It's September 12 and I'm five days into my new assignment as a forward observer with a rifle company. This is my second combat patrol.

Our strategy is two-fold. First, send Marines into the villages, embed them with the local militia, and form Combined Action Companies to protect the population. Second, saturate the upland area west of the villages with patrols to interdict Viet Cong units, which sneak into the villages at night for re-supply. Force them to stay in the mountains and starve.

My artillery battery has divided our four forward observation teams so we can now support eight infantry patrols. Typically we spend one night in base camp with hot food, showers, cots and tents, and then several days and nights with a rifle unit operating in the western highlands.

My role is to whisper numbers into a radio and like magic, death and destruction will suddenly appear. I can make the earth erupt with explosives, make the sky rain hot steel, and turn night into day. I can mark targets for other instruments of mayhem, and most terrible of all, I can burn. With white phosphorous I can touch human skin with unimaginable pain and sear to the bone, and I can ignite an inferno and burn a village to the ground. In short, if there is ever such a thing as an agent of death, it's me.

The tools of my trade include a map in my left pocket and a compass in my right. My brain becomes a global positioning system. My navigational instincts become that of a latter day Daniel Boone, and I am not allowed to be lost. I know my precise location on a 1:50000 meter map, and speak a new language with words like "fire for effect" and "drop 400."

My radio operator, David Henderson, is my constant companion for without him I am nothing. He is one of two lifelines to the rear if we call for help. Our radio has a range of eight miles, is a Korean War relic, and is prone to malfunction so Henderson always carries a spare battery and handset.

I am developing a system for carrying all the accouterments necessary for war. Each item has a precise location on my person so in the heat of combat I will not have to think.

Are my dog tags taped? Do I have my notebook with pen in my left front pocket? Is my 45-caliber automatic pistol clean and oiled? Do I have four magazines on my belt each with only seven rounds? I have already learned that over seven rounds will jam the pistol. I am an expert shot with the .45, but really want a shotgun for self- defense. It will take a few firefights to sort this issue out.

At the operations tent I pick up the patrol overlay and exchange call signs. Mine is Primrose India. We are going out for two nights and our instructions are "...for a period of 48 hours remain concealed and conduct night ambushes..." The Captain of Kilo Company, Tom Marino, will lead the patrol, which gives me a sense of confidence. I don't know him well, but he has a reputation of being calm and collected under fire.

The patrol leaves mid-afternoon, and only after we pass the last sentry do I slide a round into the chamber of my pistol. Then ever so carefully I put a finger between the hammer and the firing pin and slowly squeeze the trigger. The hammer moves forward and rests on half-cock safety. There are two ways to put the pistol on safety and this is the one I use. With one motion I can pull my pistol from the holster, cock the hammer, aim, and squeeze the trigger.

Trucks take us part way, and then we disembark and walk due south through the villages along Route One. Nighttime falls, the moon has yet to rise, and blackness and silence engulf the column. Dog tags, canteens and anything that can make a sound is wrapped as we proceed. White tape on the back of our helmets ensures we see the Marine in front. Surrounded by darkness, the rancid smell of a village engulfs us, along with an eerie silence. We see a faint glow from a candle in a grass hut, and hear an occasional dog barking in the distance. The villagers know we're moving through, but not a sound of recognition passes between us.

I am one-third of the way down the file of Marines, and if needed by the patrol leader for consultation, a whisper "Arty Up" will pass down the column, and I will quickly move to the front.

We turn west, pass through rice paddies, cow pastures, barb wire fences, and eventually leave signs of habitation behind. We stride silently through scrub brush and open land, and continue for an hour before we reach our destination.

In front of us is a dirt road running from the mountains in the west to the villages in the east. The Marines are professional, and we construct the Killing Zone, that precise section of the road where we position the enemy before we destroy them. Machine guns are positioned at each end, and will sweep the road with interlocking bands of fire. As a coup-de grace we have attached hand grenades to detonation cord in a ditch on the far side of the road. If our quarry leaps that way, there is still no way out.

Everyone finds his spot quickly, and like apparitions we disappear into the high grass beside the road. A wire is strung snug along the ground in front of us, and we go on fifty-percent alert with every other Marine awake. Most of our ambushes consist of fruitless nights lying in the weeds where nothing happens, and we learned by trial and error that requiring everyone wide awake all the time doesn't work.

If the enemy approaches from either end, a Marine will pull the wire to alert the entire ambush. We wait until they reach the center of the killing zone, the patrol leader pulls the trigger, and then we slaughter whoever is in front.

The villagers know Marine patrols are operating in isolated areas west toward the mountains and there is a curfew in effect. All this has been cleared with the village chiefs and relayed to the local population in order to minimize the risk to civilians.

Stay off the roads at night! What could go wrong?

Henderson and I are behind Captain Marino in the center of the ambush. We are facing away from the road, and providing rear security. We have the radio between us with the hand set squished against an ear. One of us relaxes while the other keeps radio watch and peers into the blackness.

All is silent, the moon floats across the sky, shadows dance on the edge of the darkness, normal night sounds return, crickets resume chirping and whatever nocturnal creatures are around continue with their normal habits.

We wait.

Suddenly there is a pull on the wire, the world stands still for a brief moment in time, and then a roar of weaponry and explosions shatter the darkness. I crawl to Captain Marino.

"Do you want illumination, Skipper?"

"Not yet, John, let's see what develops."

Suddenly shouts of "cease fire, cease fire" penetrate the night and all firing stops abruptly. We hear moans and crying from crumpled heaps of clothing in the center of the moonlight-dappled road.

Now I believe the world runs according to the laws of science and physics. I don't believe in the supernatural, and I don't believe in miracles, but a miracle is as good an explanation as any as to what we see in the middle of the road.

Six women are on their knees, crying and wailing, all uninjured, except for one slightly wounded.

Maybe our Marines saw the women and fired high, maybe we were just plain incompetent, or maybe there really was a miracle. We treat the wounded woman, take all six of them, and move to a new defensive position in an area with high grass and trees.

Silence settles in again and soon it's as if none of this violence ever happened. A bright moon moves across the sky, shadows lengthen, a gentle breeze is blowing, and moonlit grass waves in front of me as I struggle to stay awake. My mind's eye snaps a warm picture with fuzzy edges that will remain with me through the years.

Comes the dawn and we move the women to a pick-up point where they are taken to the rear and turned over to the Vietnamese authorities. We never do find out their story, but surmise they may have been visiting their Viet Cong brothers and husbands in the hinterlands west of us.

I am eternally grateful we did no harm to those women, and often wonder how I would feel if we had!

Notes: 3rd Battalion 4th Marines Command Chronology, September 1965, Map Hue Sheet 6541 IV, 1st ambush position grid 931064, in position at 7:30 pm. Ambush triggered at 11:20 p.m. stream position grid 891094, 2nd ambush position grid 906096. See pages, 6, 34-35, and 64-65. I will meet up with Tom Marino again at a reunion in San Diego in 2015 and Las Vegas in 2017. Tom thinks a miracle is as good an explanation as any.

Also see India Battery Journal September 13.

Water

We prepare to move out. There is just one problem; I'm out of water. Normally I am judicious about the quantity I drink, not wanting to run out, but the excitement of the previous night had caused me to consume more than I should have. Whatever the reason, I'm out of water.

It is a hot humid day, heating up fast with temperatures heading into the hundreds. We have a long hot slog ahead of us, and I know I am in trouble. I learn we are heading toward water, but I don't know how far or how long it will take to get there.

Heat casualties are a big problem for Marines in the field. We eventually become acclimated, laugh and joke about long hot walks in the sun, learn to take salt tablets with religious zeal, become judicious on drinking water, and next to ammunition we come to value a cool drink of water as a priceless commodity. But we still collapse from heat exhaustion.

The sauna-like atmosphere contributes to casualties from booby traps and land mines. Our flak jackets are heavy and hot, and there is always a temptation to unzip the front for coolness. Unfortunately this exposes the throat and thorax area to damage from shrapnel, and more than a few Marines pay the price for this temptation.

Many a time when the going gets rough I daydream about sitting in the backyard of my girlfriend's parents' house in Waynesboro, Virginia, sipping a cold glass of ice tea, hearing the ice cubes tinkle and looking at the Blue Ridge Mountains. At the same time I will be forcing myself to keep putting one foot in front of the other. On my Vietnam tour I will be pushed to the limits of my physical endurance twice. Both times I am out of water and this is one of those times. I will remember this trek in my old age.

It's now mid- morning and the coolness of the night has long since disappeared. The sky is a deep blue, the heat is crushing, the air so humid it drips, and my canteens are bone-dry. I hold them to my lips to insure I have drained the last drop. I'm in column, ten feet behind the Marine in front, I keep my eyes focused on the back of his helmet and don't think of anything else. I tell my feet to keep moving.

He's starting to bob and weave and I don't know whether it's him or me. I feel myself start to waver then jerk myself upright and think: I'm an Officer. Marines look up to me. If I fall out they will too. Keep moving. I think of Officer Candidate School and the Hill Trail. If I can survive that I can survive this. I lose track of time, but finally word is passed down the column, "water ahead."

I break through the underbrush and see a sparkling clear stream gurgling over rocks and pebbles as it hurries further to the east. As the scene unfolds I think of Gideon in the Old Testament Bible as he selects his warriors on how they drink water, "…and the number of them that drank putting their hand to their mouth …" The Marines tight discipline and professionalism come natural, as we cross the stream, set up guards and ever alert, wait by squads, weapons at the ready, until it's our turn to water.

I have halazone tablets to purify water, and when our turn comes I don't remember whether I used them or just drank straight from the stream. What I do remember is I drop my gear, walk to the middle of the stream, lie on my stomach, and let the water run into my face and over me. I then turn over, let the water lap all around me, look up at the beautiful blue sky and fluffy white clouds, and think "life is good-I'm happy."

Henderson does the same. We set up a defensive perimeter, well hidden in the underbrush. We rig a poncho on a bush, crawl underneath it, put the radio between us and "crap out". I have a paperback novel and we alternate between reading, sleeping, and radio watch.

We spend the day here. Night comes and we set up another ambush, and the next morning meet trucks on the road and return to base camp.

Long hot walks in the sun cause casualties as well as the Viet Cong.

And so continues my education in the war.

Notes: 3rd Battalion 4th Marines Command Chronology, July 1965. Terrain and Weather. "The weather is predominately hot and humid. Daytime highs range from 85 to 115 degrees Fahrenheit with an average humidity of 85%." The chart shows what that was like in what we called "a long hot walk in the sun." We operated in the Danger and Extreme Danger Zone and the sun was an additional enemy.

NOAA's National Weather Service
Heat Index
Temperature (°F)

Likelihood of Heat Disorders with Prolonged Exposure or Strenuous Activity

Caution   Extreme Caution   Danger   Extreme Danger

RIVER CROSSING

The heavens that September of 1965 suddenly opened with a deluge of water that made the biblical flood pale by comparison. It was as if I had been resting on a sunny beach when a tsunami abruptly rises up from the sea and swallows me. I didn't know water could fall in such quantity and so fast. I'm a 2nd lieutenant forward observer with a Marine rifle company in Vietnam and the monsoon season has arrived. In addition to the Viet Cong, Mother Nature has also joined the ranks of the enemy.

The deluge was accompanied by a howling wind thirty to forty miles per hour. Rain blew sideways left to right, and then right to left. It blew upside down and then right side up.

From the India Battery Journal: *The long expected and awaited monsoon season has arrived with 48 hours of rain and no letup in sight.*

From a letter home: *Dear Mom and Dad...rainy season is really on us. It has rained straight for the last 36 hours like I've never seen before-guess this is only the beginning. Life could really start to get miserable-roads washing out, no dry clothes...*

Our world was transformed. Farmers' pastures and rice paddies where we patrolled became a vast inland sea. Rivers and streams rose up out of their banks, and we were never quite sure if our next step in knee deep water would suddenly plunge us over our heads. We now had to worry about drowning. In Vietnam death stalked us constantly in a variety of guises.

It's September 16 and once again I'm out with another platoon of Kilo Company with instructions, "*for a period of 48 hours remain concealed and conduct night ambushes.*" The executive officer, 1st Lieutenant Gil Bronson, leads the patrol of forty Marines, and intelligence has indicated Viet Cong activity in our vicinity. During September there will be several firefights with both Viet Cong and Marines killed and wounded in this area.

I'm slogging through an inland sea that was once a farmer's field. My constant companion and radio operator Lance Corporal David Henderson is an arm's length away, and if I need to call in fire I merely reach for the handset. Water is knee deep, could suddenly plunge to over–our-head-deep, and none of us are sure of our footing. We are proceeding slowly and methodically. A foggy mist floats through the air and a cloudy sky spits rain intermittently. Heavy clouds hug the ground toward the mountains to our west. Muddy water intermixed with vegetation swirls around our legs and a small intermittent current wanders in no particular direction. Water snakes glide through leaving small v-shaped ripples as evidence of their passing.

I hold a map as I attempt to keep our bearings. I know the Nong River is ahead with a precipice drop of fifteen feet. Earlier I had scrambled up and down its near-vertical banks with almost impenetrable vegetation when it was just a shallow gurgling stream. Today that benign stream has overflowed its banks and is now a silent, swift, malevolent river. Where ground drops away and river begins is a mystery.

A hand signal from ahead and the patrol stops. Everyone faces outboard and we feel vulnerable. There is nagging fear of both drowning and gunfire. Word filters down the column that we have found the river and will start to cross.

"Mr. Booth, if we take fire from Mr. Charles, there's no place to hide. We certainly can't hug the ground."

"I agree, Henderson, I want to get across this river and be done with it."

Now a river crossing without bridges or boats is a hazardous undertaking at best, much less under combat conditions. The objective is to get everyone across quickly and safely, and at the same time maintain security on both sides of the river. Your unit is vulnerable as it is split in two with unequal strength as one side gains and the other loses.

All Marines have some degree of water training. In Basic School as young officers we had to jump into a pool with rifle held high, swim to the other side, and emerge with rifle dry. We had abandon ship drill where we leaped from a high diving board, with one hand clasping our nose and the other clasping our gonads, whereupon we rose to the surface and swam to the end.

I was an Eagle Scout and certified as a Senior Lifesaver with the American Red Cross and Explorer Scouts. At age eighteen I had a summer job as a lifeguard. I still remember the terrible claustrophobic feeling in a lifesaving exercise in ten feet of black impenetrable water at age fourteen. I could not see my hand in front of my face, and it took several attempts before I could overcome my fears, swim to the bottom, and retrieve a garbage can lid.

I'm standing thigh deep in water somewhere before the invisible drop off. I can tell it's the river though, because a few yards in front there is a swift silent current where branches, leaves and vegetation swirl as they rush downstream, and periodically small bushes and trees will rise to the surface only to be sucked under again. Whirlpools appear and disappear. Toward the bank the current ebbs and flows in circles as it makes its way through the small trees standing upright in the water. I visualize the branches and vines beneath the surface, and imagine being sucked under and entrapped, never to surface again.

I hear cursing behind me. "We have to cross that."

To say that the river was evil is like saying a man-eating tiger is evil. A tiger's not evil, it's just a tiger and it does what tigers sometimes do when they're hungry. But I can't think of another word to describe that scene and the sense of foreboding it projected.

It's dusk. A Marine swims a rope across the river and ties it to a tree on the other side. On our side the rope is anchored to a small tree leaning out over swirling water. We cannot see the drop off beneath us but we now it's there. In turn each Marine moves deeper into the swollen river, places his pack and rifle on an air mattress, and either pulls himself hand over hand on the rope, or keeps one hand on the rope and swims across. The air mattress is pulled over and back by another rope, and the next Marine takes his turn.

Henderson comments, "Mr. Booth, I think the river is still rising."

In front of me, PFC William Henry, a member of a machine gun crew, is on the rope and starting to cross. Draped across both shoulders are belts of machine gun ammunition in addition to his personal weapon and gear. I'm next and I think it wise to unbuckle the belt that supports my web gear. I'm not worried about drowning, but if I go beneath the surface, at least that weight won't be dragging me down.

Suddenly, the tree anchor snaps loose in front of me, the unleashed rope coils like a whip, and PFC William Henry drops and disappears like a stone into an abyss, fifteen feet to the bottom in a swift-flowing river.

Memory does not recall the timing and sequence of what happens next as there is a quick scramble away from the bank as we make sense of what happened. My first conscious thought is that it is beyond a reasonable doubt that Henry is dead in fifteen feet of water, held down by the weight of ammunition-belts and his gear. He has been under far too long to survive, and I do not need to entertain any thoughts of diving after him.

With Henry dead the first priority is to get the patrol on the same side of the river. The rope crossing is re-established and I swim side stroke through the swirling water, holding on to the rope to keep from being swept downstream, kicking with my feet, boots still on. The water isn't cold which is a surprise. I reach the far bank, which is higher, and hands and voices reach down to pull me up.

"Give me your hand, Lieutenant."

"Glad to see you, Mr. Booth."

We stop the patrol, and go into a defensive position as night falls. We do not get the entire patrol across the river before dark, and now we are split in two. I am standing on the riverside with Lieutenant Gil Bronson, and am calling in continuous illumination, as we make an attempt to find and recover Henry's body.

Illumination shells burst over top of one another every thirty seconds. The resemble roman candles stacked one atop the other in the dark sky. They slowly drift to the ground, illuminating the night. If the timing and altitude are correct the shell extinguishes just as it hits the ground. The light patterns and shadows dance all around, and the only sound is the hiss of the flames as the shells descend beneath their parachute. This is a fruitless attempt and after a while we quit and await help to arrive in the daylight.

In the early morning the weather clears slightly and South Vietnam Army troops and Captain Tom Marino arrive in sampans with long poles and grappling hooks. We find Henry after several hours and his body is heli-lifted to base camp.

Later, after all this is over, it occurs to me that I was next in line, and had the rope pulled free on me I would have been in difficulty. I'm a strong swimmer and had unbuckled my belt to drop my gear so I don't think I would have drowned, but you never know.

I didn't bring back any demons from the War, but I must admit that when the wind howls in the night and the rain beats against the side of the house, I think of that river crossing. I would leave Vietnam ten months later in July of 1966. I would lose twenty pounds, have more close calls and see more death. I would have no regrets,

except one.

I should have dived for PFC William James Henry, and maybe, just maybe, I might have brought him back alive.

Notes:

1. Command Chronology 3rd Battalion, 4th Marines, September 1965. See pages; 7, 34, 67, 68, 92. Henry's body was found over 1000 feet from where he entered the water, which indicates a strong current, in spite of the much entangling underbrush. In writing and researching this story decades later I think I did the right thing, but I must admit I'm not 100% sure.

2. India Battery Journal. See September 16-19.

3. On September 19, 1965, Chaplain Roswog held a memorial service for PFC Henry.

4. I did not know PFC Henry personally as I had been with Kilo Company only eight days. He was from Long Island City, New York, was born on December 21, 1943 and was Roman Catholic. He is memorialized on the Vietnam Wall on Panel 02E line 84.

5. I would cross paths with Gil Bronson in the Marine Reserves in the 1970's and 1990's. I would meet up with both him and Tom Marino at a reunion in Las Vegas, Nevada in May of 2017. Tom is living in San Diego, California, and Gil in Williamsburg, Virginia.

ARMAGEDDON

It's early morning on September 27, and our helicopter, flitting like a dragonfly on a stifling day, suddenly swoops to the ground only to bounce up and make one more jump before finally landing, whereupon we quickly leap from the door, and run into the surrounding ten-foot-high elephant grass.   The chopper instantly becomes airborne as we move swiftly away from the landing zone where we pause and briefly listen. Silence settles in and the sun beats down.

I'm the leader of a ten-Marine patrol sent to an observation post on Hill 153 overlooking the Ta Trach River, deep in Indian country. The two pretend landings and third actual landing were to confuse any Viet Cong patrols in the area. There is no way to hide our entry into this no mans land, but at least the enemy will be confused as to where we actually disembark. Ours is a small patrol and depends on stealth to reach our objective.

This area along the river has seen plenty of enemy activity. Small firefights and sightings have occurred in previous months, and in September four different contacts resulted in twenty-five Viet Cong dead. Intelligence puts a Viet Cong battalion and two infantry companies in close proximity. We have been inserted into the thick of it and hope to sneak onto our objective and kill a few more. Like overturning a rock and watching roaches scurry, if one poked around the Ta Trach River something would happen. Well, we were poking.

We are part of a larger artillery-led operation and are to set up one of three observations posts, positioned on high hills along the river. Three and one-half miles southeast on Hill 207, 2nd Lieutenant Steve Brown, the forward observer with a reconnaissance platoon, has been in position since last night. Two miles southeast on Hill 163, 2nd Lieutenants Wayne Hawkins and Dick Cavagnol and their teams are also moving into position. The mortar battery has been heli-lifted to the base of Hill 163, and in the evening a rifle platoon will be located close by to provide support if necessary. A howitzer battery has also been moved forward. We are under a broad umbrella of artillery support and can strike suddenly like a snake.

Well hidden in the tall elephant grass and intermittent patches of underbrush, I take a compass bearing, and silently and stealthily our patrol winds its way upward until we reach the crest of Hill 153. On top I find an elevation marker installed by a French survey crew when Vietnam was part of French Indochina. The number 153 represents the height in meters above sea level so Hill 153 is 502 feet high, and presents a commanding view of the terrain for miles in all directions. No wonder the French put a survey marker up here.

We make a careful search for trip wires or any other signs of booby traps from Mr. Charles, and also find c-ration trash so we are not the first Marines to occupy these heights. The sides of the hill are at a 45-degree angle, which gives us an added degree of safety. We position our machine guns, set up local security and settle in to the business at hand – which is "observing."

Even though we have the added zing of being isolated on the western edge of our area, we really don't expect anything to happen. The top of the hill is devoid of any vegetation and we anticipate this will be another boring, hot, sweltering, little water day.

One issue that is understated is how much time we spent doing "nothing" when manning an observation post or lying in ambush. By "nothing" I mean:

Sitting all night wrapped in your poncho, rain beating in your face, water dripping down your neck, a radio headset squished to your ear, and staring at the darkness. Or sitting all day under a scorching sun, little water, no shade, binoculars to your eyes and scanning the terrain.

Hill 225 and Hill 180 were permanent observation posts we all took turns manning, but they were closer to our base camp, secure, civilized, with infantry support, bunkers, barbwire, and cover from the sun. But even though we were in a combat zone, each of the above examples had one thing in common.

It was all very boring, 98% of the time.

Now, Dear Reader, if you want a comparable experience go up on an asphalt roof on a hot summer day with a set of binoculars, spy on your neighbors, and observe the street in front of your house. Stay there all day and do not come down for any reason.

Sometime after our arrival our artillery battalion commander, Lieutenant Colonel Edwin Rudzis, joins us with his small entourage. I do not remember how or when he arrived, and I think, "Lots of radio antennas up here now. What small chance we had of being unnoticed is gone." However, he is very personable and I enjoy talking to him.

In mid-morning roaches start scurrying.

Hawkins on Hill 163 observes Viet Cong in a village across the river and calls in fire. Two adjusting rounds bracket a structure, and three Viet Cong attempt to sneak out. However, they didn't sneak out quickly enough, for Hawkins calls Fire for Effect and devastates the area.

At 11:50 am, Brown on Hill 207 catches eight Viet Cong crossing the river on a boat, blows the boat out of the water, and chases the Viet Cong into the underbrush. He then pulverizes the area with 200 rounds of high explosives, whereupon the quick reaction platoon led by Lieutenant Jack Downing, is heli-lifted into the area to search for bodies. Later Downing reports the area is so overgrown it would be possible to have 100 bodies there and never find a one.

Meanwhile back on Hill 153, I have no knowledge of these events, and am bored stiff. It's 2:20 pm and I am scanning the river yet again. My arms are tired from holding the binoculars so I drop my arms to rest. Lieutenant Colonel Rudzis, sitting beside me scanning the river, drops his binoculars, says nothing, and points to the Ta Trach River five hundred feet below and one mile west.

Binoculars quickly to my eyes again and:

The river and its banks are crawling with Viet Cong, and at least twenty- five are crossing the river in boats. The enemy is so numerous they resemble a swarm of wasps.

My first reaction is embarrassment as my battalion commander spotted them first. I was just looking at this same area and didn't see a thing. My instantaneous second reaction is "get over it and put your brain in gear." Quickly I speak the magic words into the radio.

"Bearmat, this is Primrose India, fire mission, 25 Victor Charlie Crossing River, grid 782099, direction 4250, Victor Tango in effect. Out."

Translation: I have identified the target and transmitted their map coordinates with a compass direction. I have also requested airbursts, and will shower them with a rain of molten steel when I adjust the rounds on target. Every number is repeated back to insure no mistakes.

Five miles away in the battery, those six and four-digit numbers stream into the fire direction center, are quickly translated into four and three-digit numbers and rushed to the gun line. Commands are shouted; "Fire Mission" and gun crews drop whatever they are doing and race to the cannons. Two howitzers quickly roar in response.

After an eternity, but probably three minutes, back comes, "shot out." Two rounds are on their way, and I stick my head back up.

When artillery flies in an arc over your head, the shells roar like a freight train, not subtle like a mortar which drops vertically and will catch you by surprise. My quarry is unaware they are being observed, and that life as they know it is about to change. They are leisurely paddling across the river. Suddenly, they pause, look up, and quickly resume paddling with an urgency like there is no tomorrow.

As expected, the first two shells are over, explode long, and my friends on the boats are about to disappear around a bend in the river. I have a choice. Make another adjustment with only two rounds for a more precise location or make a broad guess and call fire and brimstone from the heavens. I opt for the latter.

"Drop 400, fire for effect."

Immediately the entire battery roars, air- bursts blanket a broad area, and I observe steel shrapnel pepper the river like rain. The Viet Cong have now disappeared around the bend, and probably into the village. The area is designated a Free Fire Zone and the village is abandoned. I call for more volleys and use every shell and fuse in our arsenal. Earth erupts, the sky rains shrapnel, and most terrible of all, the heavens pour burning white phosphorous. Fires ignite, an inferno blazes, flames lick over rooftops, and smoke billows toward the clouds. I call for more high explosives and white phosphorous, and for a brief moment in time I transform several acres of earth into Armageddon.

I probably killed and wounded a bunch of Viet Cong, but I don't really know. This is early in the war and McNamara's body count is not yet the all-encompassing foolish metric it will become to measure success. I did not see any enemy bodies thrown into the air, was unable to observe if any were lying about, and was not about to descend from our perch for a damage assessment and to count enemy dead. If we had done so, I would not be writing these words.

Of more immediate concern was that our position is probably compromised for sure. The Viet Cong aren't stupid, and we need to move. If they figure out where we are, which is likely, they will come after us, and reinforcements are over two miles away over rough terrain. We are alone and isolated.

Soon, Viet Cong are sighted at the base of our hill and are taken under fire. They scatter. Twilight approaches, we pack our gear and like the Longfellow poem, "…fold our tents like the Arabs and silently steal away." We stealthily descend from our perch and find a finger of land abutting the hill with dense vegetation and a steep drop off on three sides, a perfect place to hide. We quietly eat cold C-rations, go on 50% alert, and settle in for the night.

It's dark. A hand shakes my shoulder and a voice whispers in my ear. "Mr. Booth, Mr. Booth, I think people are moving outside our lines." The Marine and I crawl over to the edge, and sure enough, we hear movement and discern a dark shadow in the blackness. Suddenly without warning, the shadow breaks into movement and runs away. Whether it was a Viet Cong trying to get a fix on our position or a monkey, we never know. The rest of the night passes uneventfully and at early dawn we descend and a helicopter extracts us to base camp.

Epilogue

Until I read the declassified documents decades later, I did not pull all the threads of this yarn together. This was an artillery-led operation without infantry involvement. I think our artillery commander was on to a good strategy because in one day this "artillery sniping" did more damage to the Viet Cong than many infantry ambushes over many weeks combined. From my purview of many documents I think I sighted more Viet Cong than ever seen in one place at one time in the last six months.

If the infantry and by extension their communication network had been with us we could have launched an air observer immediately and who knows what we may have uncovered. Maybe we could have piled on rifle companies into the area and really torn the enemy apart.

Our commander wanted to do more of these "artillery sniping" operations, but to my knowledge we never did, and I don't know why.

Anyone who thinks fighting a war is a sane and organized activity is crazy!

Top Left: Forward Observer on Hill 153. I don't remember his name, but he was a cannoneer who wanted to learn to be an FO, so I took him on my team. He worked in a steel mill in Pittsburg, PA. He had a good- looking sister!

Top Right: Same Marine and our battalion commander, Lieutenant Colonel Rudzis on Hill 153. Note Ta Trach River at bottom of hills.

Middle Left: White Phosphorus shells. Fired as marking rounds as well as to start fires.

Middle Right: 2nd Lt. John Booth on observation post.

Bottom Left: Radio Operator on Hill 153. Note South China Sea in background. We could see for miles.

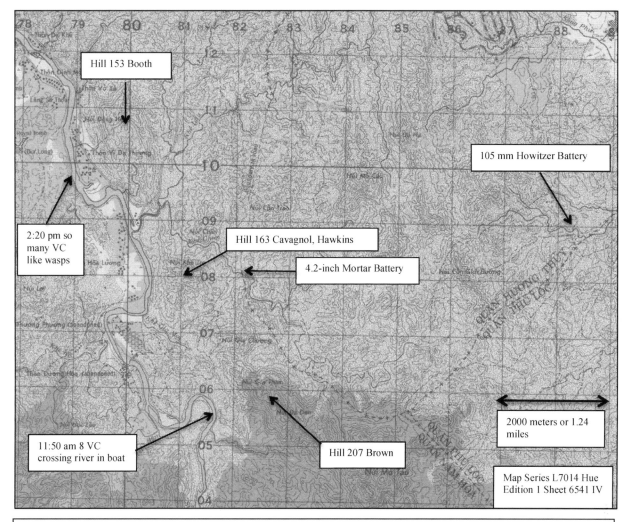

Information taken from September 1965 Command chronologies of: 3rd Bn. 4th Marines; pages 6, 19-20, 42, 47, 49, 76, 83; 4th Bn. 12th Marines; pages 6-7; India Battery Journal; September 22-October 10, pages 78-80.

Early in the am on September 27, the 4.2-inch Mortar Battery was heli-lifted to the base of Hill 163 grid 820082.

On the evening of September 27, the 1st platoon of India Company set up an ambush at Hill 107 grid 815092 to support the 4.2-inch Battery and the observation posts.

On the morning of September 27 India Battery displaced four 105-mm howitzers to grid 883092.

2nd Lieutenant Steve Brown was the forward observer with the 3rd platoon of the Reconnaissance Company located on Hill 207 grid 825059. He fired at 8 Viet Cong crossing the river at grid 815058 at 11:50am.

1st Lieutenant Jack Downing commanded the reaction force, the 1st platoon of India Company. Later Jack and I would spend 41 days together on Hill 41, a combat outpost south of Da Nang.

2nd Lieutenants Dick Cavagnol and Wayne Hawkins with their observation teams were located on Hill 163 grid 812079.

2nd Lieutenant John Booth with his observation team were located on Hill 153 grid 797108 and fired on numerous Viet Cong at grid 788099 at 2:20 pm.

THE VILLAGERS

"Rob, what's going on?" I ask.

I'm returning from an overnight ambush and have just entered the junior officers' tent where the 2nd lieutenant forward observers reside. I've spent another boring night huddled in the high grass beside some upland trail waiting to blast a Viet Cong patrol into oblivion. My fellow comrade in arms and forward observer, 2nd Lieutenant Rob Kelly is sitting on his cot looking glum.

"Captain Harmon put me in hock and restricted me to the mess hall, our tent and the latrine."

I grin and think this is going to be a good yarn. Captain Harman was a real character. He kept goats outside his tent among other things. I hadn't had a run-in with him yet, but others had.

Our battery has some imaginative thinkers, and we constructed a role for our howitzers in the counterinsurgency campaign we are waging in the countryside with the concept of preplanned fire. Vietnamese village chiefs on certain surveyed targets can call in artillery fire without the presence of a Marine forward observer. A trail intersection is a good example.

This concept demanded absolute accuracy on the first rounds. No adjustments. Our forward observers and survey crew would go out ahead of time and measure in the exact target location, and then with exquisite detail adjust artillery fire to these precise coordinates.

When you fire artillery close to your position, it's dangerous work, as consecutive shells fired from the same howitzer with the same data do not land in the same location. They impact the earth in a statistical pattern called a normal distribution curve. Consequently, to lessen the risk of injury from shrapnel we would fire base-ejection smoke rounds instead of high-explosive rounds. Smoke, not shrapnel, would then flood the air when the shell burst. Simple, eh? Even an idiot can to this.

When you have bullets cracking past your ears and you call in artillery for help, you are anxious and impatient. You want explosions immediately, like now. Not five minutes from now. Consequently, to shorten the process and relieve infantry anxiety, a certain sequence of words is used to convey information. The words are short, brief, and it is assumed unless the spotter specifies otherwise, the shell is high explosive. All this had been drilled into us in artillery school as well as tales of confused stupid spotters who called high explosives on themselves.

Rob continues, "I was calling in fire on a preplanned registration outside a village. Captain Harman was trying to impress Vietnamese officials and senior Marine officers with our artillery prowess."

"So what?" I ask.

"I forgot to change the shell request to smoke and we got high explosives instead" Rob responds. "Shrapnel was buzzing 'round our ears and we had to grovel in the mud. No one was hurt though."

Now a war with all its violence can change your sense of humor, and the thought of all those senior officers and dignitaries wallowing in the mud struck me as hilarious and I couldn't stop laughing. Rob didn't think it was so funny though. I did what I could to cheer him up and his quarantine was soon lifted.

I still remember the screams of terror that emanated from the radio when a fellow Marine, snuggling into the grass on some woebegone ambush discovered a rather large serpent occupying the same real estate. The snake didn't like it one bit and sunk his fangs into the unfortunate Marine. As I was currently going to work every day doing the same thing, that struck me as hilarious also. The Marine survived.

We had other interesting and hilarious encounters with wildlife, as there are documented accounts of tigers chomping on some surprised Marine and attempting to drag him away for supper. The tigers must not have liked the taste of Marine because there were no fatalities that I know of.

Rob and I would cross paths again eight months later in Operation Cherokee in a conventional war up north close to the DMZ. By then I would be twenty pounds lighter after weeks of continuous combat, but that's another story.

*****

In the early dawn when returning from an ambush in the western hinterlands we would wait in the hamlets astride Route One for our trucks to return us to base camp. I have an image frozen in memory of the early morning light displaying a rainbow of colors framing a fisherman silently polling his dugout on a still river. These were moments for reflection and I came to appreciate the beauty of the countryside and the quiet dignity of the Vietnamese people.

I had purchased a language book in Hue and attempted to haltingly speak some words and phrases, and I delighted in watching the interactions of children which reminded me of home. After a while the Marines and villagers came to trust one another, and we would purchase cold drinks from the small hamlet vendors.

Part of the Marine strategy was just plain acting nice to people. The villages were always overflowing with children so one day I tried an experiment. I had candy from home and I remembered a game my father taught me as a young lad. Two players place twenty-one stones in a pile between them, and each player then removes one, two or three stones in turn. The object is to force your opponent to be stuck with the last stone. The game involves a mathematical trick, and I never lost.

Through our interpreter I convince a young boy to play the game, and I promise him candy if he beats me. The lad is somewhat dubious at first, looks at me askance, but he agrees to play.

"You go first," I say, and we proceed to pick the pile of stones.

"Ah ha," I win. "No candy," I say. "Play again?"

He looks at me, leans his head to the side, and then grins, and I know I have him hooked. He reminds me of a squirrel studying a problem. He grabs one of his mates, they talk, and then we play again, and I win again. By this time a crowd has gathered and there is much talk and excitement.

"Who can beat this Marine?"

I figure whether I win or lose I better distribute candy, which I do accompanied by much laughter and frivolity. Parents wander over to see what the excitement is all about, and through halting Vietnamese and gestures I match up one father with his son and his mates and persuade them to let me take their picture. I would play this game in several hamlets, and after a while the villagers came to recognize me and would greet me with a shy smile and grin.

My fellow Marines noticed and one commented, "Mr. Booth, you certainly do like children." I would guess so, for as I write these words my wife and I have five daughters and eight grandchildren. I have played this game with my grandchildren and I lose every   time.

*****

"Lieutenant Booth, your scout sergeant Bob Jones has volunteered for a CAP team, so your going to be short-handed for a while."

"Fine, we'll just suck it up."

We are patrolling and ambushing so much that my forward observation section is split in two so we can support more infantry operations.

The Viet Cong hide in the mountains to the west and must travel to the lowland villages in the east for rice resupply. We have saturated the highlands between those areas with so many patrols and ambushes that the Viet Cong are running a gauntlet to reach their rice resupply. Consequently between Marines in the highlands, and CAP teams in the villages, the Viet Cong are slowly starving.

The CAP team is a Combined Action Platoon, a concept invented by our battalion. Insert a squad of Marines into a platoon of village militia, or as they are more commonly called, Popular Forces, under the command of a Marine officer. The platoons live in the villages among the Vietnamese population and combine the loyalty and local knowledge of the Popular Forces with the professional skill of the Marines.

The Marines live totally immersed in Vietnamese village life. They teach the Popular Forces how to fight and in turn are taught Vietnamese customs, culture and language. With our sustained presence, the Marines developed a familiarity and trust with the local populace that enable them to understand local living conditions and what is normal and what is not. The Viet Cong infrastructure is rooted out of the village, and ongoing intelligence about Viet Cong activities is obtained. Combined with this the Marines send medical teams into the villages, dig wells, build bridges, repair roads as well as other civic action programs.

The strategy is officially adopted by the Marine Corps and is so successful that no village ever protected by one of the CAP teams is ever reoccupied by the Viet Cong, and 60% of the Marines who volunteer for these units also volunteer to extend their Vietnam tour another six months.

Top picture: Village chief showing General Walt (2 stars on right collar) how he is able to call in fire. My battery commander Captain Don Harmon is behind General Walt. 2nd Lt. Wayne Hawkins, a fellow forward observer is at the right rear.

Left and bottom pictures show artillery being fired in on a precise location on the ground on a likely approach to the village, the dirt trail. This was dangerous work so we used base ejection smoke shells instead of high explosive shells. If the observer didn't specifically request smoke shells, the default was high explosives.

I came to appreciate the beauty of the countryside and the quiet dignity of the Vietnamese people.

Pictures taken along the Nong River south of Phu Bai. I am returning from a night ambush in the western uplands and caught the villagers as they start the affairs of the day.

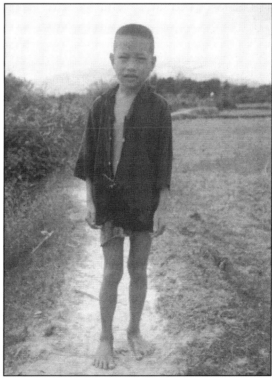

63

Sentinel at the Bridge

Took me 2 shots to get them grinning!

Big Sister and Little Brother

Father and Son

A village militiaman, otherwise known as the Popular Forces. We taught them how to fight.   They taught us all things Vietnamese.

The Marketplace

Village Huts. This is how they lived. Little concept of sanitation or cleanliness.

We came to trust one another and upon returning from night patrols would buy drinks like Coke or Tiger Beer provided the tops were sealed.

"Hey, Mr. Booth, I have a message from division headquarters that says you are to report to Da Nang. A Mr. Dan Daniel would like to meet with you."

I'm talking to our administrative chief, Sergeant Ed Shannon. In civilian terms he's our office manager. He keeps our paychecks coming, makes sure we get our mail, handles correspondence, and all the other miniscule tasks necessary to keep India Battery Marines content and functioning. He's on his second enlistment and is wise in the ways of the Marine Corps that 2nd lieutenants are not. He reports to Carl Satterfield, the Battery 1st Sergeant, our senior enlisted Marine, and both are widely respected within the enlisted and officer ranks.

"Shannon," I reply, "I don't know any Mr. Dan Daniel. The Marine Corps has made a mistake. Send a message back telling them that, plus I don't want to go to Da Nang anyway. That's fifty miles south of us and Division doesn't want to waste a helicopter flying me down there for nothing."

Shannon tilts his head to the side, looks at me askance and replies, "I'm not so sure about that, Lieutenant. I don't think you should argue, just go."

"Shannon, it will be immediately obvious they have made a mistake when this Mr. Daniel says he doesn't know me either. The Marine Corps will thank me."

Shannon grins, shakes his head and walks away with a parting shot, "Well, I'll give it a try, Mr. Booth."

Shortly thereafter, Shannon, running and grinning from ear to ear, tracks me down holding in his hand a fresh piece of paper. "Mr. Booth, I have here another message from division." Shannon knows he is vindicated but remains polite to this boot 2nd Lieutenant. I don't remember the exact wording of the second message but it was a bit sharper and said in essence, "2nd lieutenants should do what they're told. Quit arguing and get your butt down here ASAP."

So, like a good Marine officer following orders, the necessary paperwork is prepared, a just-for-me helicopter is obtained, and I am launched on an air journey to the 1st 8-inch Howitzer Battery in Da Nang where I am to meet the mythical Mr. Daniel. Upon arriving and introducing myself to the Battery Commander, Major Paul Kelly, I learn he doesn't know any more than I do, other than important dignitaries are arriving on the morrow.

The next morning, October 10, Major Kelly and I are waiting in the Landing Zone at 10:00 a.m. when a helicopter lands and our dignitaries deplane. General Walt, our division commander, leads a delegation of four civilians and all is soon made clear.

The mythical Mr. Daniel is actually a Mr. Dan Daniel, currently a member of the Virginia House of Delegates, a senior executive with the textile firm of Dan River Mills, a senior executive with the American Legion, and most importantly a friend of my uncle and mother's brother, Bill

Ashley, currently a vice-president also with Dan River Mills. My uncle upon learning that his friend and business associate is going to Vietnam comments,

"Make sure you say hello to my nephew."

Delegate Daniel dutifully makes that request to the Department of Defense, and it is relayed down the chain of command, with the result that 2nd Lieutenant John Booth is now making small talk with his Commanding General Lew Walt and Delegate Dan Daniel. The ensuing conversation consumes about fifteen minutes whereupon our dignitaries re-board the chopper and lift off to their next destination. What a welcome handshake and hello from my Uncle Bill back home!

Everyone quickly resumes the affairs of the day. Except me! I'm left standing all alone.

With all the command interest and urgency to facilitate my arrival in Da Nang not one person has asked nor planned how I am to return to Phu Bai. Well, I'm pretty self- reliant and had somewhat thought of how I might go about that. Hitchhike on a helicopter.

"Major Kelly, could I borrow a driver and jeep to run me over to the helicopter base at Marble Mountain?"

"Sure, Lieutenant, have at it."

This will work fine if nothing happens, but I am now off the radar, in a war zone, and no one officially knows where I am, but that doesn't occur to me. I'll be chewed out for doing this exact same thing ten months from now. In any event, I arrive at Marble Mountain, find the operations section, seek out the officer in charge and explain my situation.

"I need to go back north to Phu Bai and you guys have choppers coming in and out of here all hours of the day. Can I hang around and grab a seat on the next bird going north?"

"Sure, Lieutenant, grab a cot in the next tent in case you need to spend the night, and by the way the chow hall is the next tent over."

I drop my gear on a vacant cot, have lunch, and then hang around the landing zone as helicopters come and go. When one lands, blades still swirling overhead, I run out and shout at the crew chief above the engine roar,

"Hey, are you going to Phu Bai and do you have room for me?"

I get lucky and on my second try manage to hitch a ride.

"Hop aboard, Lieutenant, and join us and our 150 cases of beer."

Once on board I inquire about the purpose of their trip and yes indeed, it was strictly a beer run. Oh, the aviators lead a rough life! After a thirty-minute helo ride I arrive back home in India

Battery and am greeted with the same nonchalance when I was high-lined back to the USS Matthews after she left port without me.

"Where you been Booth, goofing off?"

Epilogue:

Mr. Dan Daniel was active in Virginia and national politics and was elected to the US House of Representatives in 1968 where he would have an illustrious career serving on the Armed Services Committee. He prodded the military into creating forces adept at terrorism and brushfire wars. He died of a heart attack on January 23, 1988.

My uncle, William (Bill) Earl Ashley, was a Marine in World War II participating in the campaigns of Tarawa, Saipan, Tinian and Okinawa. Next to my father I admired him greatly and his inspiration to me as a young lad was instrumental in my volunteering for the Marines. He left this world on October 18, 2009.

USMC 3rd Mar. Div. Photo 2-685-65. Right to Left: 2nd Lt. John Booth, Mr. Dan Daniel, Major General Lew Walt, 3 civilians from the American Legion, Major Paul Kelly is 2nd from left.

Crew Chief and me sampling the cargo.

Helos always traveled in twos for safety reasons, either crash or enemy fire.

Da Nang was a 30 - minute helo ride.

Navigation

"1, 2, 3, 4, 5,….." I'm counting to 100, and when I reach 100 I will take one small stone from the 48 in my right pocket and put it in my left pocket, and no, I'm not crazy. As a forward observer with a rifle company I'm acting as a pathfinder. I'm a latter-day Daniel Boone.

Tonight, with no moon and darkness such that we can barely see our hand in front of our face, we must trek 4800 meters on a compass heading of 4800 mils to reach a dry stream bed, then turn to a heading of 5300 mils and continue until we reach a road whereupon we will set up an ambush and hope to waylay some hapless Viet Cong patrol heading east from the mountains. They aim for the villages where they can resupply.

It's important to turn at the correct stream bed for the countryside is hilly, has several ups and downs that could fool us, and we must pivot at the correct spot in order to arrive at the precise location beside the road. Our ambush will be plotted to six-digit precision on a 1:50000-meter scale map in the combat operations center five miles away.

My pace is one meter per step and having done the calculations I will put 48 stones in my right pocket, and when my right pocket is empty we will have walked 4800 meters or about three miles. Navigation this way is not an exact science, but it's close enough.

My right pocket is empty, has been empty for several minutes, and I'm starting to sweat.

Oh crap! Have I screwed up the navigation and we've become lost? These guys depend on me to know where we're going, and I depend on me to know where we are so I don't call artillery on top of us.

Suddenly, I fall into a ditch, and I'm so relieved. My navigation was spot on. We pivot to our new compass heading and keep on going. I'm a bit bruised but that's OK, just another night at the office.

On another blackened moonless night I get into an argument with the platoon sergeant over our location. I know exactly what he's thinking.

"This boot Lieutenant doesn't know what's he's doing and is going to get us killed."

"Sergeant Jones," I explain. "Here's how I did the calculations, and here's where we are on the map."

All to no avail, but I don't worry, for if I call in artillery it's coming in by my coordinates and not his. I'm feeling pretty good with my navigation skills at the tradecraft of a forward observer.

A Good Nights Sleep

A wind-driven rain lashes the side of our tent and strains the ropes holding it down. It's blowing thirty miles per hour, and howls and moans as it capriciously changes direction. Our base camp at Phu Bai is in the throes of an October monsoon and the landscape around us has become a vast inland sea.

The tent is dark and empty, except for me. All my compatriots are out on patrol, and by the luck of the draw this is my night to stay back in the junior officers' tent. I'm fully clothed, minus my boots, and lying on an air mattress atop a canvas cot. My 45-caliber pistol is stuck in my boots, a hand's reach away. Over me is draped the canvas of a regulation pup tent and my pillow is some wadded up something piece of canvas.

I am dry, warm, safe, and drifting off into the wonderful dreamland of sleep. I am completely in the moment, and care not that tomorrow night will be a repeat of last night, and I will be back out on some miserable ambush lying on my stomach beside some path waiting to kill some hapless Viet Cong who wander down the road.

All that worry is for tomorrow, not tonight, not now.

Pleasant dreams, Lieutenant Booth.

A Moonlit Night

I'm crawling on my hands and knees through a graveyard. Around me dark burial stones stand in stark contrast against glistening white sands on a bright moonlit night. Ahead I hear the chatter of machine-gun fire coupled with explosions of hand grenades and the shouts and screams of men engaged in close combat. The sounds, borne by a gentle breeze, drift through the night. The Viet Cong are attacking a Voice of America Radio Station guarded by forces of the South Vietnamese Army.

I'm a forward observer embedded in a Marine rifle platoon and our goal is to lie in wait along a grassy path and ambush the enemy as they exit the scene of battle. Suddenly up ahead a lead Marine stirs up a bee's nest buried beneath the sand for angry hornets now buzz round my ears. I cringe expecting to be painfully stung for years earlier as a Boy Scout at night in the Virginia woods the exact same thing happened, and I remember vividly the sharp stings from the angry wasps.

Curses roll from my lips.

"How could that idiot Marine be so stupid?"

But wait, these hornets have a metallic twang and a sharp crack as they whistle past my ears, and it abruptly dawns on me as I turn and remark to my radio operator, crawling by my side, with what is probably the understatement of the year,

"These are real bullets, we could be shot!"

The ending is anticlimactic. We crawl into position aside a piedmont trail and wait, but the Viet Cong leave another way, and we spend another wasted night lying in the weeds.

I SEE THE ELEPHANT

In the American Civil War, a soldier would say to his comrades-in-arms "Reckon we'll see the elephant today, boys." It was a common phrase then, a euphemism for coming in contact with the enemy, and feeling the fear and touch of the Grim Reaper.

Nine thirty at night on October 16 and I'm immersed in total darkness. I am a forward observer with a Marine rifle company on an ambush in an area with plenty of Viet Cong activity. Their patrols carry back rice from the villages in the east to the mountains in the west, and collective ambushes like ours are successfully depriving them of food. In the month of October we have disrupted three patrols and killed four Viet Cong.

Lance Corporal David Henderson, my trusty radio operator, and I, are hidden in the bushes and tall grass. We are providing rear security for our ambush, which is immediately behind us spread out along the road. He's stretched out beside me, half asleep. I've got the radio watch and I'm staring into the blackness looking for movement with the headset squished against my ear listening to static at the same time. Every so often a faint disconnected voice speaks, "Primrose India radio check." I dutifully respond by squeezing my handset twice, which breaks the static and once again the fire direction center knows we are still alive and still awake.

The monsoon drenches us and the night brings a mean wind and driving rain interspersed with blowing mist. Visibility is zero. We had arrived at our position hours ago by following a compass heading and stumbling through the dark until we hit the road.

Earlier I had gone into a village outside of base camp and had a seamstress make me a rain jacket in another fruitless attempt to stay dry. It's a nice jacket with nylon camouflage that has a distinct but not unpleasant smell. Unfortunately, it leaks and I'm soaking wet and miserable. I've learned to accept it for we're never dry and the best we can hope for is a warm dampness. My eyes ache from staring at nothing but blackness, and I fight to stay awake.

Suddenly, off to my left I hear voices. My first reaction: What idiot Marine has broken silence? My second reaction: The voices are Vietnamese and the operations section has routed a Vietnamese Army patrol on top of us, and we're about to have an intramural fire fight. Silence is broken, and I start to curse.

Suddenly, I get it. It's a Viet Cong patrol stumbling into our rear, mere feet away, and on top of Henderson and me. We discover one another at the same time, and the night erupts into confusion, gunfire and flashes.

Bullets buzz past my ears. Their weapons and ours have different and distinct sounds at night. Orange flashes and crackles signal muzzle blasts from Viet Cong carbines answered by the roar of Marine rifles. No one can see and everyone fires at sounds. Confusion reigns. I call for illumination to turn night into day so we can make sense of what's happening. I relay to the Command Center; "Contact, Viet Cong hit us in the rear."

"Illumination on the way," a faint voice emerges amid static from our lifeline to the rear, our radio, carried by Lance Corporal Henderson.

I hear a faint sound in the black sky, a shell bursts open, a parachute pops out, and a burning candle descends earthward from 3,000 feet in the clouds, but the low ceiling masks the light. I will have to lower the shell trajectory and time the fuse so it pops at a lower elevation, hopefully, just beneath the cloud cover but not yet on the ground. This will be tricky business and will require precise fuse adjustments so I will make small elevation changes. In artillery tradecraft we speak technical shorthand based on the metric system.

"Drop 100," a short pause, another shell pops, still no light and still black as midnight. Our candle is still burning above the clouds.

Another "Drop 100," and another and another until finally, success. The clouds touch the earth, the shell pops on the ground, phosphorous ignites, and light reflects from boiling clouds. The scene is unworldly, surreal, as if on stage from Dante's inferno. Light dances and shimmers in the low rainy mists as dark silhouettes of Marines run back and forth.

At my feet sprawls a dead Viet Cong, arms askew, eyes and mouth wide open as if to say, "What happened?" On my left lie four Marines clinging to life and crying in agony.

"Mom, it hurts so bad."

"Oh God, I don't want to die." and

"Jeanie, where are you?"

I'm chilled to the bone from the rain and wind and so scared I'm shaking like a wet dog. "Come the dawn, I will not be alive," I think, but I continue to give commands over the radio, Henderson still steadfast at my side.

"On target, continuous illumination." It's strange though; the voice from my mouth is not me. It's calm and rock steady.

An eternity passes and gunfire ceases. The thwack of blades signals the arrival of the med-evac chopper, which whisks away the wounded.

I search enemy dead for intelligence. The mist has washed away the gore and through a large cavity in his chest I observe his rib cage. I unbutton his blouse and run my hands over his still warm body and examine him with clinical detachment. He's a young man, stocky and muscular, which is surprising because most Vietnamese are smaller and slighter.

Over his belt is strung a nylon camouflage cloth that has the identical look and smell as my rain jacket. He and I have probably been to the same seamstress in the village! He has a distinct communist belt buckle, with a raised hammer and sickle that would be a great souvenir.

"I think I'll take it," and start to unbuckle his belt. A voice speaks inside me.

"Let him be, John, don't desecrate the dead. It could be him searching you."

I look for his weapon, can't find it, and conclude I couldn't get it back into the United States anyway, so I take a Chinese hand grenade off his belt. I also find papers, which I turn over to the platoon commander.

At sunrise we string him up like a trussed pig and carry his body, slung between two rifles, to a helicopter evacuation point, and then we hike to the road, climb aboard trucks and return to base camp.

I get a compliment from my battery commander, 1st Lieutenant Bill Schaeffer, who was in the command center when my message came in. "We didn't know what was happening, and you kept us informed. Good job, Lieutenant Booth."

Major Hawkins, the operations officer in the gunnery section, and I have a technical discussion on how to adjust illumination in low visibility and low altitude. The shell bursts were so low to the ground that the gunnery crew could not read the fuse settings off the slide rule, and had to scramble to find the numbers in the gunnery tables. He also compliments me, "Well done, John."

I reflect a bit on what I've learned. The Marine who shot this guy probably saved my life. The enemy stumbled on top of Henderson and me, and as a forward observer my first instinct was to stay on the radio, not go for my pistol. He would have had the first shot unless I got real lucky and drew my pistol in time. I kept my cool under fire and am learning my trade, that of a forward observer.

The wounded Marines live to fight another day and all return to duty. Months later I am standing in formation in Okinawa when several Marines are called to the front for medals. Stirring words describe their valiant actions, and as I listen I think, "Wow, that sounds like a hell of a fight. How come I didn't hear about it?" Then it dawns on me. "That's the fight I was in. What are they talking about? Events didn't happen that way, and if they got a medal, why not me?"

Welcome to the war, Booth. Sometimes the best reward for seeing the elephant is living to tell about it!

Epilogue

I take the grenade back to the junior officers' tent in base camp.

"What you got there, Booth?"

"Just a Chi Com grenade off a dead VC."

"You shoot him?"

"Nah, they stumbled onto Henderson and me, and someone else shot him. Things happened so fast I didn't even get my 45 out of my holster, and when I figured out what was happening I went for the radio instead."

We have a discussion and then a decision. There's a reason young men win medals in war. They do stupid things that people in their right mind wouldn't think of doing, like "Let's disarm the grenade!" How stupid can you get?

The Chinese hand grenade is shaped like an iron pineapple with serrated grooves in the sides. A wooden plug attached to a string is stuck into a hole in the top. Pull the string and explosives fracture the iron along the serrations and shrapnel sprays and kills. I look over 2nd Lieutenant Dick Cavagnol's shoulder and think there is nothing unusual about disarming explosives in our tent.

The hand grenade was the only souvenir I would bring home from the war. I use the word souvenir instead of trophy because "trophy" conveys a different meaning, like a sporting event or big game hunting. When I saw a dead Marine, I felt a sense of sadness. When I saw a dead Viet Cong, I felt indifferent, but I did recognize him as a fellow human being. I didn't hate him.

I would keep the grenade in my garage in a duffle bag full of Marine gear. It would survive several corporate moves until 1983 when we moved from Cleveland, Mississippi to Chicago, Illinois. Several months later I looked and couldn't find it. My conclusion, the movers stole it. They were a seedy-looking lot!

Notes:

1. All information taken from the 3rd Battalion 4th Marines Command Chronology October 1965, Section and pages, intelligence 6, close combat 21, 22, S-3 Journal 55. I was the forward observer for Kilo Company.

2. The map series is HUE Sheet 6541 IV. The ambush happened at 9:30 p.m. on October 16, 1965 at grid 807158. After the shooting was over we moved to an alternate position at grid 812158 and wrapped things up by midnight.

3. Other combat in the area. 1 October, grid 801146, 2 Viet Cong KIA; 10 October, grid 814125, 1 Viet Cong KIA, 1 Viet Cong WIA; 10 October, Grid 838137, 1 Viet Cong KIA; 22 October, grid 839152, Truck hits mine, 7 Marines WIA.

Two of my Marine buddies. Holding the grenade is 2nd Lt. Dick Cavagnol and in front is our Naval Gunfire Spotter, 1st Lt. Steve Soechtig. I took the picture in October 1965 during the monsoon season. We are in the junior officers' tent of India Battery. We have connected again at reunions in later years.

2nd Lt. John Booth serving as Forward Observer of Kilo Company 3rd Bn. 4th Marines. Picture taken in October 1965 during the monsoon season. Picture taken same place as one on left. We were never dry.

THE GATES OF HELL

Ginter Park Baptist Church   September 20, 2001
1200 Wilmington Avenue
Richmond, Virginia, 23227

Dear Reverend Gorman and John Franks,

Thank you for the anniversary letter from the church. It took some sleuthing on someone's part to find our current address and I suspect Jim and Mary Brevard did the detective work. Please convey to them my warm regards. Older members of the church will certainly remember my parents Howard and Ellen Booth. Dad passed away in 1990 and Mom followed in 1998. The letter asked for a brief account of an event that impacted them from the church. I have many warm feelings and stories about the church but one time in particular stands out.

In 1965 and 1966 I was a 2nd Lieutenant in the US Marine Corps serving as a forward observer with a rifle company in Vietnam. The church put me on their mailing list for the weekly bulletin, so wherever I was when the mail caught up with me, I would receive one or several bulletins. Besides being an anchor from home the words on the front stuck in my mind so I cut them out and had them beside my cot back in base camp.

> There shall always be the church and the world
> > And the heart of man
> > > Shivering and fluttering between them choosing and chosen
> > > > Valiant, ignoble, dark and full of light
> > > > > Swinging between hell gate and heaven gate
> > > > > > And the gates of hell shall not prevail

Every now and then when things got pretty rough I would think about "the gates of hell shall not prevail" and it would help. Although I was and am by no means fatalistic and didn't really think about this until I was much older, I had a rock-hard faith that if I were killed in action there was life everlasting and I credit that to Ginter Park Baptist Church.

I received many letters from the congregation and Mom told me later that when I arrived back in the USA safe and sound it was announced in Sunday morning worship and the congregation burst into applause.

I am now happily retired from two careers, one as a business executive and the other as a Marine Corps officer. Please convey warm regards to everyone in Ginter Park.

John Booth

Notes: It was in Phu Bai that I placed the church bulletin beside my cot.

PART 3 HILL 41
COUNTERINSURGENCY AMONG THE VILLAGES

A COMBAT OUTPOST SOUTH OF DA NANG
NOVEMBER 15, 1965 THRU DECEMBER 24, 1965

Picture: Forward Observer 2nd Lieutenant John Booth and his Radio Operator Lance Corporal David Henderson returning from patrol on Hill 41 November-December 1965.

DON'T STACK YOUR DEAD AROUND YOUR TANK

"I'm lucky to be alive, John."

I'm squatting in my buddy Ron Cushman's hooch on Hill 22, five miles south of the Da Nang airfield and two miles south of the Tuy Loan River. Ron is the forward observer with Alpha Company, we had become friends in artillery school, and Ron is detailing a blow-by-blow account of the recent Viet Cong attack on their position.

On November 14 I was reassigned to India Company, and we were transferred fifty miles south to Da Nang, and placed under operational control of the 1st Battalion of the 1st Marine Regiment. My company is dug in on Hill 41, one mile west of Ron, and I've led a patrol over to get the details of what happened two weeks prior. All I know is: On October 30 Alpha Company was overrun, Marines were killed, and they could not get fire support. As the artillery expert and spotter for my rifle company, it behooves me to find out what happened.

That the Viet Cong would attack us is no surprise. Our two clay knob hills stick out like flashing neon signs and thrust like a spear into the main route used by the Viet Cong to seize supplies from the villages. We are isolated south of the Tuy Loan River and from the rear we have only one road for resupply and that crosses the Tuy Loan on a vulnerable wooden bridge. Blow the bridge, which the Viet Cong continually attempt to do, and we're stuck! After the October 30 attack our battalion receives amphibious tractors as a contingency to evacuate us via the Yen River in case we are cut off.

The two-mile stretch of road between our position and the bridge is frequently mined and in the coming weeks six Marines will be killed and ten wounded along that road. Our closest support is over the river and four miles to our rear. Think isolated U. S Army outposts in our American west in the 19th century.

Being on the wrong side of the river is worth the risk though. Our two rifle companies on Hill 41 and Hill 22 are major obstructions to the Viet Cong units to our mountainous west. They depend on resupply from the well-populated low lands to our east. Our numerous patrols and ambushes extend over four miles south and west and intelligence sources report that we are disrupting the Viet Cong big time. They are continually making plans to attack Hill 41 and Hill 22 and kill us all. From a Viet Cong prisoner:

"The Marines are everywhere."

Our vigorous patrolling and ambushes have disrupted several attempted attacks, but this one somehow slipped through the cracks and hit us by surprise. As tall, lanky Ron calmly details the events of that night, my eyes are drawn to a diagonal line of bullet holes neatly stitched in the canvas behind his head.

"How did they get through the wire, Ron?"

A well dug-in rifle company is a formidable adversary against much higher odds especially when surrounded with multi-layered barbwire, interlocking bands of fire, and pre-planned artillery strikes.

"Our listening post was asleep, John, and their throats were slit."

"Wow, that's a sobering thought. Alpha Company, caught by surprise!"

"They came through the wire in a human wave, and fought their way unto our command post and ammunition bunkers before we knew what happened. They also had mortars and recoilless rifles."

"Why couldn't you get fire support?"

"We couldn't get clearance to shoot. Shells were loaded in the howitzers, gunners had their hands on the lanyards, and all they needed was the command to fire, but we had to go up the Vietnamese chain of command for permission and it took forever."

Wow, that's the second surprise. A rifle company overrun, Marines killed, and we have to get permission to return fire? No one commander in charge?

"We also mistakenly stacked our dead and wounded around our tank, so we couldn't use it to maneuver and fire back."

The attack on October 30 unfolds as follows:

This saga begins shortly after midnight when a squad from Alpha Company springs an ambush one mile south of Hill 22 and kills three Viet Cong. The Marines then make a terrible mistake, they should have moved but didn't. The squad's Korean War radio relics don't work so the command post on Hill 22 had no knowledge of the ambush, nor the presence of a sizable enemy force.

02:10 a.m. The Viet Cong double back and attack the squad again, killing three Marines and wounding six. Two more Viet Cong are killed.

02.20 a.m. Both Hill 41 and Hill 22 are attacked by mortar and small arms fire wounding four Marines on Hill 41. The tank commander on Hill 41 requested permission to return fire, which was denied, whereupon he feigned a communications failure, and blasted away at the mortar flashes forcing the enemy to move and ultimately cease-fire completely. The back blast and pressure from the tank shells would have smashed the eardrums of those nearby.

02:22 a.m. The main attack commenced and a human tsunami, estimated at 300-400 Viet Cong, overran and smashed Alpha Company. The sights and sounds would have been horrific what with screams, shouts, the chatter of automatic weapons and explosions from hand grenades. Intermingled were the cries and moans of the wounded. The sky would have resembled 4th of July fireworks with interlocking tracers overhead in every direction. All this was in darkness as illumination and high explosive shells were requested, but didn't appear until twenty-five minutes later.

02:45 a.m. "Situation bad"

02:54 a.m. "Situation desperate"

03:00 a.m. "Request emergency drop of ammo"

03:10 a.m. "Don't need med-evac; too late" (*This was from Hill 41, and one wounded Marine was now one dead Marine*)

03:20 a.m. "VC mostly out of our CP…"

03:30 a.m. "VC have pulled back. Ring our position with artillery and let us walk it in."

Hill 22 continued to receive intermittent small arms fire for another thirty minutes, and then all enemy activity ceased. The Viet Cong disappeared like a tsunami settles back into the sea. The main fight was now over. The next twenty-four hours was a response of air strikes, artillery missions, and patrol insertions in an attempt to trap, find, and kill any of the enemy left behind. Marines on Hill 41 and Vietnamese villages were bombed in error. War is messy and mistakes happen.

What a night! Ron and I exchange pleasantries and talk about how the war is screwed up. We laugh!

"I'm glad you're alive, Ron."

"I'm glad I'm alive too, John."

I say good-bye, we shake hands and I return to Hill 41 and debrief my company, which included:

Don't stack our dead and wounded around our tank.

Epilogue

The Viet Cong Battalion had recently been filled up with recruits and had just completed training. This attack had been carefully planned as critical defense bunkers were hit initially with the ammunition bunker receiving the main attack. The enemy commander was noted for his intelligence and audacity and to cap it off the attack was apparently a graduation exercise!

Sixteen Marines were killed and forty-five wounded. Forty-seven Viet Cong were confirmed killed by body count, but later intelligence indicated the number was between 150 and 200 or about fifty-percent of the attacking force. Attacks against the Da Nang facilities were always suicide missions for the Viet Cong and they would take horrendous casualties. Ho Chi Minh made a famous statement: "You will kill ten of us, we will kill one of you. We will still win." I must admit our adversaries had guts and were committed to their cause.

The Korean War relic radios were the primary cause of this debacle and I can personally attest to their unreliability. As forward observers we used the identical radio only with a different frequency. I always required my radio Marine to carry a second battery and a second handset, the two most likely reasons for failure. When on patrol we only had two lifelines to the rear, the platoon commander with his radio and me with mine. This failure contributed to the issuance of a new improved radio shortly thereafter.

Sleeping Marines on outpost duty were also a contributory cause. This is a court-martial offense and the Roman Legions executed their soldiers for the same. How, you ask, could a Marine go to sleep on an outpost in combat? Shouldn't fear keep him awake? Let me tell you how, Dear Reader, and this will tell of the life we lived.

We were continually sleep deprived, never-ending days under a broiling sun or monsoon rains, unremitting heat, stifling humidity and never enough water. No bathing, C-rations only, and no relief in a rest area. Constant patrolling, ambushes, booby traps and sniper fire with Marines killed and wounded by ones and twos. All this added up to a physically demanding life. One night I slept in shallow water.

The best we could hope for was to put everyone on fifty-percent alert, and depend on discipline and common sense to keep one of the Marine pair alert and awake. On many an ambush I spent the darkness with a headset squished against my ear, staring into blackness, listening and looking, with my radio operator asleep at my side. When my two hours were up I would gently nudge him awake, and we would reverse roles.

Howitzers oriented in the wrong direction were another contributory factor. My battery at Phu Bai had perfected a technique where howitzers could be shifted in thirty seconds and fired 180 degrees in a new direction. I guess our innovative procedure hadn't filtered up to the rest of the division.

General Lew Walt delved into the command relationships with the Vietnamese Army and we did not have the "no permission to fire" problem again.

Notes:

1. Command Chronology 1st Battalion 1st Marines October 1965 Volume 1; Significant Events; pages7, 8, 9, 10, 12, 14, Close Combat; 26-28, Fire Support; page 28, S-2 / S-3 Journal; pages 57-73, Narrative; pages 169-173.

2. *U.S. Marines in Vietnam The Landing and the Buildup 1965,* Jack Shulimson, 1978; pages 125-129.

3. I remember as if it were yesterday the interview with 2nd Lieutenant Ron Cushman, forward observer with Alpha Company on Hill 22. In the fall of 2012, after forty-six years I reunite with

2nd Lieutenant Dan Morley, forward observer with Mike Company on Hill 41. Dan and I were in the same battery and would spend time together in Okinawa in early 1966. He and his wife live in Charlotte, North Carolina. We talk for over six hours.

4. General Westmoreland was not the Theater Commander and the South Vietnamese Forces were not under his command. This explains why we had to seek their permission to fire.

LIFE WITH A RIFLE COMPANY

I'm sleeping in a cave, well it just seems like a cave. It's a large hole with canvas spread over the top propped up in the middle with a pole. The soil is wet, the air is musty, frogs hop on the floor, and dirt falls on my head. I'm sharing these luxurious accommodations with three other Marines, but it's not working, so I give up and move out to fresh air.

However, that doesn't work either as thirty mile per hour winds and a blinding monsoon deluge that drives sideways, floods my feeble attempts with a pup tent. I re-pitch the tent, throw a tarp over the top, stake everything hard to the ground, dig drainage ditches and manage to construct a small island where I stay dry. The monsoon is like the biblical flood alternating with days of boiling sun.

At Phu Bai, when back in base camp, we had showers, and strong-back tents with wood floors, but here, nothing. Well, this miserable combat outpost on a clay hill is a base camp of sorts, so once again I'm bathing out of my helmet, never changing clothes, and smelling like a goat. Somewhere is a rain-filled hole I will dive into if we are attacked.

However, I write Mom and Dad: "I'm doing fine. Life is good!"

First Lieutenant Bill Parker shares a tent with another platoon commander, Staff Sergeant Smith, and he invites me to move in with them, which I do with alacrity, and wind up sleeping on a cot, moving slightly back up the food chain!

Bill entered the Marine Corps later than most young officers, and brags that at age thirty-three he is the oldest platoon commander in the Marines. He was a former policeman and regales us with tales of chasing miscreants throughout Oklahoma City. All three of us become friends and would often laugh and joke about the events of the day while we drank an occasional Vietnamese Tiger beer.

Our palatial residence was a nondescript, non-regulation rectangular tent, which stuck out like a flashing-light on an already visible clay knob and for sure, wasn't tactical, but since no one shot at us except once, we didn't care. The tent was pitched on a slope, and if we weren't careful we could roll off our cots. When the wind howled, and the rain beat against the side, the tent would shake and threaten to fly off into the night, but it never did.

Our tent had one thing going for it however. It was dry. Outside was a water-filled trench we planned to dive into if mortared. However, I must say I don't know what we would have done if put to the test. When I wasn't out at night on an ambush, I slept on that cot fully clothed, boots on, and pistol at my fingertips.

Our company commander was Dave Usher, a 1st Lieutenant and 1962 Dartmouth graduate, not much older than I, from New England, tall, lanky, quiet and an art lover. The executive officer, also a 1st Lieutenant, was Jack Downing, a Harvard graduate who spoke Mandarin Chinese and as he explained to me: "Vietnamese is a tonal language, John, like Chinese," and Jack could communicate with the local populace. Bill Parker, Dave Usher and Jack Downing had been together since the battalion was stationed in Hawaii nine months ago. Dave, Jack and the company 1st Sergeant slept on cots in a hollowed out hole covered with a tarp, dug into the side of the hill. We held company meetings there in nighttime darkness to receive instructions, discuss tactics and other affairs of the day.

The other newcomer, besides me, was 1st Lieutenant Steve Ek, a platoon commander from the Seventh Marines. His transfer was a result of Secretary of Defense Robert McNamara's misguided policy, titled Operation Mixmaster, of moving individuals so not every one in the unit had the same rotation date. Forget the bonding and friendships needed for a cohesive unit in combat. Steve and I would start from scratch learning our new comrades. Steve's platoon, however, was on a small low-lying outpost almost in the rice paddies one-eighth of a mile away. As a result Steve and his Marines stayed wet a good deal of the time and due to the distance I didn't see much of Steve. I instantly liked them all, and since we were all in the same miserable mess, that further helped to bond us.

A water buffalo, which is what we called a 400 gallon water tank on wheels, was placed at the northeast base of the hill outside the wire, and every few days a two and one-half ton four-wheel drive Marine Corps truck would labor out to our position and exchange the empty buffalo for a full one. We would refill our canteens here, and such washing that we did was out of our helmets back up on the hill.

We stayed clean-shaven, and I remember many a morning scraping my face looking into a blurred small aluminum mirror and dipping my razor into a half-filled helmet. We did not use aftershave because the smell would give you away when in the bush stalking our adversaries. Staying clean-shaven was part of our Marine culture, and distinguished us as a disciplined fighting force instead of an unruly mob. Though I must admit that when examining the hill from afar, what with the tents, holes, sandbags, barb-wire and the other paraphernalia of war, one got the impression there could be some outlaws up here.

At the west end of the hill was a wooden box with four holes open to the entire world, which was our latrine or head in Marine Speak. Having a four-holer was the height of luxury as we didn't have to squat in the weeds. Once ensconced here with our trousers down around our ankles, we had a wonderful scenic view for miles. Of course, we were also visible for miles, and I suppose a sniper could have shot at us, but none ever did, so we didn't worry about it.

The place was no respecter of rank, as an officer would often share space with the lowest ranking enlisted. A morning exchange would be as follows:

"Good morning, Mr. Booth."

"Good morning to you, PFC Jones," I would reply.

Every so often the box would be moved aside, fuel oil poured into the abyss, "Fire in the hole," would be shouted, a match tossed down, a whoosh with flames shooting into the air, and the contents incinerated.

As I write these words a memory floats to mind:

I'm on the back of a two and one-half ton truck with a platoon of Marines barreling down Route One. The company executive officer, Jack Downing is up front with the driver. Suddenly, Mr. Dysentery lands on my shoulder, grabs my guts, and whispers in my ear, "Welcome back to Vietnam, Lieutenant Booth."

Over the roar of the wind and engine I pound on the cab, and shout:

" Jack, I've got to take a crap!"

"Can't you hold it till we get to base-camp?"

"I'll either crap all over the back of this truck, or you can stop and I'll go in the weeds, take your pick."

Laughter and hoots from my fellow Marines, a groan from Jack as he stops the truck, grabs a rifle, and follows me as I head for the bushes. A Marine on his haunches with his rear-end flashing white to the world is a tempting target for a sniper. Parallel to Route One is a railroad and during this brief moment in time a passenger train barrels by and I look up and see women peering out the windows. Jack stands guard over me, rifle at the ready, while I squat and do my business. Forget modesty in combat.

Our food was C-rations in which we all shared equally, but some C-rations are more equal than others. A non-commissioned officer would slice a box open with his k-bar knife, turn it upside down, drop it in our midst, and then contents unknown, we would pick one of the twelve available meals. Then the bargaining would begin.

"Hey, Mr. Booth, what will ya give me for a can of peaches?"

"How 'bout ham and limas?"

"No way sir" and so it would go.

If I was not available, maybe I was off at an officer meeting, some Marine would look after me and attempt to make sure I got something decent.

"Here, Mr. Booth, I tried to get you a good c-rat."

"Thanks."

I have a dim memory of a hot meal. It's Thanksgiving and I'm standing at the base of the hill in a cold driving rain, a fierce blowing wind, and mess gear in hand. My helmet is on my head, I'm covered in my poncho, and my pistol is belted around my waist. We are immersed in mud, and our hill sticks out like a sore thumb in the middle of a rice paddy inland sea. We're in line filing past a two and one-half ton truck, and from the back a Marine is ladling out portions of hot turkey and potatoes, nicely leavened with falling raindrops. Battalion is thinking of us.

Another memory floats into view. We've returned to base camp from a punishing patrol with temperatures well over one hundred degrees. Our brains are broiled from the unrelenting heat and humidity, and we have had several heat casualties. I pass a staff sergeant kneeling on one knee. With his left arm he is cradling a lance- corporal, who has collapsed from the heat, and with his right hand he is pouring water from his canteen over the face of his younger comrade in arms. The water from the canteen, and the sweat from both of them, one black Marine and one white Marine, mingles together as it drips to the ground.

Looking back on this period of time I feel a strong bond in my heart to all of these Marines, many of whom I didn't even know. We hailed from different backgrounds, were from all walks of life and came from all over the United States. The common threads that bound us together were our shared hardships and dangers, for we lay in the same mud, took the same risks, ate the same food, and guarded one another when we slept in the weeds. We didn't care if you were black, white or orange. All that mattered was that you could shoot straight and behave like a Marine. We bled together and died together. What a brotherhood!

Epilogue

Bill Parker and I would reconnect in the Marine Reserve when we served together in the 12th Marine Regiment in Dallas, Texas in 1982. Bill was the assistant dean of the College of Liberal Arts at the University of Central Oklahoma. He retired from the Marine Corps in 1993 with the rank of Colonel. He was divorced with one son. He died from a self-inflicted gunshot wound on January 9, 1996. No one would know why.

Dave Usher obtained the rank of Captain and left the Marine Corps after four years. He graduated with an MBA from the Columbia Graduate School of Business and became an art dealer. He was married with several children. He died in a tragic boating accident in Long Island Sound on March 15, 1997.

Jack Downing, Steve Ek and I would reunite more than forty years later at a reunion, and it was like we were all back on Hill 41. Both had successful careers, respectively, in the CIA and FBI.

It's 2007 and I am attending a business meeting at a Marine reunion in Savannah, Georgia. Two former Marines, now old men like me, are arguing. It's obvious they don't like one another and the conversation is getting heated. Our treasurer, Chuck Larson, raises his hand for silence. If there was ever a Marine to be bitter about the war it was he, having lost an arm and a leg from a short round by Marine artillery in Operation Hastings in August of 1966.

"You know," says Chuck, "We didn't all like one another when we served together in Vietnam. So what makes us think we all will like one another now?"

"Yeah, so what?" we think, and then,

"But you know, we would have given our lives for one another."

Dead silence, you could have heard a pin drop, and we all think back to some place and time in Vietnam where we helped a fellow Marine.

Then some wag breaks the silence, "Well, I wouldn't go that far." And we all dissolve in laughter and get back to business.

Shakespeare had it right with his words preceding the Battle of Agincourt and the unlikely English victory against an overwhelming French Army.

"We few, we happy few, we band of brothers: For he to-day that sheds his blood with me Shall be my brother; be he ne're so vile, This day shall gentle his condition; and gentlemen in England now-a bed shall think themselves accursed they were not here, and hold their manhoods cheap while any speaks that fought with us upon Saint Crispin's day".

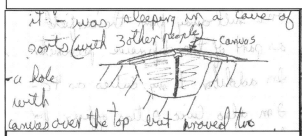

November 16 1965: "I was sleeping in a cave of sorts (with 3 other people) a hole with canvas over the top but proved too crowded, musty and damp. Dirt falling on my head, frogs hopping around on the floor so I moved out to fresh air."

"Finally got this monsoon season figured out. Days of boiling sun interrupted by days of pouring rain. When it rains hard there's about a 20-30 mph wind blowing with it."

The move to fresh air didn't work either. So I tried a pup tent with a tarp spread over top. See upper right picture. The pup tent with the tarp over the top proved a little better, but not much.

2nd Lieutenant Bill Parker (pictured below) invited me to move in with him and a fellow platoon commander. We slept on cots in lopsided hooch on the side of a hill. When the wind howled the tent flapped and attempted to fly away, but never did. Outside was a water- filled trench to dive into if mortared. We never were. Bill and I would meet again in the USMC Reserves after the war.

91

View west toward mountains. Our strategy: Patrol lowlands, interdict Viet Cong coming down from mountains to seek supplies. Starve them. It worked.

On the left is an Ontos, an anti-tank weapon. Not much use to us but came into its own in the Battle of Hue in 68. "All the rice paddies around our hill are flooded."

81 mm mortar. We had two of them.

India Co. had 1 tank. High velocity shell had high overpressure. Right ear closed up once.

Vehicle is known as an "Otter." What it took to resupply us in the monsoon.

Command Post on Hill 41. Note ketchup bottle on the right.

NICE

I'm standing in the middle of a dusty dirt road on a sweltering humid day trying hard to act nice. Dear Reader, you heard correctly. The word is nice, N-I-C-E. I certainly don't smell nice as bathing water has not touched my person for several days, and I certainly don't look nice as I'm armed with a pistol and wearing helmet and flak jacket. I'm looking down at a small group of local villagers and asking with halting Vietnamese and hand gestures for identification.

On November 3 under cover of darkness, Viet Cong entered two hamlets less than a mile from our position and at gunpoint stole the government identification issued to all legitimate residents. Slightly west of that incident on November 7 in afternoon broad daylight two Viet Cong attempted to steal identification cards from farmers working the rice paddies. They were surprised by a Marine patrol and one Viet Cong tried to throw a hand grenade. He was promptly killed whereupon the other quickly surrendered. The dead guerrilla had sixty-three cards in his possession.

Requiring government identification was a tactic to identify and root out the Viet Cong infrastructure embedded in the villages. This was all in accordance with the Mao Tse-tung doctrine that in a War of National Liberation the guerrillas need the support of the local population so they can move around like fish in the sea. We certainly can't tell the difference between the good guys and the bad guys, and the fact that this is happening practically beneath our noses indicates how deeply imbedded and how long the enemy has been in this area. We Marines have only been here a few months so we have our work cut out for us in making the villagers feel secure.

Two weeks later some official discovers that Vietnamese Popular Forces aren't checking the locals for identification, so in typical bureaucratic fashion word goes out that Marines will now start checking villagers for the same.

We normally did this anyway whenever we scooped up innocent bystanders inadvertently caught in our firefights with the local Viet Cong, but now this meant a more formal procedure. We were very sensitive to our relations with the local Vietnamese, and our objective was to win their allegiance, so "making nice" when asking someone for their identification was part of our job.

A few months earlier I had gone into the city of Hue and purchased a Vietnamese language book, but that made little difference, none of us spoke Vietnamese. The company executive officer, 1st Lieutenant Jack Downing, spoke Mandarin Chinese, which as I've said before is a tonal language as Vietnamese is and that gave Jack an edge, and he could make himself understood.

As for me, I stumbled around with a few Vietnamese phrases and hand gestures, trying desperately to wrap my Anglo Saxon tongue around these strange sounds, and all the while trying to be nice to some beetle-nut chewing, wrinkled old grandmother who wanted nothing more than to make it to the local village market. I asked our interpreter to teach me the phrases "Please show me your identification" and "Thank you."

Surprisingly it was easier than it sounds as the population generally supported this procedure. They didn't like the Viet Cong because they were brutal, stole food, extorted money and sometimes killed and kidnapped. Young healthy civilian males were always suspect because most of the male population was in uniform, and if you were not, the question was why not. One search tactic was to see if the young men had callouses on their shoulders, and if they did that could be a sign they were carrying mortar shells for the Viet Cong in their spare time.

When we identified suspects, we treated them well, and turned them over to the local Vietnamese authorities. We tried very hard to conduct all our operations in such a manner as to gain the loyalty and cooperation of the people and create conditions that permitted them to go about their normal routine in peace and security.

Notes: Command Chronology Volume 1, 1st Battalion 1st Marines, November 1965, pages 49 hamlets of Duyen Son (4) grid 943664 and La Chau (4) grid 942653 and page 56 hamlet of La Chau (5) grid 961669 for Viet Cong stealing identification cards, pages 77 and 83 for Popular Forces not checking for identification and Marines ordered to check all civilians encountered on patrol. See page 6 for last sentence which is in Mission Statement.

GHOSTS

We adopted a baby.

The youngster was born in the hamlet of Duyen Son (1) on November 2 in a house located just a quarter of a mile from the base of our hill. On the evening of November 19th we heard crying and wailing coming from the baby's house, and the next morning Jack Downing, the company executive officer, a corpsman and an interpreter went to the house to investigate.

Upon arriving, they found the baby's mother was very ill with an infected womb. The corpsman attempted to give medical assistance to the mother, but her husband and an old woman attending, refused to let the corpsman treat her, stating she was possessed by evil spirits and would soon die. After explaining to the family that the mother should be evacuated to the hospital in Da Nang and that evil spirits and ghosts wouldn't be able to bother her once in the hospital, the husband and the woman finally allowed the corpsman to give the mother a shot of penicillin. Milk and sugar was given to the baby, who was in excellent health.

Although the husband and the old woman did permit the corpsman to administer penicillin they still refused to let her go to the hospital, but after further talking they finally agreed to let the mother go on November 29. The husband and the old woman explained that spirits and ghosts would get to the woman on November 29 and she would die on that date. However, if she were still alive, then they would let her go to Da Nang for medical treatment. Everyday thereafter, the corpsman brought milk and sugar for the baby and examined the woman who seemed to become worse each day. And everyday, the Marines on Hill 41 could see villagers chasing ghosts with white sheets and other devices like bamboo sticks.

On the evening of November 29, crying and wailing was once again heard from the woman's house, Jack and the interpreter went once again to investigate, and upon arrival they found the mother had died. The husband and old lady's prediction had come true.

On November 30, the funeral was held for the mother. Jack attended the funeral and learned the villagers were planning to bury the baby with her mother because there wasn't anyone to care for the child. Jack intervened, said we would informally adopt the baby, and that the Marines from India Company would provide clothing, food and milk for the youngster. The villagers seemed very grateful and now India Company has another mouth to feed.

I wish I could give a definite conclusion to this yarn, but I can't. I assume the child was turned over to the proper Vietnamese authorities.

Notes: Command Chronology, 1st Battalion 1st Marine Regiment, December 1965, Volume 3, page 68. The village of Duyen Son was composed of five hamlets numbered (1) through (5). The hamlet of Duyen Son (1) was located at Grid 938660 and was at the base of Hill 41.

IMMERSED IN THE VILLAGES

Soap

I'm staring at a dog. It's a light tan colored, shorthaired, mangy cur about medium size and it's listlessly sniffing the ashes of a village cook fire. Judging from the dog's movements it probably has several diseases, which would be expected given the general condition of the village. Trails of wood smoke meander into air ripe with the pungent odor of the surroundings, which is a combination of everything that goes in and out of a human being. Thatch huts sit astride dirt paths, which are overrun with garbage, dogs, chickens and children.

In addition to my forward observer duties I'm also the civic action officer of our rifle company, and have led yet another patrol into a small Vietnamese hamlet with a name like Duyen Son (3) or La Chau (2). A village is a collection of hamlets and will have a single name like La Chau for example. Each hamlet within the village will have the same name in addition to a number. I have been to so many hamlets now that the names all run together. This area south of Da Nang and roughly fifteen-mile-wide stretch of land between the South China Sea and mountainous lowlands is some of the most fertile land for rice growing in South Vietnam. It's also densely populated so there are many hamlets and many civilians.

My job is to lead patrols to village hamlets and provide security while the medical team holds sick call and the intelligence team questions villagers regarding the Viet Cong. I've gotten pretty good at this and enjoy being immersed in the Vietnamese population. Medical assistance is a tactic in our counterinsurgency strategy, and is second in importance after offering protection from the Viet Cong. General Walt aims to use this strategy as a weapon to sever the population from Viet Cong control and induce and solidify loyalty to the government.

Medical teams operating in Phu Bai noticed a drop in medical cases and came to the startling conclusion that the reason was the distribution and use of soap! Marines operating in one village demonstrated the proper method of washing infants. As the mothers presented their children one Marine undressed the child, one washed, one rinsed, and another dried and redressed the infant. The demonstration was successful, enhanced the image of the Marines and convinced battalion medical officers that improved sanitation and hygiene could reduce the sickness in the area seventy to eighty percent. Imagine that, the Marines who raised the flag on Iwo Jima, now washing babies.

Medical teams operating around Da Nang simultaneously came to the same conclusion. Numerous Vietnamese suffered from rashes and sores that in many instances could be cured simply by keeping the infected area clean. The Marines ordered tons of soap to pass out locally as part of their Combined Action Program. The villagers really were living in the Middle Ages and had no concept of sanitation. Soap was considered a luxury and to use it needlessly was considered wasteful. Statistics were kept on Civic Action and in December 1965 the 3rd Marine Division distributed 28,000 bars of soap.

A mother brings her baby to the Navy Corpsman before me and lays him down on a pallet. Flies crawl over the infant, who is listless, dirty and covered with infected sores. The corpsman offers the mother a bar of soap and through the interpreter explains how to wash the baby and how often to do so. That's all the corpsman does. No shots are given nor pills dispensed.

One week later we return to this same village, and the same mother again brings her baby to the corpsman. A miracle has occurred and the infant does not resemble the same child. The sores are gone, the baby is bright, cheerful, and the mother is ecstatic. I am astounded and conclude the Marine Corps has made a friend for life. That mother will tell her family, her friends, and the village chief about the Marines and that bar of soap.

About the same time this was going on, General Westmoreland was asked how he planned to win the war. He responded "Firepower." The Army strategy was attrition with overwhelming firepower. The Marine strategy was counterinsurgency, with tolerance, sympathy, and kindness to the locals.

The Radio

On another occasion our interactions are not so noble. Our patrol is passing through a village and Vietnamese officials are off to the side scanning our column looking for someone in charge when all of a sudden they spot me. How they know I'm an officer I'm not entirely sure for on patrol we wear no rank insignia. None of us are anxious to be an easy target for a sniper. Perhaps it's because they observe I'm only armed with a pistol and have a radio operator by my side. Or maybe it's the subtlety of body language both spoken and unspoken on how we interact. Or maybe it's because of how we "look."

One way or another, if you hang around Marines in combat, you can always spot the officers even if we don't wear rank. As a twenty-three year old 2nd lieutenant immersed in a sea of enlisted Marines only a few years younger, I was always treated with utmost respect and was always Mr. Booth or Lieutenant Booth.

"Dai-uy," that's Vietnamese for Captain, "One your Marine steal radio from village boy," the hamlet chief says to me in halting English.

Being swarmed by children when we pass through village hamlets is not unusual. Children are everywhere and are always trying to sell us everything from soft drinks to their sisters. I'm thinking,

"What idiot Marine would steal from a kid as it's in our own best interest to have a friendship with the villagers. If there is an ambush ahead we want the locals to tip us off."

"Show me the Marine," I say.

I'm led up the column until we confront a big surly Marine over six feet tall and in fact taller than I am. I look up to him and command,

"Did you steal the radio?"

"Yes Sir." Well, that's surprising, he admits the theft, but now comes the hard part, what to do?

"Give him back the radio" is the first thing, but after that what?

I'm still new learning my way in command of Marines. I'm not in his chain of command as I'm the forward observer, and as I'm not his platoon commander, I don't even know how good a Marine he is. We are in active combat, so any punishment will not have much effect. There's not much more you can do to a Marine when he gets little sleep and goes on patrol every day dodging mines, booby traps and sniper rounds. I decide it's not my job to decide and go in search of our company 1st Sergeant. I explain what happened and let him handle the miscreant Marine.

In retrospect, I wish I had given him a public tongue-lashing and explained how his actions endangered us all. While it might not influence his future behavior, it could have had a positive impact on those around him. Our daily actions with Vietnamese civilians are important for the success of our counterinsurgency strategy. As explained in our battalion operating procedures;

"Simple everyday contacts, whether it is helping a man push a heavy cart, helping a woman with a heavy load, or picking up a child who has fallen, all are important. Many Vietnamese have invited the Marines to eat with them or offered them food for their use."

From my personal experience all of the interactions by the Marines with whom I served were positive and would make one proud of the Marine Corps. This instance was a rare exception.

Notes:

1. Command Chronology, 3rd Battalion, 4th Marines, September 1965, see pages 95-103 for civic action in the villages in the Phu Bai area and the story about Marines washing babies.

2. Robert Coram, *Brute, The Life of Victor Krulak,* 2010, Hachette Book Group, pages 289-290 and Lewis Sorley, *Westmoreland, The General Who Lost Vietnam,* 2011, Hughton Mifflin Harcourt, page 218, for the difference in strategy between the Army and the Marines and Westmoreland's comment on firepower.

3. Command Chronology, 3rd Marine Division, December 1965, see pages 24-25 for statistics on soap distribution.

4. *U.S Marines in Vietnam, The Landing and Buildup 1965,* Jack Shulimson, 1978, pages 142-143 for comments by General Walt about using civic action as a strategy and weapon.

5. Command Chronology 1st Battalion, 1st Marines, November and December 1965, see Mission Statements for how Marines are supposed to behave. These stories are from my memory.

The Marine Corps had a counterinsurgency program that worked. First provide security then medical help. Villages south of Da Nang and Hill 41 December 1965.

Tom Sawyer, Huck Finn and his mates.

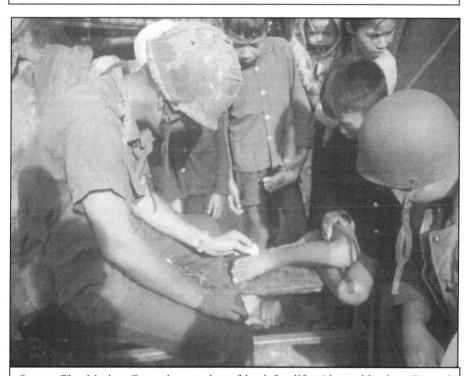

Soap. The Marine Corps has made a friend for life. About this time General Westmoreland is asked how he plans to win the war and he responds "firepower." The shadow to the left is me taking this picture.

Top: This young lad wanted to wear my helmet. Notice the cigarettes in his pocket.

Right: Command Chronology, 1st Battalion, 1st Marine Regiment, December 1965, page 43.

Now No Bullets

The civil affairs team of the 1st Bn., First Marine Regiment, 3rd Marine Division, is not a timid crew. In performing their function of giving medical help to Vietnamese villagers and distributing gifts of clothing and food from the United States, they do not limit themselves to safe areas of the countryside.

Recently, accompanied by a squad of Marines, the team penetrated into an area normally seen only by heavily armed patrols.

In a small hamlet near Da Nang, Vietnamese interpreters announced the presence of the "bocsi" (doctors) over a loud speaker.

Despite pouring rain, a crowd soon gathered around the Americans to receive treatment from the Navy corpsman.

After the medical team finished their work, Marines passed out clothing and canned foods to the Vietnamese.

The team members are convinced that their audacity is paying off. Navy corpsman Robert LeBlanc (Windsor, Ontario, Canada) feels their work is effecting a permanent change in the people's attitude toward health and cleanliness.

The daily visits to the countryside are showing definite results, according to 1stLt. Jim Keeley, battalion civil affairs officer. "In the beginning, nobody waved at you on the road, and you couldn't go out without getting shot at."

Now the team is greeted by friendly waves and shouts almost anywhere they go in the battalion area.

THE VIEW

People have misconceptions about combat and think you're under fire all the time or some other such thing. The reality was much different as it consisted of numerous long hot walks in broiling sun or long wet walks in monsoon rains where nothing happened and you fought the elements. This is interspersed with periods of great boredom and even briefer periods of intense fear and enemy fire. This was one of those less intense periods, and while I wasn't bored, I didn't have a whole lot to do.

It's mid-day, and I'm lounging beneath a poncho to shield me from the sun on top of our combat outpost, 135 feet above sea level. It's clear, visibility is excellent and I can see for miles. Off to the east is the deep radiant blue of the South China Sea, to the south is a mix of rice paddies neatly dissected by dikes and verdant green rolling piedmont, which rises to greet the jungle mountains to the west.

I'm sitting cross-legged engrossed in reading *Uhuru* by Robert Roark. The book, published in 1962, is about the Mau Mau uprising by Kenyan African rebels against British rule. Since childhood I have been a voracious reader, and in fact have a pleasant memory from another lifetime of Ms. Bottom, my 2nd grade teacher, fussing at me for surreptitiously reading a book on my lap. *The Adventures of Freddy the Pig* was more appealing than whatever she was teaching. So, now I always have a paperback stuck in my pack.

I came by *Uhuru* from a recommended reading list at the Marine Corps Basic School in Quantico Virginia, where all new 2nd lieutenants are trained. In 1961 the Soviet premier Nikita Khrushchev voiced his support for a guerrilla warfare rural insurgency which he called "wars of national liberation." President John Kennedy had responded by developing our own counterinsurgency strategies, one of which was the formation of Special Forces within the United States Army. The Marine Corps knew we would be involved in the emerging counterinsurgency in Southeast Asia and had shifted its training accordingly, hence the recommended reading list.

I had also read *Street Without Joy* by Bernard Fall, which is the story of the French experience in Indochina, and also, works by Sir Robert Thompson, which deal with the defeat of the communist insurgency in Malaysia. Thompson was a British military officer who was widely regarded as the leading expert on how to defeat this Mao Tse Tung concept of a rural guerrilla insurgency.

Uhuru was a good yarn, had captured my interest, and was a primer on how not to fight a guerrilla insurgency, as the British did not prevail. But with the blue sky, a light breeze, and the view, life for the moment was good.

Suddenly, there is a whiz and a sharp "*kapow*" over my head, high enough that I don't grovel in the dirt, but someone doesn't like me! An enemy sniper has just taken a shot at a lounging Marine on top of a hill. Me!

I wait, and nothing happens, just one round. I settle back in and resume reading. This guy must be some amateur.

On yet another day I am having a gourmet's delight of C-rations atop our hill and taking in again the delightful and relaxing view, when suddenly I hear shouts to the northwest of our position. In the distance I observe a lone Vietnamese male, dressed in civilian clothes, frantically running along a dike between two rice paddies. In hot pursuit, with frenzied shouting and much arm waving are the "Keystone Cops," or at least that's the image that comes to mind. Some are in uniform and armed, and the overall impression is they want to capture him, not shoot him. This is interesting. Can this guy outrace his pursuers for about 1000 yards, and escape into the underbrush on a hillside? It's shaping up to be an exciting chase!

Suddenly, another group of pursuers appears on a dike that will intersect our escapee's route. If they get to the intersection first, our man will be trapped and have to surrender. Now the question becomes: Who will get to the intersection first, the escapee or the pursuers? Oh, if this were a horse race on whom would you bet!

Now, Dear Reader, you may ask, why didn't he jump into the paddy and head off in another direction? If he had, he would have been caught for sure. The paddies were knee-deep water and mud. The mud stuck to your boots and your feet became like lead. Leeches infested the water, attached to your legs, crawled up your thighs, and when discovered, were burned off with a match. We tied our trousers around our boots to prevent such an occurrence.

An image comes to mind. I'm slogging through a paddy, and I look down at the rippled water, which reflects dancing sunlight and squirming leeches, all trying to attach themselves to my ankles. I look up and keep on going. It's generally a death sentence for a Marine patrol to be caught in the middle of a rice paddy, and I have another memory of a mud-slinging, leg-wrenching, gut-tightening slog across a paddy, and how relieved I felt when we finally reached the other side.

Back to the story. Who wins: the escapee or the pursuers?

The Keystone Cops reach the intersection first; our man surrenders and is led away. I find out later he was a Viet Cong agent who lived in the village, and someone turned him in.

On November 23, we have a partial eclipse of the sun preceded by an urgent message from higher headquarters: "Looking at the sun through binoculars may cause permanent damage to the eyes."

At night, the view from our hill was worthy of a cinematography award for the pyrotechnic display to our southeast. The countryside south of the Cau Do River and east of the Yen River, was densely populated, and had been under Viet Cong control for years. Only within the past few months had the Marines, with the assistance of the Vietnamese Army, moved into the area and begun the slow process of pacification. Nightly firefights with the Viet Cong were frequent and yellow tracer rounds from machine guns would launch upward into the night and cross one another with a moving display worthy of the 4th of July. The fights were far enough away so we could not hear the sounds of machine-gun fire, but only see the visual effects of the streaming tracers.

In mid-December, Operation Harvest Moon was launched miles to our south, and from our perch at night we could see streams of yellow dragon fire flicker down from a black sky and ignite fires on the hills in the rising piedmont. The dragon fire was from a close support airplane with the nickname of Puff the Magic Dragon, enhanced with special armaments that could kill on a vast scale. All this with no sound, and only a visual display of yellow and orange set against a black night background, was a gourmet's feast for the eyes.

Only when you thought about it did you realize it was death and destruction for those on the ground, and no, I didn't think it was terrible, for I had concluded our adversaries, the Viet Cong and the North Vietnamese, were vicious and savage terrorists.

MY PISTOL

In the Marine Corps weapons are holy things to be cherished and respected. It's true, every Marine is a rifleman first and in Basic School all of us were trained on every hand-held weapon in the Marine Corps from the .45-caliber pistol to the M-60 machine gun. We could disassemble and reassemble them all at the drop of a hat and developed an instinct and expertise with firearms that was a second nature with us. I became an expert marksman with both the M-14 rifle and .45-caliber pistol.

We became familiar with larger weapons such as the bazooka and 60 millimeter and 81 millimeter mortars. We held hand grenades, pulled the pin and threw them. We shot flamethrowers, and I still remember with awe and fear the heat on my face and strain on my arms when I aimed that hose of molten flame down range. That's how we cleaned out our fanatical foe, the Japanese, in World War II.

As an officer in Vietnam my official weapon is the .45-caliber pistol. We are armed twenty-four hours a day, seven days a week and my pistol becomes as much a part of me as my right arm. The three-pound constant weight on my right hip is a source of comfort. In Marine Corps parlance its official name is the M1911A1, single action, semi-automatic, magazine-fed, recoil-operated, .45-caliber pistol. It kicks like a mule, shoots a heavy slug, and if it hits anywhere on your body, will knock you down. It was developed to stop drug-crazed Moro guerrillas during the Philippine Insurrection in the early 1900's.

However, with its short range it is a defensive weapon only, and when I was assigned to a rifle company as a forward observer, I went through a shakedown period as to what weapon I should carry. I needed more firepower, or so I thought.

For a while I carried the M-2 carbine, which I borrowed from the battery gunnery sergeant Carl Satterfield. I remember Carl's laughing admonition on handing me the weapon.

"Mr. Booth, if you get shot, please fall so you don't damage the stock."

However, the carbine's disadvantages soon became apparent. It required rounds not stocked in the supply chain, so you had to scrounge ammunition. In addition each weapon has its own distinct sound when fired, and as the Viet Cong were frequently armed with carbines, you were at risk of being mistaken for the enemy in a firefight, especially at night. I quit carrying the M-2 carbine.

Next I migrated to the M-14 rifle, which was the mainstay individual weapon in a rifle company. However it was heavy and cumbersome, and I soon discovered I didn't have enough hands to both carry a rifle, and do my job as a forward observer. My trade skill was to continually know our precise location on a 1:50000 scale map and to accurately call in high explosives at a moment's notice. I was often either reading a map or sighting a compass on a distant landmark, and when rounds were snapping overhead I was on the radio. While it was my job to kill the bad guys it was with artillery, and not a rifle. So, I quit carrying the M-14 and focused on becoming the best forward observer in the Marine Corps.

It's a bright sunshiny day and I'm relaxing. In front of me I have cleaning solvent, oil, rags, and I'm going to clean Old Faithful, my pistol. We keep our arms spotless, as rice paddy mud and dirt road dust can easily jam our weapons. I'm turning Old Faithful upside down and sideways, and in preparation for disassembling the barrel I pull the slide to the rear when suddenly, surprise, surprise, out pops a .45-caliber round. I forgot to unload my weapon, and thankfully did not shoot myself!

"What an idiot I am. How could I have been so careless? I could have blown my head off!"

Much chastised I double check to insure my pistol is really empty and finish the cleaning job.

I'm not the only one who has become careless. Our rifle company institutes the following procedure:

Each Marine, when returning to Hill 41 and before passing through the wire, will slide the bolt of his rifle to the rear, and the patrol leader will slip a finger into the breech to insure the weapon does not have a round in the chamber. We do not wish any accidental shootings, of which there have been a few. I remember messages like:

"PFC Smith has shot himself in the foot. Request evacuation."

During my tour in Vietnam I would have my pistol out twice to defend myself.

I'm chest deep in stagnant black water, and attempting to avoid entrapment in the sucking mud and clinging vines on the bottom. My pistol is in my right hand with my finger on the trigger. With my left hand I am pushing away vines to peer into the leaf-shaded darkness and muck of the bank. Marines on my right and left are doing the same. Our patrol has chased a lone Viet Cong guerrilla into a deep ravine filled with vile water, and like magic he disappeared. He undoubtedly is hiding in a cave with maybe an underwater entrance, and we're hoping to smoke him out. I expect to suddenly come upon some crouching Viet Cong holding a rifle, and then it will be a question of who shoots first, him or me.

We really hadn't thought this through. The smart thing to do would have been to shout down and give him an opportunity to surrender. None of us spoke Vietnamese, and I don't remember if we had an interpreter with us or not. If he felt we were going to kill him regardless of what he did, I'm sure he would have sold his life dearly and shot one or two of us before we dispatched him. That would not have been an equitable exchange, but nothing happens. He's hidden himself so well we eventually give up, and proceed with our patrol. I have an expensive pair of binoculars on my belt and discover that water has entered the lens and ruined them. Oh, well.

On another occasion rounds are snapping and cracking overhead, my heart is in my throat, and I'm crouched on a village path holding Old Faithful with both hands ready to blast away, but more on that story later.

Some things stay with you a long time. In 1982, sixteen years after I left Vietnam, I'm a business executive walking through the front office. Suddenly that three-pound weight that was once upon a time my constant companion appears yet again on my right hip. The sensation is so real that my right hand instinctively reaches for my pistol, only to discover an empty pocket. I have no idea from whence this feeling came. I regain my composure and continue with the affairs of the day.

In my old age I still like to shoot and will occasionally go to a range and plink away trying to convince myself I'm still the dead-eye marksman I once was in my youth.

H & I FIRES

"Skipper, the Viet Cong didn't do this, we did."

I'm standing in an ankle deep mix of mud and buffalo dung in the village hamlet of Phu Son (1) while a slow rain pelts my shoulder and face. My poncho is draped over me holding in a rank odor that I have come to recognize as mine. This is what I smell like when I haven't bathed for several days and body heat is confined within my poncho. Water drips off my helmet onto my neck and slides further down my back. This is yet another normal day in the life of Marine 2nd Lieutenant John Booth.

I'm with my company commander, 1st Lieutenant Dave Usher and beside us stand our interpreter and a village farmer. In front of us are several water buffalo confined within a pen. One buffalo has a large hole in his side, and I'm able to look directly into his stomach and observe the digestion process. The buffalo doesn't seem to mind as he's contentedly munching hay with drooling spittle and hay strands hanging from his mouth. He looks at me with dark wide mournful eyes.

I am trying to convince Dave that the hole in the buffalo is due to shrapnel from an errant artillery high explosive shell, and not by actions of the Viet Cong. In other words we, the United States Marine Corps, will owe this farmer compensation for messing up his water boo.

A tactic that was used in our counterinsurgency strategy was unobserved artillery fire. Shells were fired at random twenty-four hours a day, but especially in darkness, at specific targets, such as trail junctions and possible assembly areas. The theory was this would keep the enemy off balance, would occasionally kill or wound one or two, which would then keep them further off balance. This technique was called H&I Fires or Harassing and Interdiction Fires. It was used widely in World War II and Korea.

I was well aware of how we threw high explosives of all kinds throughout our area of operations and quite frankly was not that all impressed with our accuracy. My knowledge of gunnery, statistics and shell dispersion only added to my conclusion that this was caused by "us and not them."

In addition for various reasons, there seemed to be a lot of unexploded ordnance lying on the ground, which the Viet Cong would promptly salvage and throw back at us in the form of mines and booby traps. On patrols combat engineers would often accompany us and blow unexploded ordnance where it lay on the ground.

On November 6 a jeep was blown up by a mine one mile to our rear on the road to the bridge and two Marines were killed and two wounded. On the same day an errant mortar round killed a civilian and wounded his wife and child three miles to our rear. It was impossible to determine if the round was from the Viet Cong or us. On November 18 another mine was detonated one-half mile south of us, but fortunately no one was hurt. On December 6 one Vietnamese child was wounded and one killed one-half mile south of us. Both were playing with unexploded ordnance. On December 19, two Marines were killed and three wounded from my company by a booby trap.   During November and December, Marines, civilians and Viet Cong were killed and wounded by ones and twos in a steady drumbeat of mines, booby traps, and unexploded ordnance. There was only one mention of a Viet Cong killed by H & I fires. This doesn't count the casualties from firefights and accidental shootings.

General Harold K. Johnson, Assistant Chief of Staff of the Army, was dismayed by this tactic as he felt there was not much good to show for it and potentially a lot of negative impact on South Vietnamese peasants. At the time I wondered about this since we were immersed among many villages and hamlets, but I wasn't in charge of strategy, so I just tried to be careful. This would not be the case in 1966 when we were up North in an isolated area in search of the North Vietnamese Army.

"Skipper, we really screwed up on this one," I say.

"OK, John, I agree with you. I'll instruct headquarters to compensate him."

We send a message to battalion. "Marine artillery hit at coordinates (AT 943652) wounded two (2) cows, threw shrapnel through village huts. Suggest you cancel H&I fires at these coordinates."

We're lucky no civilians were killed.

Notes:

1. Command Chronology Volume 1, 1st Battalion 1st Marines, December 1965, Volume 1 page 76, Volume 2 page 136. Incident happened December 9th at 11:25 am, One mile south of Hill 41 along the road at Phu Son (1)

2. *Westmoreland, The General Who Lost Vietnam,* Lewis Sorley, Houghton Mifflin Harcourt New York, 2011, page 101 for General Johnson comment on Harassing and Interdiction Fires.

3. One has only to scroll through several hundred pages of the Command Chronologies of the 1st Battalion 1st Marines for the months of November and December 1965 to get a sense of the number of casualties suffered by all from mines, booby traps, errant artillery shells, accidental shootings, and firefights. At least 118 KIA and at least 269 WIA. See pages 126-129.

ANOTHER NIGHT AT THE OFFICE

It's pitch black, moonrise not for another four hours, and I'm huddled in a hole next to my company commander, Dave Usher. In my hand is a map, a shielded red light, and my heart is pounding. A Viet Cong force is advancing stealthily to attack our position, and I'm developing the coordinates for a high explosive fire mission to obliterate them. This will be an "all or nothing," on the first salvo. If I use precision adjustments under illumination, they'll scatter like roaches. Throw the book at 'em the first time, and hope to kill a few is what I'm planning.

We have a seismic detection system that gives us early warning if someone approaches our position. Metal stakes are sunk into the earth on avenues of approach, and long wires extend back to a control panel where a Marine sits with earphones. Footsteps on the ground, whether animal or human, are magnified, sound like booming drumbeats, and are transmitted to the operator. It takes some skill to distinguish between a water buffalo and a human, but there is no doubt that what is out in front of us tonight is a mass of enemy of undetermined size approaching our position. I briefly wore the headphones, and the approaching noise is deafening.

We have nicknamed this seismic device The Animal and its official designation is AN/TPS-21. We are the most exposed rifle company in our battalion, stick out like a sore thumb into Indian country, and have really messed up Viet Cong access to the villages. They keep running into our patrols and ambushes, are unable to resupply and consequently are starving. Enemy intelligence repeatedly indicates they intend to wipe us out. As we have only one of these devices in our battalion, it's allocated to us.

A village is close to the base of our hill, but fortunately the enemy is approaching from the jungle foothills in a different direction and is on unsheltered open ground, so civilian casualties are not a concern. We are on high alert. Marines are crouching over M-60 machine guns and sighting down M-14 rifles. Our mortar squad is waiting with shells in hand to drop down tubes. Our tank is locked and loaded with its 90-millimeter tube sighted into the darkness. An artillery battery stands by with high explosives loaded, waiting an order from me. We know they are approaching, but they don't know we know. The situation is far different than the devastating attack on Hill 22 when Alpha Company was caught by surprise. All is silent, and we await orders from our company commander.

"Fire," yells Usher and we unleash our death and destruction. Artillery explodes in the air and hot shrapnel rains over the earth below. If we are remotely on target, hopefully we killed a few. Five minutes later I follow up with illumination, and the night landscape is bathed in a flickering ghostly glow and barely audible hiss as the illumination shells descend via parachute. Shadows dance along the ground. We detect no movement and cannot determine if there are any dead or wounded.

Thirty minutes later, with no further action, we send out our normal night ambushes. At the dawn, we send a patrol to check the area, and they report no blood or bodies. They do find a straw hat with a hole possibly caused by shrapnel, markers made of stones and sticks, and many footprints up and down the hill. The stones and sticks were probably direction markers for the attack on our position. Viet Cong tactics are to evacuate all their dead and wounded so we will never know how many we killed, if any. Later, it occurs to me that maybe we should have not fired at all and given them a chance to hit us first. We would have given a devastating response, although we may have incurred casualties ourselves. Oh well, I'm not the company commander.

In the context of the five rifle companies in our battalion spread out over five miles south of Da Nang, this is just another normal event in the daily routine of fighting our counterinsurgency war. So passes another night at the office.

Notes:

1. This incident happened on December 15, 1965. At 7:15 p.m. high explosives shells fired on grid 928653. At 7:20 p.m. illumination shells fired on grid 936657. The Animal (AN/TPS-21) had target 10 degrees wide or 583 feet, at a range of 1000 meters. The target was identified as 20 Viet Cong, which I think is wrong. This means a spacing of 30 feet between individuals, which is too much. I think 5 feet is more likely which would equate to over 100 Viet Cong. Whatever the number I believe we foiled an attack of a very large number of the enemy.

2. Command Chronology 1st Battalion 1st Marines December 1965. Volume 1, pages 10, 23, 99, 100, 102, Volume 2, pages 32, 35, Volume 3, pages 4, 5.

3. Command Chronology 3rd Marine Regiment December 1965, pages 21, 22.

4. Command Chronology 1st Battalion 12th Marines, December 1965, page 5. The time is wrong. At 2015 (it was 1915) Battery A fired high explosives at grid 928653. At 2020 (it was 1920) Battery A fired illumination at grid 936657.

THE FINAL JOURNEY HOME

Death by ones and twos finally caught up with us on the evening of December 18 at 7:15 pm. The Grim Reaper was waiting astride the road in the village hamlet of La Chau (2), practically in our back yard, and less than a mile from Hill 41. The culprit was a simple explosive device that a child could construct, four of our own hand grenades, purloined by the Viet Cong, placed upside down in holes with the pin removed and connected to a trip wire across the trail.

It's the morning of December 19 and I'm sitting on the edge of my cot, having just returned from another fruitless night lying in the weeds. The sky is cloudy and pregnant with rain for another monsoon deluge. I've only been with India Company one month, and I'm still learning names and faces of the one hundred and thirty Marines who comprise my comrades in arms. Only five of us are officers, I'm the forward observer, so they all know me, while I'm still learning them.

Suddenly, Bill Parker, fellow officer and platoon commander, storms into our hooch.

"I told Usher not to send that patrol into the same area twice!" Dave Usher is our company commander.

Parker has just returned from the division mortuary where he identified the body of Corporal Tommie Garrett, a squad leader in Parker's platoon. Garrett, a tall slender light-skinned African American with a pencil-thin mustache from Augusta, Georgia, had a reputation as a squared-away leader of the thirteen Marines under his command, and as I write these words his picture is in my mind's eye. He had my trust and confidence. I hope I had his.

This was one of our nightly squad ambushes with this one along the road to La Chau (2) and the bridge across the Tuy Loan River. Tactical policy was not to send an ambush to the same location twice. The Viet Cong were observant and more apt to set booby traps in locations you frequented. Evidently that's what happened. Corporal Garrett tripped the wire and was killed instantly. Four other Marines were wounded, of whom three were evacuated. Three days later on December 21, Corporal Ronald Mullinax from Shelby, North Carolina, died of wounds sustained in the blast.

All Marines killed in Vietnam were routed through the division mortuary in Da Nang where their earthly remains were cleaned and embalmed. Information was sent to the United States, an officer was dispatched to notify the next-of-kin, their personal affairs and effects were taken care of as best the Marine Corps knew how, and when all was said and done, they were launched on their final journey home.

Later in the afternoon of December 19 we host a Christmas Party at the base of Hill 41, and about 800 villagers attend from the surrounding area, some from the hamlet of La Chau where Garrett and Mullinax were killed. We distribute clothing, soap, medicine, canned milk and toys, and our battalion surgeon holds sick call.

Corporals Tommie Garrett and Ronald Mullinax are memorialized on the Vietnam Wall, panel 4E and lines twenty-three and thirty-three, respectively. Corporal Garrett is laid to rest in South View Cemetery, Augusta Georgia and Corporal Mullinax is laid to rest in Cleveland Memorial Park in Shelby, North Carolina. Rest in peace, my comrades.

Notes:

1. Command Chronology 1st Battalion 1st Marines, December 1965: Volume 1, Ambush site grid 943677 page 24, S-1 log, pages 105-106, 108-109; Volume 2 Intelligence summary page 37; Volume 3, details on Christmas party page 101.

AN OFFICER OF MARINES

For his actions in the village of An My on July 12, 1965, Lieutenant Frank Reasoner was posthumously awarded the Medal of Honor. His small patrol came under attack by a Viet Cong company, and he was subsequently killed. On December 17 a North Vietnamese Army Battalion, strength 400, moves into the same area. The An My village complex is four miles south of our outpost on Hill 41, at the outermost limit of our artillery range, and offers the Viet Cong a forward operating area in close proximity to their jungle bases.

It's December 20 and daylight has peeked above the South China Sea. Our platoon is outside the wire at the base of Hill 41 and going through our normal shakedown procedures as we prepare for a patrol south to the village of An My, deep in Indian Territory. We know nothing of Frank Reasoner's Medal of Honor and the North Vietnamese Army battalion.

Now 2nd lieutenants are the brunt of jokes. We're young. We're inexperienced. We don't know a thing. And the list of our sins goes on! The facts were most of us held leadership positions during our college years, and the Marine Corps had immersed us in nine months of intense training in how to become an officer. Having said that, there was still a grain of truth in the comments. All of us knew that once placed in command, we still had to earn the respect of our men. The crowning story went something like this.

"There will come a time, Lieutenant, when you're up to your neck in alligators, bullets cracking overhead, and you're the only officer left alive. Some grizzled sergeant, old enough to be your father, will turn to you and ask, what do we do next, Lieutenant?"

We also heard stories about what happens when the infantry leader is killed, and suddenly you're in command. Lieutenant Harvey Barnum, serving as a forward observer with a rifle company, took over when his company commander was killed and subsequently won the Medal of Honor. This happened south of Da Nang two days earlier on December 18. Of course I know nothing of this.

Implied, but left unsaid was: If you can pass through this dark valley, you can call yourself an Officer of Marines. Well, today I will enter that valley. I just don't know it yet.

I had concerns about the command arrangements. The patrol leader was Staff Sergeant Smith, and while not in the infantry chain of command, I still outranked Smith as a 2nd lieutenant. Normally this was not an issue, as the patrol leader was usually another officer. But Smith and I knew one another. We were short of officers, and nothing was going to happen anyway.

To be successful I learned early on that the infantry officer was in charge of the patrol, and the forward observer was in charge of artillery. A few hard-charging observer lieutenants had to learn this the hard way: do not attempt to run the patrol. Privately though, artillery officers would joke that we were smarter than our infantry counterparts. Indeed, in artillery school a poster proclaimed,

"Artillery lends dignity to what would otherwise be a vulgar brawl."

The sky is cloudy with probably some light intermittent rain, but there is decent visibility if I have to call in a fire mission. Navigation is not exactly precise in the rice paddies, but I should be able to pick up enough landmarks to triangulate with my compass and map.

I go through my mental check list: two hand grenades on belt, pins secure, two magazines each with seven rounds, map in left pocket, compass in right and so forth. I check my radio operator, Lance Corporal David Henderson:

"Henderson, do you have your extra battery and handset?"

"Yes sir, Mr. Booth."

I will remind you again that our radios are Korean War relics, prone to failure, and if we need help, Henderson carries one of our two lifelines to the rear.

Only after we leave the base of the hill do I load my pistol. I pull the slide to the rear, let it go, and a round slides into the chamber. Then ever so gently squeeze the trigger until the hammer falls on my finger, and my pistol is now on half-cock safety. I can pull my weapon, cock, aim and shoot in one fluid move. This will come in handy later in the morning.

The squad leaders do the same; we all give thumbs up, form into column and move out. I'm close to the front with the point squad, machine gun fire team and Sergeant Smith ahead of me.

Our patrol is going deep and will be out from underneath the protective umbrella of our workhorse quick response 105-millimeter howitzers, for we will be out of range. I had observed 105 gun crews in action and knew one six gun battery could have thirty shells in the air in one minute and smother a football field with a rain of hot jagged steel. If I was to face fast moving Viet Cong guerrillas, I wanted a 105 battery at my back.

Our only fire support, though, will be from two longer-range eight-inch howitzers. While the eight-inch is the most accurate artillery weapon in the Marine Corps arsenal, it is slow to adjust, cumbersome to reload, and only accurate if the target is stationary. That is unlikely, because if the Viet Cong hit us, they will be like a moving swarm of bees. In addition, we only have two howitzers at our beck and call instead of the usual six.

So, I didn't have a lot of confidence in our fire support, had a vague sense of unease, and felt like we were hanging out on a limb. However, those thoughts didn't linger long, for this was just another long, hot, boring patrol where nothing happens.

We go south, stay west of the road, out of the paddies, higher up and hidden inside the edge of the piedmont scrubland. Off to our left a small group of women wearing conical hats and carrying baskets slung over their shoulders scurry north on the road like mice, as if trying to escape. From what?

For two hours we move silently through the bushes, then ease down the hillside and slip into the hamlet of An My. Strangely, we haven't seen any inhabitants since the women on the road. The village sits silent and empty as if waiting in anticipation.

Then the pot starts to boil.

10:00 a.m.

We're crouched on a village path with bullets snapping past our ears, in column, each Marine ten feet behind the other and alternately facing outward to cover our flanks, solid and professional. Up front are shouts, screams, the roar of weaponry and explosions. Cries of "corpsman" signal Marines are already down. Rounds, like hornets, buzz and crack overhead, my adrenalin, up like a rocket and my heart, pounding. My pistol, held in both hands, hammer cocked, finger on the trigger, and I am focused like a laser on my surroundings.

I'm looking at the entrance to a thatch hut, ten feet away, dark and silent. All I can think is: I don't want to get shot in the back, so I decide to search the hut. Now I'm in my seventh decade with five daughters and eight grandchildren, and with the wisdom that's supposed to accumulate with old age and hindsight, that may not have been the wisest decision. All I can say is at age 23 and an officer in the Marines; it seemed like the right thing to do at the time.

I enter the hut, pistol held in front by both hands, finger tight on the trigger, ready to kill anything that moves. I slowly place one foot in front of the other, eyes searching, heart pounding, when suddenly at my feet there is noise and movement.

A chicken jumps up squawking and quickly runs outside.

Why I didn't empty my pistol at the chicken I'll never know, because it survived to cluck another day. I retrieve heart from throat, leave the hut and run toward the sounds of gunfire.

A mass of Viet Cong in white blouses and carrying weapons are walking away in waist high grass at a distance of two hundred yards. They're in a wide-open field, an easy target, and if I had a quick action 105 battery on call it would be like shooting fish in a barrel. But I'll do the best I can with what I have.

I look for Sergeant Smith and discover he is clearly panicked with a white face and wild eyes, and the patrol has dissolved into chaos. The noise is deafening. There is a staccato roar of machine guns and explosions from hand grenades. Well, I guess this is my time. Smith has lost control and we could soon be in dire straights.

I'm in command!

I'm quickly on the radio talking to artillery Marines and request variable time fuses on high explosive shells, which will automatically explode at ninety feet and cover the field below with hot raining shrapnel. I don't think I'll have much luck with only two tubes of eight-inch but I'll give it my best shot!

Marines are shouting and running forward without direction. Some one screams, "Stop, stop, arty coming in." There is a danger of being cut down by our own artillery fire! At least one Marine lies wounded in the confusion.

Training and a controlled rage take over. I stand tall so everyone can see me, oblivious of any rounds snapping overhead. Oaths and profanity roll from my lips the gist of which is: "Smith, put some control on your men, and cease fire on the machine guns."

A freight train rumbles as incoming shells roar overhead.

"KABOOM!"

Deafening explosions rain shrapnel and dapple the blowing grass on the fields in front. A clean miss, the Viet Cong are still walking away unperturbed. I'm trying to kill flies with a sledgehammer. They can move faster than the time for adjustments so I give up with the eight-inch. I make one big adjustment, smother the area with shells, and hope I'll get lucky and kill a few.

"Up 100, fire for effect, two volleys."

The din of small arms fire continues, soon interspersed with airburst explosions and once again shrapnel rains on the grass. However, the result is the same, a clear miss. The Viet Cong are still ambling away with an "I could care less attitude" toward the distant tree line.

"Use your rifles, take well-aimed shots," I shout. "Marines are the best marksmen in the world!"

A Marine near by, who doesn't know I hear him, mutters, "That Lieutenant doesn't know what he's talking about, those Viet Cong are too far away."

I don't think they're too far away and I'm a crack shot. I almost shout back at him, "If you can't hit 'em, at least make 'em duck." As I write these words I wish I had.

Another comment floats through the air amid the roar of fire, "The Lieutenant seems to know how to run a firefight."

Eventually we cease-fire when the enemy disappears into the distant tree line. Instinct tells me that now is not the time or place to pursue our adversaries.

I straighten out a garbled message to Jack Downing, our company executive officer four miles behind me on Hill 41. The company thinks we're pinned down by fire and is preparing to come to our assistance.

"No, we're not pinned down, things are under control, Smith panicked, I'll tell you about it when I come in."

11:00 a.m.

I'm standing in an open field calling in a medical evacuation over the radio. I carried a small waterproof card in my left front pocket with written instructions for emergency evacuations by helicopter. I had lost the original card, but thought the information so valuable that I wrote the instructions on a piece of cardboard and wrapped it with scotch tape so it was waterproof. The instructions are simple, but in a firefight, you forget even simple things.

Switch to the air evacuation frequency and encode all information. Encryption sheets were changed daily. The Viet Cong knew the radio frequency but if everything was encrypted it made no difference. Then give the following information in this precise order, which I still remember, all these many years later.

"Number of dead, zero,"

"Number of wounded, one,"

"Map coordinates of evacuation, 920603,"

"Condition of the landing zone, hot, expect enemy fire when you come in."

We hear the "thowp, thowp" of choppers in the distance. Someone throws a smoke grenade to mark the landing zone and determine wind direction and soon one bird swoops low. There is a picture in my mind's eye of a helicopter hovering slightly above the ground, a gray sky and tree line in the background and another bird hovering overhead providing cover. Four Marines rush to the chopper door carrying our comrade on a poncho. Arms reach out to take him and our wounded Marine is whisked away.

Instructions are relayed from battalion headquarters.

"India, switch to the command frequency and use call sign Tar Bush 41 to speak to an air observer who will be overhead shortly."

I'm thinking, "Wow, we have the attention of the brass in the rear. We must be on to something big for they're worried about us."

12:00 p.m.

I can't remember if I'm standing up or lying down. The snap and crack of enemy fire is overhead and I'm mad at myself. I'm looking at a bamboo arch directly astride the dirt road at the hamlet of An My. On both sides of the arch is barbed wire interspersed with punji stakes. A table and chairs are set up, and it is obvious that anyone traveling the dirt road will be forced to pass through the arch, stand in front of the table, at which time Viet Cong tax collectors will extort money from the travelers.

Above the arch is a flag, and I am mad at myself because I cannot remember whom the flag represents, and I should know. It could represent the National Liberation Front, which is the political arm of the Viet Cong, but it also could represent the flag of the North Vietnamese Army in which case we could be in deep trouble.

I'm talking to Jack Downing, the company executive officer; "The flag is red at the top, blue at the bottom with a yellow star in the middle."

He confirms, " It's the flag of the National Liberation Front." A sigh of relief, "One less thing to worry about."

2:00 p.m.

Our patrol is returning to Hill 41 and we have picked up nineteen civilians in the vicinity of An My. They do not have proper identification so we treat them as Viet Cong suspects and will turn them over to Vietnamese officials. All but one will be cleared and he will be held for further questioning. We see many new dug-in positions such as mantraps and punji pits.

What drove my instinct that told me that now was not the time and place to pursue our adversaries? We've shot up half our ammunition and could shoot it all to no avail. If the Viet Cong have reinforcements in that distant tree line they could outnumber us, turn around and overwhelm us. The closest two rifle companies are four miles to our rear and at least one hour away. Getting help will be difficult and air support probably impossible. And to top it off I have absolutely no confidence in our artillery support. Going after these guys is not the smart thing to do. Not today.

It's over. The Viet Cong live to fight another day, but so do we. I feel drained. I'm exhausted and let sergeants run the patrol back home. Smith is somewhere in the column.

I notice a change in the men. A Marine approaches with his canteen in hand,

"Care for a drink Lieutenant?" I know he doesn't have enough water for himself.

Sergeant West, a squad leader, walks up, offers me some snuff, and then a high compliment,

"I'm glad you were with us today, Mr. Booth."

Then it dawns on me and I'm almost overcome with emotion:

"These Marines entrust me with their lives and will follow me under fire."

What an awesome feeling and what awesome responsibility. In a no-name firefight in an obscure hamlet south of Da Nang, I truly become an Officer of Marines.

Epilogue

Months later I pass a battalion aid station and see Marines stretched out, arms over their foreheads, sleeping peacefully, a corpsman rubbing one with alcohol, and rock music playing softly in the background. But they will nevermore wake this side of heaven.

"What happened?" I ask.

"Old Indian trick, Lieutenant. They got suckered in and then picked off one by one."

Years later I remember I didn't get suckered in that day and articulate a leadership principle. Great personal courage and lack of judgment are a deadly combination in a Marine officer.

The final pieces of information for this yarn do not come to me until decades later when I am researching the official records. I was unaware of the circumstances of Frank Reasoner's Medal of Honor and the close proximity of the North Vietnamese Army battalion. The North Vietnamese were across the Yen River and in the operational sector of another Marine battalion. They moved into position on December 17 and our battalion did not receive this intelligence until December 20. Our patrol was on the same day, and the fact that for whatever reason we did not receive that information could have been very costly!

It's reasonable to assume the enemy we encountered was associated with that North Vietnamese Army Battalion, and if we had pursued them, we would have been greatly outnumbered, and like Custer and the Battle of the Little Bighorn, I might not be writing these words! My instincts in my youth on December 20, 1965, were spot on.

Notes:

1. Information obtained from command chronologies of the 1st Battalion, 1st Marines Regiment, December 1965, Volume 1, Intelligence page 12, Close Combat page 20, S-1 pages 111-112, Volume 2, Intelligence Summary, page 39-41. Volume 3, S-2/S-3 pages 14-15. 12th Marine Regiment, December 1965, and the 3rd Reconnaissance Battalion July 1965, pages 35-40.

2. I was a Forward Observer with India Battery, 3rd Battalion, 12th Marine Regiment assigned to India Company 3rd Battalion, 4th Marine Regiment. The battery and battalion were in Phu Bai. Our company was transferred south to Da Nang and under operational control of 1st Battalion, 1st Marine Regiment.

3. The enemy unit was the 44th Battalion of the North Vietnamese Army (People's Army of Vietnam or PAVN for short) and was commanded by a Lieutenant Colonel La Den who was part Vietnamese and part Indian. The strength of the unit was 400 and they moved into position on December 17 at grid 955587, 953570, 947598 and 943598.

4. The air observer reported at 3:20 p.m. that there was plenty of fresh digging at grids 947607 and 957604. This was the air observer of whom we were notified earlier, but we had left the area by 3:20 p.m. and never had contact with him.

5. The village of An My is composed of four hamlets numbered (1) thru (4). For simplicity of this story all locations are treated as a single village. Lieutenant Reasoner and our patrol were engaged at the hamlet of An My (3) at grid 923608. The bamboo arch I observed for the tax collectors was at grid 927610.

6. The 105 mm battery that supported us was A Battery, 1st Battalion 12th Marine Regiment and was located at grid 939722 and had a range of 7 miles. The eight-inch battery was located at grid 955755. It fired a two hundred pound projectile with a range of 10 to 15 miles. We were at the maximum range of the eight-inch howitzer in the hamlets of An My.

7. First Lieutenant Frank Reasoner was posthumously awarded the Medal of Honor for actions on July 12, 1965, in An My (3) grid 927608. Five months later we are involved in a firefight in the same location where Frank was killed. I did not know Frank personally but he had been in the 1st Marine Brigade in Hawaii and landed in South Vietnam with the 3rd Battalion 4th Marines, my unit in Phu Bai. Many of the officers knew Frank and spoke highly of him. Frank was transferred south to the Recon Battalion in Da Nang and was subsequently killed in action.

8. The operations log indicates we collided with ten to twelve Viet Cong firing a machine gun and possibly wounded one Viet Cong.

9. This entire incident is in the vicinity of Hill 55, which the Marines occupied in 1966. The book *Marine Sniper* by Charles Henderson details the exploits of legendary Marine marksman Carlos Hathcock, some of which occurred in the vicinity of Hill 55. The Marines will experience extensive combat with the Viet Cong around Hill 55 in 1966.

10. The Marine dead I reference in the Epilogue were from the 1st Battalion 4th Marine Regiment and were killed in Operation Oregon on March 20-22, 1966. Total KIA were twelve Marines. I would join this Battalion on April 11, 1966.

11. The Marine wounded and evacuated on our patrol was air evacuated to the US Naval Hospital in Oakland, California. He suffered a gunshot wound to the left leg with a fractured femur.

2nd Lieutenant John Booth and L/Cpl David Henderson returning from patrol outside the wire at the base of Hill 41. I quit carrying an M-14 rifle. I didn't have enough hands to do everything in a firefight. Note hand grenades on belt.

Artillery Lends Dignity To What Would Otherwise Be A Vulgar Brawl

Artillery Lends Dignity To What Would Otherwise Be A Vulgar Brawl. Poster that proves artillery officers are smarter than anyone else!

105 mm gun crew in action. Quick and agile to adjust and can smother a football field sized area with explosives quickly. Range of 7 miles.

8 inch howitzer. Most accurate weapon in USMC arsenal if target is stationary. Cumbersome and slow to load and adjust. On December 20 had only two howitzers in support and at maximum range. "Felt like we were hanging out on a limb."

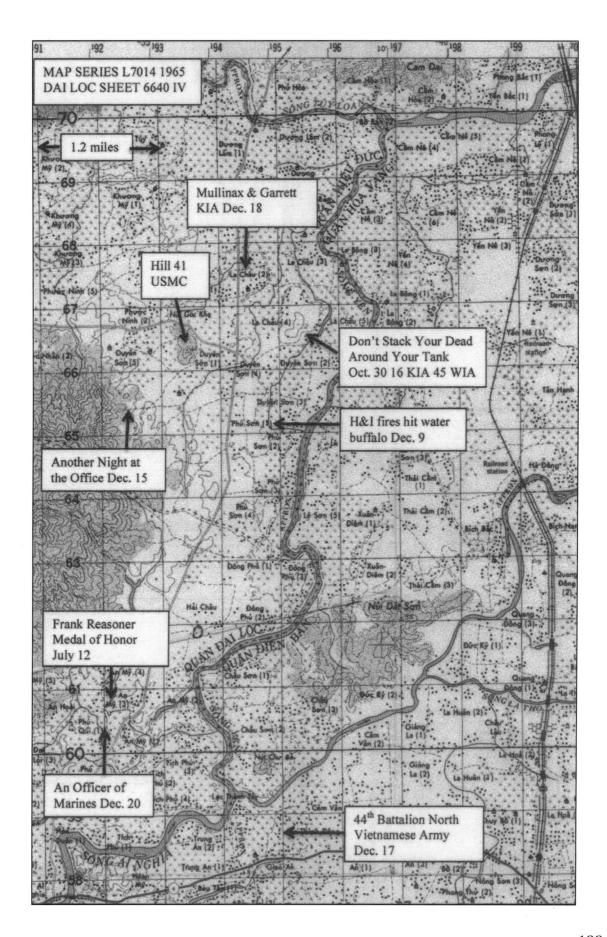

MAP SERIES L7014 1965
DAI LOC SHEET 6640 IV

1.2 miles

Mullinax & Garrett
KIA Dec. 18

Hill 41
USMC

Don't Stack Your Dead
Around Your Tank
Oct. 30 16 KIA 45 WIA

H&I fires hit water
buffalo Dec. 9

Another Night at
the Office Dec. 15

Frank Reasoner
Medal of Honor
July 12

An Officer of
Marines Dec. 20

44th Battalion North
Vietnamese Army
Dec. 17

ALWAYS FAITHFUL

Relationships are important, and if you have ever served in combat with the Marines there is a fidelity that bonds beyond all understanding. We all had emblazoned on our hearts, Semper Fidelis, Always Faithful. Shakespeare had it right. "We few, we happy few, we band of brothers: For he today that sheds his blood with me shall be my brother be he ever so vile."

Earlier in December our company received notice that our battalion would rotate back to Okinawa. In addition to receiving replacements and new equipment, it would mean some welcome rest and relaxation. My battalion had been in Vietnam since April of 1965, nine months. I had been in Vietnam six months, had spent the first two as a gunnery officer with an artillery battery, the last four as a forward observer with two rifle companies, and specifically these last six weeks on Hill 41, living in the mud, surviving under boiling sun and monsoon rains, patrolling rice paddies, protecting Vietnamese civilians, fighting Viet Cong, and dodging land mines and booby traps. I was ready for a rest.

The plan was to spend sixty days in Okinawa, and then return to Vietnam as the Special Landing Force where we would stay embarked on ships, and land and fight where needed at hot spots up and down the coast. On December 21 our replacements arrive, and at 3:25 p.m. our company is heli-lifted back north to Phu Bai to join our parent battalion.

However, there was a problem. The new company did not have a forward observation team. So guess what?

We stay behind!

I felt we would eventually catch up with our rifle company, knew it could take a week or two, but had also observed how screwed up things became in combat, so this also had the smell of a permanent transfer.

I was losing the camaraderie of my rifle company, and yes it was my company. My fellow officers, Dave Usher, Jack Downing, Steve Ek and "Whisky Bill" Parker had become like brothers. I remembered the compliment from Sergeant West, "Glad you were with us today, Mr. Booth," after our firefight in An My, the Marine who offered me a drink from his canteen when he didn't have enough water for himself, and other Marines whose names I do not remember who said either by their actions or words; "We trust you with our lives, Mr. Booth, and will follow you under fire, so trust us to look after you."

The idea of starting this bonding process all over again with a new rifle company was not appealing. On my first patrol my doubts were reinforced as they did not appear to be as professional as my company, or so I thought. Too much bunching up at stream crossings was one example, and I concluded that things could get hazardous for my long-term health. However, after the appropriate oaths, gnashing of teeth, and calling down curses upon the Marine Corps we settled in to getting to know our new comrades-in-arms.

Meanwhile unknown to me and up north at Hue our battalion embarks on a flotilla of three US Navy ships, The Valley Forge, The Monticello, and The Montrose, and on the morning of Christmas Eve they up anchor and steam from the mouth of the Perfume River toward Okinawa 1500 miles away. Unless something happens quickly, my forward observation team and I will not rejoin our outfit anytime soon.

Again unknown to me, a message arrives on the Valley Forge that says in essence:

"Proceed to Da Nang harbor. Pick up forward observation team commanded by 2nd Lieutenant John R. Booth on Hill 41. Rejoin convoy."

The Valley Forge was a 27,100-ton Ticonderoga class aircraft carrier that was commissioned in November 1946, too late to join the Pacific fleet in WW II, but saw extensive action in the Korean War. As her flight deck was of WW II design she was unable to handle the new high-performance aircraft of the post-Korean War era, and in June of 1961 was given a new mission as an amphibious assault ship for the Marine Corps. Instead of launching jet aircraft with bombs, she launches helicopters with Marines for a vertical assault from the air.

The Valley Forge slowly turns her bow to the south, and proceeds to Da Nang harbor.

That same morning we are slogging north on a dirt road returning to Hill 41 when an urgent message is received over the radio with my name in the clear, a serious breach of security protocol. Something must be very important, and someone must be very excited.

"Tell Lieutenant Booth his replacement has arrived."

Through my binoculars, and way off in the distance on top of Hill 41, I see an old buddy from artillery school, Jim Daughtry, jumping up and down and waving his arms. Upon reaching the hill we exchange greetings, I brief him on our situation, and we prepare to leave. My feelings were of excitement and gratitude, and at dusk the chopper arrives. The Marine Corps has not forgotten us!

I still remember that helicopter ride in my old age. A quick landing, we throw our gear through the door, clamber aboard, cram our flak jackets beneath us as we strap in, and the chopper shoots straight up fast. The bird strains for altitude, and in the dusk a bright yellow stream of enemy fire chases us as we hurry toward the South China Sea, and a waiting US Navy warship. The tracers are beautiful, and remind me of Christmas lights. I almost forget they're aimed at us.

An image has stayed with me through the years. We land on the flight deck in the fading light, and sailors stand in awe as filthy, unwashed Marines come tumbling out of the chopper. I didn't kiss the deck literally, but sure felt like I had. Minutes after we are aboard, I hear the shudder and feel the shake as engines crank up, and the Valley Forge gets underway to rejoin the convoy.

Entering the bowels of the ship, I stand in wonder at its vastness, and estimate the crew at well over one thousand sailors. I marvel at the stainless steel showers and flush toilets. In the officers' wardroom I order a juicy hamburger from the galley, and after a few ravenous gulps surprisingly observe the shock on the galley cook's face, and it suddenly dawns on me:

"He thinks I'm a starving wolf. I need to clean up my act as I re-enter civilization." The hot food, hot showers, clean sheets, and safe surroundings all combine into feelings so unreal that I do not sleep that first night.

December 25

Dear Mom and Dad
Merry Christmas from the USS Valley Forge. Christmas came here at 6:00 p.m. on December 24 when we were heli-lifted aboard. Last night I slept between sheets for the first time since June 27-also for the first time in 42 days I'm sleeping where I can take my boots off at night.

If we ever got in trouble we knew our comrades would come after us. Whether on some woe be-gone battered hilltop, or some God-forsaken rice paddy with half our comrades dead and wounded, we knew the Marine Corps would move heaven and earth to extract us. Don't ask us how we knew, we just knew.

It wasn't until decades later as I write these words that I connected the diverting of a 27,000 ton aircraft carrier with over one thousand sailors to extract six Marines from that scarred hilltop in Vietnam as actions that would build that trust.

Semper Fidelis. Always Faithful.

Notes:

1. When we were heli-lifted into a landing zone we always wore our flak jackets. We never knew whether our landing site would be under enemy fire. If we were going into an area we knew was safe, like that ride to the USS Valley Forge, we sat on our flak jackets to protect ourselves from fire from below. As virile young men, we didn't want our testicles shot off!

2. I was a forward observer with India Company, 3rd Battalion 4th Marines. Our company was sent south and under operation control of 1st Battalion, 1st Marines on Hill 41 south of Da Nang.

3. Command Chronology, 3rd Battalion 4th Marines, December, 1965, page 3 for ship information and dates.

4. Command Chronology, 1st Battalion 1st Marines, December 1965. See S-1 and S-2/S-3 logs from the dates December 22 through December 25. I researched those dates in an attempt to determine exactly when my replacement arrived and what messages transpired with the USS Valley Forge. The messages were confusing and I gave up. Something like the message I wrote transpired and the Valley Forge picked us up.

KILLED, INJURED AND WOUNDED VICINITY HILL 41 OCT 30 THU DEC 31 1965

One has to scroll through several hundred pages of the Command Chronologies of the 1st Battalion 1st Marines and the 3rd Battalion 3rd Marines for the months of November and December 1965 to get a sense of the steady drumbeat of casualties suffered by all from mines, booby traps, errant artillery shells, accidental shootings and firefights. This is what I have done below. War is a messy business. We all, Marines, Vietnamese civilians and Viet Cong died by ones, twos, and threes. In a counterinsurgency we cannot nor do we seek to kill our way to victory.

Date	Name-Rank-Age-Hometown	USMC KIA	USMC WIA	Civilian KIA	Civilian WIA	Viet Cong KIA	Viet Cong WIA	CAP	Location	
Oct 30	A Co 3rd Engineer Battalion									The October 30th date lists the number and best guesses for all the killed and wounded on the attack on Hill 22 to include Marines,
	Robert S Ruch Cpl 28 Bethlehem PA	1							955666	Vietnamese civilians, and Viet Cong. All Marines KIA at same location.
	Seymour P Sadberry Pfc 20 Boston MA	1								
	Ronald V Bacca Pvt 20 Magna UT	1								Two weeks later I am on Hill 41 one mile to the west of Hill 22.
	A Co 1st Battalion 1st Marines									During the attack the Marines could not get artillery support. I lead a patrol to Hill 22 and interview my forward observer buddy from
	Frank A Gagliardo* Sgt 31 Deer Park NY	1								artillery school to find out what went wrong.
	Marcos Herandez Sgt 28 El Paso TX	1								
	Richard A Cesar Cpl 20 Corydon IA	1								
	Gerald L Feltner HN 21 Carroll IA	1								
	Phillip M Sens Cpl 22 Newark OH	1								
	Dennis Smith Cpl 27 Columbus OH	1								
	Robert P Jordan LCpl 18 New York NY	1								
	Harold Schock*LCpl 21 Mamaroneck NY	1								One of the two Marines with an asterisk is from Mike Co. 3rd Bn. 4th Marines. Misidentification in KIA records.
	Richard D Sharp LCpl 19 Dayton OH	1								
	Richard A Crawford* 19 Godfrey IL	1								
	Gary E Elford Pfc 18 Newark OR	1								
	Rayes C Flores Pfc 21 Abilene TX	1								
	H&S Co. 1st Battalion 1st Marines									Will never know for sure how many Viet Cong killed and wounded because they dragged their dead and wounded away. Intelligence
	Grant L Clark Cpl 20 Pocatello ID	1								guesses 100-200. Number of civilians probably killed and wounded in the response to the attack by artillery and airstrikes also unknown.
	Marines KIA & WIA	16	45							
	Viet Cong killed, 100-200					47	150	1		
	Vietnamese civilians killed & wounded			?	?					
	November									
Nov 1	Marine from D/1/1		1						920690	Grenade booby trap. Wounds to leg, left hand. Not serious. Medevac
Nov 3	A/1/1 exchanges 30-40 rds. with VC								958668	No casualties
Nov 5	Civilian 2 children 1 woman KIA			3					952647	Booby-trapped artillery shell south of Hill 22 near spillway on Yen River. Hamlet of Phu Son (2)
	Civilians 4 WIA				4					
	Viet Cong 3 KIA					3			915704	Mortar round near An Tan
Nov 6	Civilian male KIA wife and 2 yr. child WIA			1	2				925705	81 mortar H&I fire, Viet Cong wounded by same shell
	Viet Cong 3 wounded by same shell						3			

126

Date		USMC KIA	USMC WIA	Civilian KIA	Civilian WIA	Viet Cong KIA	Viet Cong WIA	CAP	Location	Notes
Nov 6	**A Co 1st Battalion 1st Marines**								943672	4 Marines in a mighty mite (jeep) hit mine. Also received automatic weapons fire. Jensen died of wounds on Nov 23. 3 KIA 1 WIA. On road to rear of Hill 41 near hamlet of La Chau (2).
	William L Hunt Pfc 20 Indianapolis IN	1								
	Richard Jensen HN 22 Warren OH	1								
	Gerald Metott LCpl 18 Springwater NY		1							
Nov 7	A/1/1 kill 1 VC and capture 3					1		3	947670	Hamlet of La Chau (2).
	A/1/1 capture 1 VC inside cave.							1	945678	Hamlet of La Chau (2).
Nov 8	A/1/1 kill 12-year old girl by accident.			1					947670	Hamlet of La Chau (2) children running and did not stop on command.
	A/1/1 kill 1 VC & wound 1. 1D card theft					1	1		961669	Hamlet of Duyen Son (2). Dead Viet Cong had 63 1D cards.
Nov 9	C/1/1 kill civilian boy by accident.			1					978737	Hiding in bushes. Collected cash donation and gave to family. 918737?
Nov 12	Popular Force (PF) 1 KIA, 1 WIA			1 PF	1 PF				924706	Died later. Viet Cong headed west along bank of Tuy Loan River
Nov 13	D/1/1, 1 WIA from booby trap.		1						920703	Grenade booby trap. Shrapnel legs and arms. Medevac.
Nov 14	D/1/1, 2 WIA from booby trap.		2						915679	Grenade booby trap. Multiple shrapnel wounds. Medevac. 909696.
	I/3/4 replaces M/3/4 on Hill 41								**934664**	I arrive on Hill 41
Nov 17	I/3/4 reports woman hit by shrapnel.				1				947638	Artillery shell hit near house
	1/3/4 captures 3 VC.							3	933667	
Nov 17	Two Viet Cong killed, one was a nurse.					2			8771	Killed by H&I fire. Nurse lived La Chau complex. Other lived 914722
Nov 18	I/3/4 close call.	0							931671	Mine detonated prematurely 98 feet away. Found electric wires.
	2 bridges burned 943677, 943679.								943677	Repaired by evening
Nov 19	A/1/1 L/Cpl falls into punji pit.		1						965668	Not seriously wounded. Corpsman treated with 2 stitches.
	I/3/4 captures 3 Viet Cong.							3	925677	
Nov 21	I/3/4 kills one Viet Cong.					1			919678	
	B/1/1 Marine bitten by snake.		1						921725	Medevac.
	B/1/1 sentry fires on Marine from F Btry.		1							Marine went forward to relieve himself. Hit right leg. Not serious.
	D/1/1 capture 3 VCS.							3	968699	VCS = Viet Cong suspects
Nov 24	Local VC given orders to ambush,									assassinate and kidnap pacification cadre.
	Woman in Binh Thai village with								875709	orders to make love to PF's and extract information.
Nov 25	I/3/4 LP exchange fire 8-10 Viet Cong.								934658	No casualties either side.
	Each family in Hoa Thuong forced to give								910692	food to feed 3 Viet Cong.
	L/3/3 exchanges fire with Viet Cong								969645	No casualties.
Nov 26	A/1/1 2 WIA minor flesh wounds.		2						956668	Grenade booby trap. No medevac.
Nov 27	A/1/1 fired on Viet Cong						1		936622	Viet Cong medevac.
	B/1/1 Viet Cong threw hand grenade		1						962718	Wounded in shoulder. Medevac.
Nov 30	A/1/1 conducts sick call for 25 villagers								950630	Big deal! 1st time civic action held this far south. VC control area. Past 4 yrs
Nov	**1/1 Command Chronology shows 2 KIA and 11 WIA for November**	3	11	7	8	8	5	13		**1/1 Medical records show 3 KIA and 14 WIA for November**

Date	December	USMC KIA	USMC WIA	Civilian KIA	Civilian WIA	Viet Cong KIA	Viet Cong WIA	CAP	Location	
Dec 1	1/3/4 patrols An My (1) and (4).								927610	VC tax collection at 927610. I am in same village on Dec 20. Firefight.
Dec 2	1/3/4 Viet Cong throws hand grenade.		2						928674	Minor wounds from grenade fragments. No medevac.
	Marine in B/1/1 in 81 mortars shoots himself.		1							In leg with .45 cal. pistol. Medevac required
Dec 3	B/1/1 squad leader shot in chest.		1						924601 or	Viet Cong fired 10 rounds auto fire, medevac.
	One Viet Cong wounded and escaped.						1		921694	
Dec 3	1/3/4 two children playing with dud.			1	1				927653	1000 meters south of Hill 41.
Dec 3	**K/3/3 relieves A/1/1 on Hill 22**								955666	**1/1 boundary with 3/3 changes**
	K/3/3 kill two Viet Cong.					2			955662	Hill 22.
	1/3/3 kills one Viet Cong.					1			968489	I think coordinates are wrong.
	1/3/3 kill one female Viet Cong.					1			973645	Buried in Le Son (3).
Dec 5	1/3/3 patrol discovers rice cache.								969650	Arty stopped all VC fire.
Dec 6	C/1/1 2 WIA.		2						905710	Electronically detonated mine, medevac.
	Goose Alpha 6 to B3 severe head injury.		1						unknown	Injury from recoil mechanism. Medevac.
	B/1/1 reports Popular Force (PF) wounded.				1				9169	Same incident. Khuong My(2), VC KIA was from Tuy Loan
	1 VC KIA 6 escaped, 1 captured, 1 WIA.						1	1	9169	
	1/3/3 1 WIA.		1						969650	All same incident
	1/3/3 kill 2 Viet Cong.					2			965650	
	1/3/3 60mm mortar fire kills 4 Viet Cong.					4			968653	
	Platoon of PF's near Khoung My (2).					1		1	9169	
	VC held meeting to boost morale and								930609	urge increase in assassination activities.
Dec 7	1/3/3 squad ambush 2 VC KIA & 2 WIA.					2	2		971658	
Dec 9	1/3/4 water buffalo wounded by H&I fire.				2 wb				943652	Booth & Usher with farmer. wb = water buffalo.
Dec 10	**Co A 1st Battalion 1st Marines.**									
Dec 11	Charles R McFarlin Pfc 19 Sydney OH	1	2						unknown	Truck rolls over on road en-route to Operation Harvest Moon
Dec 11	B/1/1 reports 1 Regional Force (RF).				1				933693	RF wounded
Dec 12	B/1/1/Robert Brix Pfc 19 Crown Point IN	1							919690	Brix outpost duty. Other Marine left to relieve himself. VC shoot Brix
Dec 13	B1/1 Civilian male failed to stop. Shot.				1				932697	920692? Tried to evade, shot, later declared friendly. I may have seen?
Dec 14	C/1/1 8 water buffalo charge patrol			8 wb					896735	VC water buffalo according to ARVN Lt. Buffalo all KIA
Dec 14	1/3/4 shoot 1 Viet Cong. Knock him down						1		939679	Viet Cong escaped
Dec 14	**M Co 3rd Battalion 3rd Marines**									
	Richard Brunke Pfc 18 Milwaukee WI	1							unknown	Accidental homicide, non-hostile
Dec 18	**I Co 3rd Battalion 4th Marines**									
	Tommie Garrett Cpl 22 Augusta GA	1							943677	Grenade booby trap. Garrett KIA. Mullinax dies Dec 21. 2 KIA 2 WIA
	Ronald Mullinax Cpl 21 Shelby NC		2							La Chau(2)

		USMC		Civilian		Viet Cong			Location	
		KIA	WIA	KIA	WIA	KIA	WIA	CAP		
Dec 20	**K Co 3rd Battalion 3rd Marines**									
	Could not identify Marine's name	1							955664	Booby trap mortar round
Dec 20	I/3/4, surprised VC. Tax collectors.		1				1		920603	An My (3) medevac to USNH Oakland, CA. My patrol. Marine WIA
Dec 21	B/1/1 one Viet Cong killed					1			909694	Khunog My(2)
	L/3/3 one Viet Cong killed					1			979693	
	F/2/1 relieves I/3/4 on Hill 41									My FO Team gets left behind!
Dec 22	B/1/1 HN Uber shot himself in leg		1						unknown	Cleaning .45 cal. pistol, medevac
Dec 23	2nd plt/C/1/1 VC on south side of river					1	1		874713	Under operational control of D/1/1
	D/1/1 Marine with broken knee		1						874713	Medevac
Dec 24	C/1/1 1 Viet Cong killed					1			847713	Entire incident in Phil Caputo Book *Rumor of War*.
	C/1/1		9						898711	2 ½ lbs. TNT wrapped in barbed wire. Non-serious.
Dec 25	D/1/1 helilift extract from Hoi Vuc		2						872707	Marine wounded leg. Marine wounded arm. Medevac.
	Vietnamese civilians wounded				3				955666	Viet Cong booby trap, Hill 22
	K/3/3 1 Viet Cong killed					1			964658	
	1 Vietnamese child KIA			1					944670	Detonated booby trap, La Chau(2)
Dec 26	M/3/3 killed two Viet Cong					2			973660	
Dec 27	K/3/3 killed one Viet Cong					1			975613	
	M/3/3 killed two Viet Cong					2			973660	
	B/1/1 reports PF squad attacked by VC				5				946692	45 VC south of pontoon bridge.
	1st plt/B/1/1							1		Captured 1 VC
Dec 29	M/3/3 killed three Viet Cong via airstrikes					3				966650, 977653, 973650, 962641, 973642
Dec 30	D1/1		1						874705	Shrapnel in ankle. Back blast M79 grenade launcher.
	C/1/1		2						8770	Hoi Vuc
Dec31	C/1/1		1							Fever Hoi Vuc
Dec 31	1/1 Command Chronology shows 1 KIA + 29 WIA but does not show 3 /4 casualties for December	6	31	2	12	26	7	3		1/1 medical records 1 KIA + 19 WIA + 1 DOA from vehicle accident for December
	November Total	3	11	7	8	8	5	13		
	Nov. & Dec Total	9	42	9	20	34	12	16		
	Oct. 30 Attack on Hill 22 A/1/1	16	45	?	?	47	150	1		Probably 100-200 Viet Cong KIA and WIA
	Grand Total Oct 30-Dec 31	25	87	9 +	20+	84 +	162+	17		**Total KIA & WIA: At least 118 killed, at least 269 wounded.**

Abbreviations: C/1/1 = Charlie Company, 1st Battalion 1st Marine Regiment etc. KIA=killed in action, WIA=wounded in action, CAP=captured, DOA=dead on arrival, medevac=medically evacuated by helicopter. **From Oct. 30 thru Dec. 31, 25 Marines were killed and 87 wounded. At least 9 civilians were killed and 20 wounded. At least 84 Viet Cong were killed and 100-200 were wounded but the number is probably more. Killing the enemy was not a means to the end. Unfortunately General William Westmoreland did not agree our strategy.**

Đông Khánh High school.
Huế, South Vietnam.
December, 21, 1965.

Dear Sir,

I think that, you will be very surprised when receiving this letter. So I must introduce myself to you ? I am one of the students of Đông Khánh girl high school. Do you know my school ? It's the famous high school at Huế the old capital of Vietnam with many beautiful sceneries and famous temples. there is the Perfume river which flows slowly, on both sides, two lines of trees and houses reflect in the blue water, over this river there is a lovely bridge, which we call the NGUYEN HOANG Bridge. Besides the river, the Royal Tombs are also a beautiful landscape of Huế.

Those are all the special beauty of the Old capital of Vietnam. Have you ever visited Huế ? if you haven't been in Huế, How can you imagine the beauty of my city ? For me I have been living here all my life, so I have attended at this high school for 5 years, since I was eleven.

I must confess that till now, I have never written a letter for any foreign soldier, so this is the first time I am delighted to write to you and I wish that this letter will be in your hand just on Christmas day.

Christmas will come in this time millions of hearts have the same beneath, they are anxious to get the spiritual day of all people in the world. Every one is waiting for a happy Christmas day. Are you watching ? While people prepare to go shopping, for their great festival the christmas trees, holler, mistletoes, gifts and the Christmas carols for their relatives, you ought to fight in the battle. you haven't enough food to eat and missing everything. Sometimes, you are lost your life from cruel enemy

This letter was written on December 21, 1965. I do not have the slightest idea how this young lady got my name, and I assume her motivation was a high school writing project. I received this letter in early 1966 when we were temporarily sent to Okinawa for rest and resupply. As a 23 year-old Marine 2nd Lieutenant, having just left a war zone and knowing I was going back in, I didn't give it much thought. Her description of Hue is very accurate for I visited the city several times. The city was the scene of fierce fighting in the 1968 Tet offensive.

I did not respond. I wish I had.

Sincerely Yours

NGUYEN THI NHO

A student of Dong Khanh girl
high school

AIR MAIL   PAR AVION

2nd LT. BOOTH J.R.
Artillery

of course, you also have enjoyed all the interesting days.

Why are you have to leave all your loved relatives to come to this poor country in the way time to fight against the enemy. With all your heart? The answer may be resumed in "Peace". You are admired of the mankind by your noble sacrifice and I always remember your kindness.

Now, may I ask some questions about you? I want to know you well, how old are you? Are you single or married? and what state you live in United States? Are you fond of movies? For me, I like to go to the movies very much so I often go to the movies every weekend and my favourit star is Sandra Dee. do you like her?

Well, before stopping this letter, I wish you a Merry Christmas and I always hope that God will bless you. Please give my best regards to your family.

PART 4 FIND THE NORTH VIETNAMESE ARMY AND PICK A FIGHT

FIRE SUPPORT COORDINATOR WITH THE 1ST BATTALION, 4TH MARINES AND 1ST BATTALION 3RD MARINES, APRIL 11 THROUGH JULY 16, 1966.

Picture: 1st Lieutenant John R. Booth USMC in June of 1966 in Hai Van Pass, just north of Da Nang. I am with Charlie Battery, 1st Battalion, 12th Marine Regiment and assigned to 1st Battalion, 3rd Marine Regiment as a Fire Support Coordinator. I am within thirty days of going home, and have all my arms and legs, hence my big smile.

THE FRENCH FORT

"Lieutenant Booth has been in continuous combat for 45 days under fatiguing conditions…"
thus reads my fitness report written in June, 1966.

Seen through the mist of five decades my memory of these six weeks is of a grinding existence where we survived like animals immersed in mud and filth. Our constant companions were debilitating dysentery and unrelenting heat. There was never enough water. Our worldly possessions we carried on our backs. Our feelings alternated between boredom, adrenalin driven highs, and fear. Ammunition, water and food were heli-lifted in, and dead and wounded were heli-lifted out. We fought mortar attacks, land mines, snipers, and combat with an elusive enemy we never could bring to bay. From April 1 through May 31 thirty-four Marines would be killed and close to one hundred wounded.

I would lose twenty pounds and when I resurface in Da Nang on June 1, my uniform hangs on me like a rag, and I resemble a scarecrow.

****

It started like this. On April 11 I am transferred and promoted to an infantry battalion staff as fire support coordinator. In this job I also function as the liaison officer between my artillery battery and the infantry battalion we support. This move entails a new artillery battery, a new infantry battalion and a new location. My new home is twenty-three miles north, north of Hue City, the old imperial capital, almost in Quang Tri Province, and forty miles south of the Demilitarized Zone and North Vietnam.

All Marine traffic is banned from the city of Hue and surrounding roads so travel will be by air. There is political unrest caused by the removal of General Thi, the South Vietnamese Army commander of I Corps and a native of Hue. The central government fears a coup.

A chopper lands in our position. My eyes are almost blinded by the sand thrown into the air by the whirling blades. The noise is deafening. I've said my goodbyes. I run beneath the moving blades toward the shaking chopper and throw my duffel bag and pack through the door. I climb aboard, the bird ascends, and I start my new adventure. The ride is all too brief. The cool air at one thousand feet is a welcome relief from the humid and dusty conditions on the ground.

We arrive at my new unit, Charlie Battery of the 1st Battalion 12th Marine Regiment, and I meet my new commanding officer, Captain Ralph Kramer. He briefs me on my new assignment with the infantry, the 1st Battalion of the 4th Marine Regiment. On April 6, a Viet Cong mortar unit one-half mile away, attacked the battery and battalion headquarters with forty high explosive shells. In running from the sleeping area to mortar bunkers, Private First Class James Peter Harteau, age 21, from Waukesha, Wisconsin, is killed and five of his comrades wounded.

I drop off my duffel bag, check my pack, and a jeep takes me to my new home. Dropping off my duffel bag is a bad sign. All my worldly possessions are now in a small backpack, and I know I'm in for some rough living. Things will get much worse. I just don't know that yet.

The jeep rounds a turn in the road and my new home looms in front of me. It's a concrete blockhouse, and once upon a time a French fort.

The structure is squat, ugly and jammed into a sandy landscape covered with scraggly underbrush. Scorpions and lizards crawl on concrete walls overgrown with vines. Rats slink in the shadows and graffiti is scrawled on spalling concrete. The place is overrun with cats, dogs, and chickens. Goats wander next to straw huts. A village is close by. One mile to the west is the Bo River and one half mile to the south the terrain rises into hills covered with jungle greenery. Uniformed Vietnamese soldiers stroll by holding hands, and the tonal sounds of their language fill the air. Holding hands was not that unusual by their culture's standards.

Years ago French Legionnaires had guarded these portals, but that was in another lifetime, before the French defeat at the battle of Dien Bien Phu and the partition of the country into North and South Vietnam. This old French fort is now an outpost of the South Vietnamese Army, and we Marines are temporary guests.

Fifteen miles northwest of us is the most famous road in Vietnam, formally designated as route 597, it was the *Street Without Joy*, made famous by Bernard Fall, in his book by the same name. It was a classic study of the French war in Indochina in the early 1950's. Two weeks earlier from March 20 until March 23 my battalion had been engaged in fierce fighting in Operation Oregon in the exact same location. Eleven Marines had been killed and another forty-five wounded in the fight, plus another five died as a result of a helicopter crash evacuating a Marine to the hospital in Da Nang.

In a cruel twist of fate almost eleven months later on February 21, 1967, Bernard Fall is killed accompanying the 1st Battalion of the 9th Marines on Operation Chinook II on the same road he wrote about.

While mauled the enemy escapes, remains in the area, and intends to collect rice from the lowlands and transport it to enemy forces in the mountains. On March 31st my battalion is committed to Operation Golden Fleece, which protects the local farmers during the rice harvest and prevents the Viet Cong from transporting confiscated rice from the lowland harvest areas to their mountainous jungle sanctuaries.

Supports on the bridge to our rear are eroded, and safe passage of trucks and tanks is doubtful, so consequently all supplies are heli-lifted to our position.

I am in command of the Fire Support Coordination Center, which controls all supporting arms fires to include: artillery, mortars, tanks, naval gunfire and close air support. We are co-located with the infantry Combat Operations Center, and are intimately involved with all the minute details of running a war. With all these explosives flying around there is ample opportunity for mistakes, which are our responsibility to prevent. If anything goes "boom," whether theirs or ours, we're supposed to know about it.

We are awash in targets and map coordinates from multiple sources such as: forward observers with our four rifle companies, our intelligence and operations sections, regimental and division headquarters, the South Vietnamese Army, and even the Central Intelligence Agency.

We speak a technical language that uses words like, H & I fires, prep fires, Time on Target, and Save-A-Plane. Each term requires a specific translation. We deal with weapons of different calibers, trajectories, and ranges. We have a basic knowledge of close air support and naval gunfire. All this information we filter through our sieve of technical expertise for errors. Mistakes could lead to friendly casualties.

A staff of six works for me typically led by a senior enlisted Marine with the requisite technical skills and experience, normally a gunnery or master sergeant. In short, I am the Dean in the College of Mathematics and Explosives, and my senior sergeant is a Professor. In a nutshell we deal with the science of "how to blow things up" with all the resources available in the Marine Corps arsenal.

We are one of several staff sections reporting both to the operations officer Major Gilbert, the executive officer Major Rogers, and our battalion commander Lieutenant Colonel Roger Smith. All this requires a certain amount of political and interpersonal finesse on my part for senior officers are always looking over our shoulders with lots of fingers in the pot. Somewhere in all this there is a comment from Major Rogers, and I conclude my predecessor had been fired, but for what I never do figure out. I have my work cut out for me!

In perusing the personnel records, and in introducing myself, I discover, surprise, surprise, that my senior enlisted Marine, the professor, is PFC Phil Elkins, a former gunnery sergeant who was court-martialed and busted to private first class. His subordinates even outrank him!

"Elkins, what in the world did you do to get busted to PFC?" I ask.

His reply is straight from a Rudyard Kipling yarn.

"Whiskey, women, and bad checks, Lieutenant."

"Why didn't you just get out of the Marine Corps?"

"I have a family, and I want to work my way back up to Sergeant before I retire."

As we are in combat where promotions come quickly and are controlled by the battalion commander, that's a reasonable expectation. Sometimes you have to play the hand you're dealt. I reason that if he is sincere, he will do an outstanding job. I am determined to make this upside down command relationship work, so I say:

"Well, whatever your past sins, you've got a clean slate from me. Do a good job and I'll help you any way I can." And that was that. Over the coming weeks I would not be disappointed, and the Professor and I develop an unusual friendship.

It's April 13 at 2:30 a.m. and I'm the watch officer in our combat operations center. I write a letter home to Mom, Dad and my sisters.

I was transferred into new battery as liaison officer – extremely unappealing. Good living has gone out the window and I'm back on c-rations and the works.

Currently we're on an operation north of Hue –I'm with the Bn. C.P. group-right now we're in an abandoned French Fort – Rats, scorpions, lizards crawling the walls-girls the rats were squealing so loud earlier they sounded like dogs and cats fighting. This place also serves as an outpost for ARVN troops –so we also have dogs, cats, chickens, goats, straw huts, etc. almost like a Ma & Pa Kettle movie.

My new job –I coordinate all artillery and mortar fire in our area and serve as a go between the artillery battery and the infantry battalion. Mail will take a month to get caught up with me.

****

I'm sweating like a condemned prisoner waiting to be hanged. The hiss of gas lanterns and the soft sing-song tonal sounds of Vietnamese are background noise. The heat from the lanterns and too many people in too small a space is trapped within the concrete walls. There is a stench that contributes to an overall aroma that we have come to ignore. I identify a distinct smell that is uniquely me from not having bathed for several days.

It's 9:00 p.m., I've got the night watch and I'm pouring over maps and target intelligence. Suddenly an emergency message is handed to me.

"Arc Light Strike at 142345H 4817-4916-5019-5119"

Translation:

"On April 14 at 11:45 p.m. there will be a B-52 saturation-bombing mission on the listed coordinates. Lieutenant Booth, ensure none of our patrols are close to the impact area." A quick rush of adrenalin and a quick check of our maps confirm that all units are safe.

The coordinates of the bombing area are plotted on a large map hanging on the concrete wall. The impact area is ten miles southwest of our current location, five miles from villages of Co Bi and Thanh Tan, and back in the mountainous jungle. At the moment this area means nothing to me, but in the coming days I will become intimately familiar with its entirety. It's been out of government control for years and is currently home to several Viet Cong battalions. To warrant a B-52 strike a radio intercept must have picked up something extraordinary.

I'm struck by the small size of the target area compared to the large size of the uninhabited mountainous jungle. I know this area is vast and past reports indicate tigers have attacked Marine patrols. An occasional black line wanders through the green signifying a lonely trail. A medieval map would say "Here Be Dragons."

I decide to watch the B-52 strike and have visions of a vast pyrotechnical display backed by distant explosions. Twenty minutes before the appointed hour I brush aside two dirty ragged canvases blocking the outgoing light and step into the cool darkness. What a relief from the hot fetid odors of the fort.

My eyes adjust to the darkness and my ears sensitize to the silence. The jungle makes nary a sound or peep as if waiting in anticipation of the coming conflagration. At the appointed hour I await the anticipated explosions and light show and….

Nothing happens!

I wait, and wait, and wait, and finally the ground shakes silently and briefly, and then all is still. The trees and underbrush of the jungle have absorbed these massive explosions and laugh back at us as if to say; "Try something else, Marines, that didn't work." The image of that small impact area against the vast uninhabited jungle pops into my mind and I have an epiphany.

"We're trying to kill flies with a sledgehammer. There aren't enough bombs in the United States arsenal to stomp the North Vietnamese and Viet Cong in this vast jungle."

I wonder if our leaders know what they are doing?"

****

The commanding officer of all United States forces in South Vietnam is Army General William Westmoreland, and reporting to him is Marine General Lewis Walt, commanding officer of all U.S. Marines. In the early months of 1966 there is strong disagreement between them as to the presence of North Vietnamese Army units in the two northern provinces of South Vietnam.

Westmoreland and his staff place three to four enemy regiments massing for a possible major offensive, while General Walt and his staff place only one enemy regiment in the area and see no evidence of a possible attack. Walt resists every effort to extend the Marines further into the sparsely populated north and draw Marines away from the counterinsurgency campaign in the densely populated areas of the south.

This is the first crack of the differences in strategy between the Army and the Marine Corps. Westmoreland's focus is on a strategy of attrition, massive firepower and search and destroy operations while Walt's focus is on counterinsurgency and pacification.

Me, I know nothing of the above disagreement, except since I returned for the second time to the Hue Phu Bai northern area, I know something is dramatically different. While we have had no significant contact, there are a lot more sightings of the enemy, but they refuse to fight. We concentrate on pacification, as evidenced by our current operation protecting the local rice harvest, Operation Golden Fleece.

Yes, I landed in Vietnam twice. I didn't get it right the first time, so the Marine Corps sent me back to do it all over again. I didn't get it right the second time either, so they sent me home and promoted me to Captain.

****

I attend an officers' briefing.

"Gentlemen, we're moving our command post, and we have an eight-mile trek to the northwest. There will be no trucks or choppers and all movement will be by foot. Please instruct your Marines to each carry three days of C-rations, and carry nothing in your pack unless it's absolutely essential."

I pass the word to my section and contemplate my personal load in my own pack. I'm already living pretty lean and the additional load of three days of C-rations is significant.

We have taken a significant step in moving down the food chain. We are going to be living like the cats and dogs in the old French Fort. Rumor has it our unofficial mission is to find North Vietnamese army units reputed to be in the area and pick a fight. General Walt wants to resolve this disagreement

Goodbye French Fort.

Notes:

1. Private First Class James Harteau is laid to rest in the Prairie Home Cemetery in Waukesha, Wisconsin. He is memorialized on the Vietnam Wall on Panel 6E, line 89.

2. Command Chronology, 4th Marine Regiment, April 1966, pages 89-104 for combat operations of 1st Battalion 4th Marines during April. The Command Chronology for 1st Battalion 4th Marines for April 1966 cannot be found.

3. Command Chronology, 4th Marine Regiment, G-3 Journal & File 14-18 April, page 66 for B-52 strike.

4. Command Chronology, 3rd Battalion 12th Marine Regiment, April 1966, pages 5-26.

5. Command Chronology, 1st Battalion 4th Marine Regiment, March 1966, pages 5-9,15,18,20, Operation Oregon

6. Schulimson, Jack, *U.S Marines in Vietnam An Expanding War*, History and Museums Division, Headquarters, U.S. Marine Corps, Washington, D.C., 1982, Pages 139-140 for discussion of disagreement between Walt and Westmoreland on North Vietnam Army units.

THE OPEN FIELD

Well I haven't had my legs blown off yet. But then again there's always the first time. I thought my days of humping through the boonies with a rifle company were over when I was promoted to a battalion staff, but this is the Marine Corps and this is the infantry. There is something clean about being shot, but being dismembered by a booby trap is another story. All of us had either seen or heard the various insidious scenarios with hidden explosives, and my company had lost four Marines that way last December.

They ranged from the crude and simple such as punji pits, a hole in the ground with sharpened bamboo stakes dipped in fecal matter. If they didn't penetrate your boot and punch a hole in your foot, they would stab you in the leg. While it may not be fatal, you were out of action, would require evacuation, and could have a deadly infection.

More sophisticated ones involved a trip wire connected to a hand grenade, or artillery round, and unexploded shells littered the ground like trash beside a highway. We were our own worst enemy in supplying the Viet Cong arsenal.

One device we particularly feared was a tripwire strung though the trees high enough so that you walked under it, but low enough so that the antenna from your radio operator hit it. The shell, hanging from the trees would explode with a roar and spray white-hot shrapnel twenty feet in all directions. It was goodbye Charlie with that one.

The trip wire was a clear plastic line that was invisible except when touched by dancing sunlight, and then if you were alert you would detect a faint gleam in the blowing grass that gave warning, "don't walk here." I had spotted one last October and avoided being blown apart. This was all part of developing a sixth sense on how to stay alive in a war zone.

If you had taken a poll of all Marine lieutenants on what we feared the most, land mines and booby traps would lead the list. Being killed was preferable to losing half your body parts and surviving.

At the moment I'm tramping through knee-high grass, thirsty, dirty, and sweaty. I'm wearing my flak jacket; my pack is on my back, and pistol, hand grenades, water and first-aid kit on my belt. Although the sun is scorching, there is a small breeze rustling the grass, which gives some relief. The countryside is rolling green meadows with rice paddies in the distance with a blue-sky background, and if the scene were anywhere else, it would be described as bucolic. Any faint gleam I may catch might be nothing more than a flicker, as the grass moves back and forth covering any tripwire.

We left the French Fort on the morning of April 17 to trek to our new position eight miles northwest. Our battalion will set a record for the number of days we live off our back, we just don't know it yet. Like Sherman's march to the sea in Georgia, we have severed the land link. All resupply will come in by chopper.

Most action centers around a base camp where platoons, companies, or battalions go out for a week or so, but then come back in to get refreshed, with hot chow, showers, and tents, kind of like advanced camping. This is not the case with us and is one aspect of "continuous combat" that is hard to visualize and describe. It takes a physical toll on us for we live like animals, no bathing, never enough water, eat C-rations with filth-encrusted hands, and live with debilitating dysentery. One of my buddies would tell me later how he cut out the back of his trousers, so he could relieve himself more easily. Squat, do your business, attempt to wipe yourself clean, get up and keep on going. Keep on going was the name of the game.

The grassland yields to a jungle stream. I ford it, chest deep in water, my 45 held above my head, and like Lazarus rising from the dead, I rise from the stream and keep on moving. The long column of Marines ahead winds up over the hill and beyond.

It's dusk and we're collapsed on a ridgeline above an open field, way the hell and gone from nowhere, and nothing between us and the North Vietnamese units we're trying to find. We're flat on our backs exchanging small talk and glad the trek is over. The Professor, my supposedly senior sergeant, but now private first class, rolls over, reaches into his pack and retrieves a bottle of whiskey.

"Care for a drink, Lieutenant?" I couldn't help but laugh.

"Put away the bottle and don't let me see it again."

All I wanted was a drink of cold water, which I didn't get either. The Professor is incorrigible.

A large tent has been erected on the side of a gentle sloping ridge for the junior officers in the command group. A dirt road, otherwise known as the Hoa My Trail, dissects our position. It connects to Route One three miles northeast. Route One is the main north south route in Vietnam. The artillery batteries are located fifty yards away and just over the road. The rifle companies surround us in the low hills, and our battalion command post is in the grass filled valley next to a meandering stream. The terrain is clear and grassy with light underbrush. The quiet scene reminds me of my grandfather's farm in upstate South Carolina, where I used to roam the fields as a young boy.

We throw our gear on the ground, and commence to live in our new home. We don't dig foxholes because: we haven't been told to dig foxholes and we're lazy, we don't have picks and shovels and the ground is hard, and we don't expect anything to happen. So why bother!

April 18, 2:50 a.m.

Loud explosions jolt me from a sound sleep and my body floods with adrenaline; we're under mortar attack. There is no time for fear, just grab your weapon and move. We run for the command post a hundred yards away, leap over the edge of a small cliff, and hug the ground until the explosions cease.

We receive twenty-five rounds of mortar fire, and then the enemy gun crews pull out quickly. We respond with counterbattery fire on the gun positions two miles away. No one has been wounded or killed, so no screams or moans chill my soul, and I must admit a feeling of euphoria at being shot at and missed.

Come daylight all traces of laziness disappear and we start digging in. We scrounge shovels and picks from the engineers and artillery, and soon the entire area looks like an 1849 California gold rush mining camp what with all the holes and excavated dirt.

April 19, 3:20 a.m.

We have a repeat of the previous night and the Viet Cong again lob fifty mortar rounds into our encampment. This time we're not so lucky, and five Marines are wounded. The enemy's accuracy has improved and twenty rounds land amongst the artillery. We respond again with over two hundred high explosive shells, and a daylight search reveals that the Viet Cong gunners appear yet again to have scampered away unscathed.

Our foxhole efforts continue with renewed intensity as we dig holes deep enough to walk back to the United States. I scrounge three empty wooden ammunition boxes, fill them with earth and place them over the top of my hole. It occurs to me the finished product resembles a grave and if a shell explodes on top all that will be necessary is to shovel in a little more dirt. They won't even have to ship my body home!

The operations officer, Major Gilbert, and I put together a more formalized counterbattery plan. It will consist of three parts, and speed of execution will be of the essence.

First, forward observers with the rifle companies will be on one-hundred-percent alert during nighttime hours, and their position will be plotted on the gunnery boards. They will take a compass heading on the flash of the round as it rockets into the air and radio it to the gunnery center.

Second, when two observers have forwarded compass headings, the lines will intersect on the gunnery boards, and that will be the location of the enemy. The fire direction center will then calculate the gunnery data and send it to the howitzers.

Third, the howitzers will load, aim and fire. If everything goes as planned this should take three minutes. This is a geometry problem and mathematically it will work. The question is: Can we be quick enough before the enemy gunners scoot and run? We present this plan to our battalion commander, Lieutenant Colonel Roger Smith.

I write home to Mom and Dad, say nothing of these events, and unwittingly inject some humor in my letter, *".... please send a bottle of hot sauce and one bottle of worcestershire sauce – intend to improve or kill the taste of C-rations..."*

There will come a time when I'm hungry for C-rations, but that's in the future.

April 20, 2:40 a.m.

More explosions! We're hit yet again, this time with seventy rounds. Their accuracy is continually improving as two ammunition bunkers suffer direct hits. Powder ignites, and the intense heat cooks off high explosive shells. I'm in my hole, flat on my stomach, nose in the dirt, huddled beneath my flak jacket, and trying to crawl into my helmet. I hear the *kaboom* of exploding shells and the sound of hot steel whistling overhead. I'm cursing and wondering if some stray piece of shrapnel will penetrate the back of my neck. I've three months left on my tour, and I want to emerge from this long tunnel in one piece.

We respond with forty rounds of counterbattery fire spread over four locations. We still haven't nailed them, and the Viet Cong by trial and error have figured out the location of our artillery.

We stir the anthill. At noon and at seven pm we fire two missions of over seventy rounds and kill and wound twelve Viet Cong three miles south of us in the mountain foothills.

After a huddle the artillery moves to new positions one-half mile away. Mr. Charles will now have to start over finding their precise location.

The enemy has now mortared our position three nights in a row with impunity. When you consider that each one of the mortar rounds has to be carried on the back of a North Vietnamese soldier many miles down the Ho Chi Minh, they must have tons of ammunition hidden and stashed in the mountains, and we must be in the presence of sizable enemy forces.

April 21

A rifle company finds the location of the enemy mortar site at 11:30 am. It's much closer than we thought and less than a mile away. This is a frustrating game of cat and mouse. We have overwhelming firepower yet they are able to sting us with impunity.

I write another letter home and give my parents a tantalizing glimpse of war while teasing my mother. She was always hell on dirt and would have a field day in this place. I say nothing of the shelling or why I'm sleeping in a hole in the ground!

Everything OK-doing fine. Managed to do some wash today in a stream –didn't do much but took out the smell (ha) – all clothes are now uniform light brown –this mixed with the original green dye prevents me from telling whether they're dirty or not – this arrangement works real well. Think I'll try it when I get back as it would save wear and tear on the washing machine.

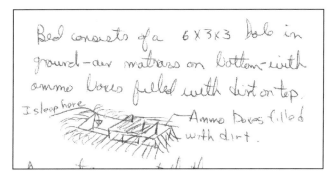

I'm sleeping in an interesting arrangement – all I need now is the rats to move in-bed consists of a 6x3x3 hole in ground –air matrass (I never could spell) on bottom-with ammo boxes filled with dirt on top. ...another request – 1 can use an aerosol bug bomb – kills mosquitoes trapped in my house..."

April 26

To better support our battalion, the artillery is split into two groups. One battery moves to a new position three miles away at the intersection of Route One and the Hoa My Trail. The other battery remains in their present position with us. Each battery can now surround the other with a broad three hundred sixty degree umbrella of indirect fire. This is more effective than direct fire, which means lowering the tubes, and firing canister rounds straight ahead at a charging enemy. Think grape shot from civil war battles.

April 27, 2:20 a.m.

Predictably the battery at the intersection of Route One and the Hoa My trail is hit again. The Viet Cong mortar men throw thirty-five rounds at the Marines but the only damage is a blown tire.

From the Phu Bai base camp twenty-three miles south; a bulldozer is dispatched on a lowboy truck along with the Counter Mortar Radar section. The bulldozer will push up dirt berms to protect the howitzers, and the Counter Mortar Radar will get an electronic fix on the enemy location next time they fire. This should further speed up our response time.

Two of our larger howitzers and their fire direction section are suddenly pulled out to support an operation north of us, upsetting our balance of mutual fire support.

April 28, 6:00 p.m.

We receive an emergency intelligence report that two battalions of Viet Cong will attack the artillery at the Route One intersection later in the evening. An emergency heli-lift from the Phu Bai base camp of additional Marines gives us some help, and there is discussion of re-locating two howitzers back to the command post to equalize the mutual artillery support now split into two locations. Darkness and the possibility of ambush preclude that decision. We have done all we can do to prepare.

We now wait.

April 29, 3:55 a.m.

The Viet Cong attack us, and not the artillery at the Route One intersection. We receive forty rounds of high explosives only this time there is a difference. The counter mortar radar quickly locates the enemy, response time is reduced, and we smother the Viet Cong with a twenty-minute barrage of over three hundred rounds of high explosives and white phosphorous. We see two large secondary explosions and tracer rounds rocketing, off into the night.

"Looks like we nailed 'em, Lieutenant."

White phosphorous is an incendiary. We used incendiaries in the firebombing of Dresden and Tokyo in World War II. One drop on human skin will burn to the bone, and pouring water on the wound will only make it worse.

Seven months ago I had chased a Viet Cong platoon into an abandoned village in a free fire zone whereupon I lost clear observation. I then unleashed Armageddon with white phosphorous and high explosives. When I finished, the village was demolished, flames reached for the heavens and smoke was visible for miles. If I thought civilians were in the area, I would not have done so. Using white phosphorous didn't bother me then and doesn't bother me now.

At 4:40 a.m. our encampment again receives four large explosions of much larger caliber than the previous attacks. What's going on, we wonder? Have the Viet Cong upped the ante? A crater analysis and investigation reveals they were artillery rounds mistakenly fired at us by the South Vietnamese Army. War is full of confusion.

Later in the day a search of the enemy position provides negative results, but that's not unusual as the standard Viet Cong tactic is to evacuate all their dead and wounded when they withdraw. Amazingly, only one Marine is wounded in the melee.

Our battalion commander, Lieutenant Colonel Roger Smith, would later write of this period of time:

"I'd bet that of all the VC-NVA mortar ammo expended in I Corps during this period, we were on the receiving end of nearly half of it."

As someone once observed: "Few things in life are as exhilarating as to be shot at with very little result."

*****

The days and nights blur together.

There is steady background chatter over the radio of fire missions from observers with the rifle companies and an air observer in a small piper cub aircraft flits in and out of the area. We monitor the traffic to insure no one is firing on friendly forces or civilian locations, which we have plotted on our maps in the operations center.

146

"Bearcat 1, this is Bird Dog 3, Fire Mission, I've got Viet Cong troops in a tree line at 547295. Direction: gun-target line"

We hear the faint hum of the aircraft as the air observer hovers to the east of us. His voice is broken by static. There is a brief moment of silence and then;

"Birddog 3, rounds on the way." intones the radio, followed shortly by the "boom, boom" of the howitzers. The sounds chase words over the radio at a speed of eleven hundred feet per second.

Another brief silence and then;

"Way to go, good effect on target, I see at least six Viet Cong dead."

And so it goes throughout the day.

****

It's night and I'm huddled over a chart beneath the glare and hiss of a gas lantern. Major Gilbert, the operations officer, is by my side. We're both stripped to T-shirts and I smell worse than a goat. Sweat runs off me in rivulets. I'm looking at a piece of paper filled with hundreds of six digit numbers. Each set of numbers represents a target, and what with the sweat and filth from my hands it is tough to keep the paper neat and readable. This is precise work and if we mess up the numbers, we kill Marines and civilians.

A priority fire mission is suddenly sent straight to us by a reconnaissance unit. An enemy company has been located at a specific set of coordinates in the mountain foothills. I glance at the map, make calculations, quickly grab numbers, and send the result to the battery. Speed is of the essence.

After a short pause we hear,

"Rounds on the way," followed by the sounds of explosions rumbling like thunder, echoing off the mountains, and speeding through the humid night air.

There is one thing wrong though. The explosions are to the south, and the enemy is to the north. Gilbert looks at me with a questioning eye, and it dawns on me with a sinking heart,

"I made a mistake."

I transposed one number wrong, and that made all the difference in the world. I calculate where the rounds really landed and discover,

"I'm lucky."

The explosives landed in an uninhabited area with no villages or Marines close by. I resend the mission and the rounds land correctly this time. The Viet Cong have been warned though and have probably moved. The only casualty is my credibility with Major Gilbert.

And so it goes throughout the night.

****

A sniper kills PFC David Evilsizer, a machine gunner in C Company, on April 15 in his company area. He is laid to rest in Richview Cemetery in Richview, Illinois and memorialized on Panel 06E Line 114 on the Vietnam Wall.

Likewise a sniper kills PFC William Denhoff, a rifleman in D company, on April 29 while on patrol. Denhoff will linger a while and dies of his wounds in the Da Nang hospital on May 4. He is laid to rest in Evergreen-Washelli Memorial Park in Seattle, Washington and memorialized on Panel 07E Line 024 on the Vietnam Wall.

During April an additional nineteen Marines are wounded either by enemy fire or booby traps.

Notes:

1. U.S. *Marines in Vietnam An Expanding War 1966*, Jack Shulimson, Headquarters and Museums Division, Headquarters U.S. Marine Corps, Washington D.C. pages 143-144 for 1st Battalion 4th Marine Operations, quote by Battalion Commander, and comments on being mortared.

2. Command Chronology, 4th Marine Regiment, April 1966, pages 89-104 for combat operations during the month of April.

3. Command Chronology, 3rd Battalion 12th Marines, April 1966, pages 5-26, 59-69 for combat operations during the month of April.

4. The Command Chronology for the 1st Battalion 4th Marines, April 1966 cannot be found so I am unable to give any more details on the deaths of PFCs David Evilsizer and William Denhoff.

OPERATION CHEROKEE

Four and one half miles due west of the old French Fort at the base of the mountains lie the Vietnamese villages of Co Bi and Thanh Tan. A dense impenetrable green jungle of trees and vines cover the mountains, which rise to a height of over three thousand feet and serve as a refuge for Viet Cong units operating in the area.

That there are large enemy units of battalion size in the area there is no doubt. For the last month aerial reconnaissance has sighted enemy units building new bunkers and trenches as well as reinforcing old fortifications. On two occasions earlier this year South Vietnamese Army forces have attempted to clear and pacify this area. They were subsequently forced out with heavy losses of personnel and equipment. Government influence in the Co Bi and Thanh Tan lowlands has been non-existent for the past few years, and local officials estimate the population in the area at approximately three thousand people.

The lowlands around the villages serve as rich rice growing area and supply Viet Cong units hiding in the mountains with a source of food. At harvest each farmer is forced to give the Viet Cong between fifteen to four hundred pounds of rice, and then forced to transport the rice deep into the mountainous jungles.

Rice is the Achilles Heel of the Viet Cong, and if the Marines can sever this logistical link we can starve the units hiding in the mountains. This was the strategy of the operations in which I had participated at Phu Bai south of Hue City, and on Hill 41 south of Da Nang in 1965.

The genesis for the operation to destroy the Viet Cong units in the Co Bi-Thanh Than vicinity and sever the food link was in late March of 1966 when our battalion was at the old French Fort engaged in Operation Golden Fleece protecting the farmers with the rice harvest. Operational commitments at the time prevented carrying the concept to completion, but now a month later things are different.

The Viet Cong are certainly well supplied with ammunition as evidenced with all the mortar rounds they have been throwing at us since April 18. All that ammunition is hauled down the Ho Chi Minh Trail from North Vietnam. Intelligence further indicates there is an enemy battalion in the Co Bi-Thanh Tan hamlets, they intend to stay and fight, and more enemy battalions are within close supporting distance. On April 14 there was a saturation B-52 bombing raid aimed at these enemy units back in the mountains. I had the watch that night in the old French Fort when the strike occurred and remember it vividly.

The Marines decide to attack with surprise and overwhelming force. The villages of Co Bi and Thanh Tan and the surrounding lowlands will be returned to government control.

The regimental headquarters puts together the concept of operations and obtains approvals from Division and South Vietnam Army headquarters. This will be a search and destroy operation. Friendly forces will serve as a blocking force on three sides of a rectangle four miles wide and six miles deep. South Vietnamese troops will block on the east bank of the Bo River and in the hills north of the Co Bi Thanh Tan lowlands. They will also evacuate civilians from the village areas. A Marine battalion will land by helicopter and establish blocking positions south along routes of egress on the ridgeline at the base of the mountains. Then two Marine battalions abreast will sweep down the rectangle. Our battalion will be on the left, brush the lowland hills and cross over Hill 51. Viet Cong units will be trapped and crushed like a hammer smashes on an anvil.

A briefing: "Each Marine will pack three days of C-rations. Carry only what you need."

I eliminate my one remaining luxury item, my air mattress, and reluctantly send it to join my duffel bag back with my artillery battery. I'm now sleeping on the ground wrapped in my poncho. I use my scouting skills from long ago as a teenager canoeing along the James River, of digging shoulder and hip holes to shape the ground to follow the contours of my body.

My personal load on a belt and suspenders arrangement, what's called 782 gear, now consists of my 45-caliber pistol, four magazines of ammunition, two hand grenades, my first aid kit including water purification tablets, and two canteens. In the small of my back and attached to the belt is my rolled-up poncho. In my pockets are a map, a compass, and pens and pencils. In my pack are an extra set of utilities, one change of underwear and socks, shaving gear, a bar of soap and a rag I use for a washcloth. Whatever space I have left in my pack and my pockets is stuffed with C-rations.

My ever-present dysentery has flared up again. I scrub my hands with dirt after I attend to my business. Water is too precious. We live in filth and it's impossible to stay clean. The days' blur together and pass like a dream.

D-Day was set for May 4 at 7:30 a.m., but rainy weather conditions forced a postponement of twenty-four hours, which will have both unfortunate and fortunate consequences depending on your point of view.

At 3:45 a.m. on May 5 the artillery leaves the Phu Bai area thirty miles south and heads north to join us. They arrive at 5:10 a.m. and are in position ready to go at 5:45 a.m. We will have twenty howitzers in direct support, and we can mass the fires of all on a single target. We will not lack for firepower.

In addition for direct line of sight fires we have five tanks and two ontos. The ontos is a powerful anti-tank weapon consisting of four recoilless rifles mounted on a tracked carriage. While we are not expecting any enemy tanks, our tanks and the ontos will prove invaluable in breaching and penetrating enemy fortifications. Engineers, medical teams, logistical groups, communications detachments, interrogation teams and aviation units will join this effort. All told over six thousand Marines and South Vietnamese soldiers will participate in Operation Cherokee.

On May 5 at 7:20 a.m. I'm with Captain Kramer, my battery commander, and the executive officer exchanging small talk amid the roar of howitzers as they fire high explosives onto Hill 51. This is a preliminary bombardment to ease the way for a rifle company to seize the hill, and drive the Viet Cong into the blocking forces. My section will leave shortly with the command group and follow in trace of that rifle company. The hill has mines, booby traps, and may be defended. The Viet Cong have told the villagers not to go anywhere near Hill 51. So once again we worry about being blown apart by explosive devices. Follow the Marine in front and keep an eye out for the faint glint of nylon lines dancing in the breeze.

The blocking forces are in designated positions on three sides of the area, and at 7:45 a.m. the two battalions that will conduct the sweep cross the Hoa My trail and Operation Cherokee begins. Imagine a jar, enclosed on all sides with the top open. My battalion will be on the left as we sweep into the jar and crush the enemy against the bottom.

Explosive devices on Hill 51 soon wound three Marines in the early morning. One mile off to our right, an ontos hits a mine at 10:15 a.m. and the driver, Private Wilbert Isom Andrews age 19, of Providence, Rhode Island, is killed instantly. Two other crewmembers are wounded but escape the vehicle before it bursts into flames. The ammunition inside the ontos explodes, and wounds the battalion executive officer. We now climb Hill 51. Not an auspicious beginning.

There is light enemy contact throughout the day, and rifle fire, and artillery shells kill several Viet Cong. There is little resistance and by 9:00 p.m. two companies are at the limit of our advance for the entire operation. We set up our battalion headquarters in a grove of trees, which will be our home for the next two days. That night it rains. At this point I'm somewhat immune to the elements, and alternate between manning the combat operations center, which is underneath a tarp, and fitful dozing.

****

"Mr. Booth, wanna join us? We found a spot to take a bath."

The sun is shining, it's the morning of May 6 and the constant rains have filled low spots in the gently rolling hills with rainwater. The ground is saturated and the water can't drain anywhere so it will just sit there and evaporate. My crew of enlisted Marines is inviting me to come along.

"You mean a real-life bath immersed in water with soap?"

"Yes sir, come join us."

The crew is buck naked except for towels wrapped around their waists and the boots on their feet. Darkly-tanned faces, necks and arms contrast with lily-white torsos. Each and every one of us, however, is heavily armed with machine guns, ammunition belts draped across shoulders, and rifles in hand. I quickly shed my clothes, grab my rag-towel, wrap it around my waist, throw my belt with pistol and two hand grenades over my shoulder, and join them.

The overall effect is quite striking, as we no longer resemble United States Marines but a gang of Mexican banditos from the 19th century. A picture is snapped and given to me, which unfortunately has been lost in all my later corporate moves.

We traipse a small distance and discover someone has indeed found a small pool of trapped rainwater hidden within some surrounding bushes. The water is silent, still, black as the ace of spades, and we don't know yet how deep. But it looks fresh and clear, or so we think, and we can see our hands when we submerge them several feet. It's also big enough for several of us to bathe at the same time. We post guards and examine our surroundings closely. Even though this is an informal occasion and they have invited me, I'm still the officer, and a dark possibility enters my brain.

"Hey fellows," I say, "this place could be booby-trapped."

Dead silence.

"You got a point, Lieutenant, what do you think we should do?"

"Well, let's search for wires, and then I'll throw a hand grenade into the pool to blow up anything that might be in there."

"Sounds good, let's have at it sir."

Everyone scours the ground around them, and then we all hunker down as I take the grenade off my belt, pull the pin, and ever so gently lob it into our soon to be bathing pool.

"KABOOM!"

A loud explosion throws water into the air, and our dark, still, placid pool is transformed into a swirling mass of water, weeds, and mud. We wait for it to settle, but it doesn't. The formally clear water now leaves our skin speckled with small dots of black mud, like the measles.

"Oh well, at least it's cool and wet."

We all laugh and dutifully take our turns guarding one another and bathing in our pool. We soon return refreshed to our duties and the challenges of the day. That would be the only hand grenade I throw in the war.

As the day wears on it becomes apparent there will be little or no resistance from our elusive enemy as they have flown the coop. The blocking battalion receives twenty-two rounds of ineffective Viet Cong mortar fire, but that provokes an artillery barrage that shuts the enemy up. Information trickles in from the rifle companies about fortifications, man-traps, freshly dug trenches, bomb shelters with apertures for machine guns, and firing positions with one-half mile cleared fields of fire. The villages are heavily fortified positions. If they had chosen to stay and fight we would have prevailed, but would have paid a heavy price. The Viet Cong, though, would have been annihilated.

At age twenty-four I'm sorry they left, and if that seems like a strange reaction, don't join the Marines. Five decades later I'm not sorry they left as I've had a wonderful life with a darling wife, five lovely daughters and eight grandchildren.

To illustrate the complexity in dealing with Vietnamese civilians, of the 1036 evacuees, 785 had relatives in the South Vietnamese forces, and 251 had relatives in the Viet Cong units or with the National Liberation Front, the political arm of the Viet Cong.

Operation Cherokee is terminated at noon on May 7. We pounced on thin air. The enemy was not there. The final score card is one Marine killed and seventeen wounded. The Viet Cong sustained nine confirmed killed plus another possible eight. We gathered 59,000 pounds of rice and turned it over to the government and local populace. Later intelligence would inform us that this was effective in helping to starve the enemy forces in the mountains.

How did we lose the element of surprise, and what caused the enemy to vanish? They had vowed to stay and fight. The most logical explanation is that we included the South Vietnamese Army in our plans and then postponed the operation for a day. This allowed time for leaks, and when it became apparent how large our force was, the Viet Cong prudently decided that discretion was the better part of valor and skedaddled to the mountainous jungles in the west. There is some indication that a Viet Cong scout observed the buildup at the logistical supply area at the intersection of the Hoa My Trail and Route One, which also helped make up their minds to leave. I would see visible evidence later that they left in a hurry.

I had served with South Vietnamese troops before and didn't have a high opinion of their fighting prowess. For these reasons and others, search and destroy operations were largely ineffective in fighting the Viet Cong. Instead of "stomping on the enemy," as espoused by one Army general, allied forces usually pounced on thin air. All that is another story.

Our battalion with some supporting elements is directed to remain in the area for at least ten days to continue the destruction of enemy fortifications, to continue the search for rice caches, to prevent the Viet Cong from reoccupying the area, and to serve as backup for Marine reconnaissance forces operating in the mountains to our west.

Notes:

1. Private Wilbert Andrews is laid to rest in the North Burial Ground, Providence, Rhode Island, and is memorialized on the Vietnam Wall Panel 7E line 29.

2. Command Chronology, 1st Battalion 4th Marine Regiment, May 1966, pages 10, 15, 16,17, 20

3. Command Chronology, 4th Marine Regiment, May 1966, page 9

4. Command Chronology, 3rd Engineer Battalion, May 1966, pages 13, 16, 34

5. Command Chronology, 3rd Tank Battalion, May 1966, pages 7-11

6. Command Chronology, 3rd Antitank Battalion, May 1966, pages 11-12

7. After Action Report, Operation Cherokee, 5 May to 7 May 1966. Submitted 24 May 1966

THE CATHOLIC CHURCH

Operation Cherokee has been a bust. Our regiment amassed three infantry battalions, twenty-four tubes of artillery, South Vietnamese Army troops, and we were going to crush the Viet Cong battalion in the Co Bi and Thanh Tan village areas. But guess what? At the last minute Mr. Charles slinks back into the mountains and we end up essentially twiddling our thumbs. Various politically correct reasons are given to avoid offending the South Vietnamese, but the bottom line is that our allies probably tipped them off.

It would have been a hard fight. Coming through some bamboo underbrush thirty feet high I suddenly stumble across an enemy trench line so freshly dug the earth is still moist, and the edges still sharp from shovels.

"Jesus, if these guys had stuck around, I'd be dead for sure."

In front of me, the western sun, retreating behind the mountains, highlights a Catholic Church, white stucco on the outside with a steeple and a cross on top. Buddhism was the predominant religion, but I knew there was a small minority of Christians, a legacy of the French colonial era. The church will be my home for the next twelve days.

The roof is half-gone, but some pews are intact, and the cross is still on the altar. I find a spot to sleep up next to the outer wall on the concrete floor where I drop my pack and can stay out of the rain. The sanctuary of the church becomes our battalion headquarters.

The South Vietnamese Army has not set foot in this area for years, the Viet Cong are in total control, and I do not know if the church is used for worship or not. This is a productive rice growing area, and the Viet Cong tax the locals heavily for their rice. South Vietnamese soldiers evacuated the civilians when we moved into the area.

Supposedly my promotion to a battalion staff as fire support coordinator has made life easier as I become an in-the-rear headquarters jerk. Except that someone forgot to tell me: there is no rear, you still stand an equal chance of having your legs blown off, and this is still the infantry.

Dysentery has been the curse of armies since time immemorial. We are no exception, and it stalks us with a vengeance. Ten months earlier I was hospitalized for a particularly bad case. I didn't know there was so much liquid in the human body, and I came to understand how early settlers in America could die of the "bloody flux." A crash diet of warm pineapple juice and no food cured me that time. I called it the Marine Corps weight loss program.

Living out of our packs and in continuous combat it is impossible to stay clean. The primary method of dealing with it is to eat all the peanut butter we can in an attempt to plug ourselves up. Some Marines keep a bottle of Kaopectate in their pocket from which they took a swig now and then. Another buddy who serves on long-range patrols near the Ho Chi Minh trail told me they solved the problem by cutting out the rear of their trousers. When they have to take a poop they step off the trail and squat in place. Simple!

Marine aviators, the cream of the officer corps as they were quick to remind us, serve as our forward air controllers, and in a fight can work magic with close air support and napalm, but they woefully miss their air-conditioned cockpits and showers back in Da Nang, and are disdainful of our primitive life style. We should be grateful they condescend to work with us lowly grunts.

One pilot explains to me how he avoids dysentery by carefully cleaning the dirt beneath his fingernails. His message goes over my head, and he comes across as a bit prissy.   One way or another we adapt.

I boil corn scraped off ears scrounged from a farmer's field, mix it with C-rations and have a gourmet meal, or so I think. Maybe that made mine worse. I don't know. Night falls, my guts are in turmoil, and my intestines are tied in knots.

We dug a slit trench in the afternoon, but I neglected to scope it out in daylight, and only an idiot would stumble around in the darkness. Our own guys would blow me away in a minute. Outside there is an occasional burst of automatic weapons fire as someone chases ghosts floating through the blackness in the paddies.

I have to poop, and I leave the church.

I'm squatting on my haunches in a rice paddy with my trousers around my ankles. Crap is pouring out of me like water flowing through a goose. My 45-pistol slung across my shoulder weighs on my chest. I've never been so miserable in all my life. I swear if I ever get out of this place alive and with all my arms and legs, I will never again complain about how I live, ever!

An illumination shell bursts overhead casting a flickering light as it drifts to the ground. Shadows dance about me, and all is silent except for the hiss of burning phosphorous. My white buttocks stand out like a beacon, a perfect target for a sniper, and I momentarily debate whether to throw myself flat in the filthy slime in which I'm crouched.

No one shoots me while I squat in the paddies. I finish my business, make some futile attempt to clean myself, and re-enter the church.   The radio is crackling. Something is happening somewhere. Another night in paradise!

Notes:

Command Chronology 1st Battalion 4th Marines May 1966. Chaplain Handley removed altar stones from desecrated Catholic churches in the area and returned them to the Archbishop of Hue. The Catholic church was located at grid 568246 on Ap Lang, Sheet 6442 II. It served as battalion headquarters from the night of May 7 through the night of May 17. I think this incident happened on the night of May 7 as I for sure located the slit trench the next day.

RAT HOLE

I'm lying on the floor of the church sanctuary near the sidewall. It's hard to relax on concrete. My pack is serving as a pillow. I'd sent my last remaining luxury, the air mattress, to the rear two weeks ago, prior to Operation Cherokee. We were warned to further lighten our load because we anticipated hard fighting, and would need extra space in our packs for ammunition, water and food. Well, Cherokee was a bust, and here I am feeling sorry for myself.

A life and death struggle crackles over a radio, around which are gathered the battalion commander and some of the staff. It's dark, night falls quickly in the tropics, and the glow from a gas lantern throws dancing shadows against the walls, and the hiss of the lantern mixes with the static and excited voices that emanate from the radio. Everyone is silent and listening, as the drama unfolds. We may be called upon to assist.

Yesterday, on May 13, a reconnaissance patrol, call sign Iron Horse, of eleven Marines had been inserted into the mountains two miles southwest of our church command post. Their mission was to observe and collect information regarding North Vietnamese Army units infiltrating from the west. We will provide security for them in event they get into trouble.

2:45 p.m.: The Marines kill one Viet Cong in an ambush in the first volley of fire. The patrol leader immediately sends out listening posts east and west along the trail.

2.55 p.m.: He hears approximately thirty to forty Viet Cong moving into the area and immediately notifies the listening posts.

3:00 p.m.: The listening posts are taken under fire, and one Marine, Lance Corporal Richard Henling, is seriously wounded. They immediately withdraw into the patrol bringing Henling with them. Two Viet Cong firing positions are located, Marines return fire, screams and groans are heard, and the Viet Cong fire ceases. The Marines are now completely surrounded by twenty Viet Cong unleashing heavy small arms fire.

3:05 p.m.: The patrol calls for a medevac and the reaction force. "Iron Horse to Motor, request Sparrow Hawk and Gold Brick, Have One Square." Translation: We need help and have one wounded. These eleven Marines are now fighting for their lives.

4:00 p.m.: The Marines call in artillery fire on twenty Viet Cong.

4:20 p.m.: The reaction force and medevac helicopters arrive on station and within fifteen minutes link up with the beleaguered Marines.

4:45 p.m.: Our battalion receives a warning order. "From Motor to Perspective. Iron Horse is in contact. Sparrow Hawk has been committed to assist. In the event additional forces are required it will be necessary to utilize your command. Have one company standby for possible helicopter lift into area. Recommend you monitor Rat Hole radio frequency."

We immediately put a company on standby.

I feel guilty I'm not with our commanding officer and battalion staff gathered at the radio as this firefight unfolds. These Marines are fighting for their lives, and the least I can do is offer moral support by listening to their plight. But I'm lethargic, don't feel like moving, and maybe I have a fever. It's not like me to feel sorry for myself, and it's not because the enemy has been trying to kill me, and it's not because I'm suffering from dysentery and have lost ten pounds, and it's not because I'm living like a pig or sleeping on concrete.

It's because I feel I don't belong.

Several things contributed to this.

It takes a while for a newcomer to bond to a unit and form friendships. This is my third artillery battery, my fourth infantry unit, and my ninth commanding officer. In eleven months I've been in three different jobs spread over six geographic locations, have had a wealth of war experience, am a seasoned combat veteran, but it seems I am forever having to learn new people, and I'm just worn out. This morning our Fire Support Coordination Team, of which I'm the leader, was left behind as our battery left for Da Nang.

"Only heaven knows if we'll see 'em again."

Unit cohesion and close friendships are made difficult by the rotation policy set by the Department of Defense. Individuals are rotated instead of units. Marines are always either joining or leaving, and there is constant personnel turnover. As new units land, they are slowly and deliberately broken up so Marines will not have the same rotation date to return to the United States. The months of training and bonds formed by combat are all for naught. If there is a way not to run a war, this is it.

It's especially tough to break into a unit that has been in continuous combat for some time. The fall of the Special Forces outpost in the A Shau valley thirty-three miles west of Phu Bai in early March opened the way for movement of enemy units into our area of operations. This was a surprise, and resulted in several Marine battalions, mine included, quickly moved north to block the threat, perceived or otherwise, of a North Vietnamese invasion through the Demilitarized Zone or from the west.

My battalion lost eleven Marines killed and forty-one wounded in Operation Oregon in late March. My predecessor was fired soon after, for what, I never did find out. I joined the battalion on April 11.

It's hard to get along with my battalion commander, Lieutenant Colonel Roger Smith. He is a former enlisted Marine who had landed in the invasion at Inchon in the Korean War. I'd heard him joke about climbing the wall at the beachhead under fire and being scared to death, so I know he had guts, but he was a screamer if he didn't like something. I remember an incident several weeks ago.

It's late afternoon and the battalion leadership is gathered for our daily combat briefing. Each of the staff officers shares pertinent information with the twenty to thirty officers and senior enlisted present, and it's my turn to speak.

"Good afternoon, I'm 1st Lieutenant John Booth, your Fire Support Coordinator, the division order concerning the 1000 meter rule is still in effect and…..,"

I'm abruptly interrupted, and shouted down by Smith, who says among other things: "Lieutenant, there is no 1000 meter rule."

"Yes Sir"…. and I continue with the rest of my briefing. Whether there is or isn't a rule makes no difference. We are way the hell and gone from nowhere, and out here his word is law. He would shout at other junior officers, so I am never sure if it's personal, or if that's just the way he is. I never do figure him out. All this adds up as to why I am reluctant to join the group at the radio, so I continue to listen from afar.

5:30 p.m.: We receive a message from Regimental Headquarters. "Motor to Perspective, Take charge of Rat Hole extraction and recovery operation. Ten helicopters are being dispatched to your location. Recommend you use one company to lift in. Take control of Iron Horse and Sparrow Hawk."

We are now in charge of the extraction. Choppers are close by to launch an assault to assist the besieged Marines in the jungle.

Henling, our wounded Marine, must be extracted up through fifty feet of jungle canopy, and it does not go well. As he is strapped into the litter, there are sudden and frantic signals from the crew chief above.

"Stop immediately. Do not tie him in."

But it's too late. The chopper suddenly ascends forty feet while moving forward, and Henling plummets to the jungle floor and lies hidden beneath the foliage. After searching thirty minutes he is found. An incoming helicopter gunship attempts to mark a Viet Cong position with a smoke grenade, but marks Henling by mistake. The patrol leader quickly notifies the gunship,

"Do not attack."

Henling is winched upward yet again and safely evacuated. Shots, screams and garbled words interspersed with static and periods of silence come over the radio.

6:00 p.m. We receive a message, "Do not commit forces unless necessary."

6:10 p.m. Another message: "It appears that Iron Horse and Sparrow Hawk can retract without committing your units. Priority of helicopters should be for retraction."

Our battalion is no longer needed to assist in the rescue.

7:35 p.m.: We send a message. "Extraction of Iron Horse and Sparrow Hawk completed. All out."

8:00 p.m.: I lead the effort to smother the area, now void of Marines, with high explosives and white phosphorus in hopes we may kill any enemy foolish enough to remain. We will either blow them up or burn them to death.

"What a hell of an evening," someone says.

Life returns to normal. I've had enough of lying on concrete and send a message to the rear to send my air mattress on the next re-supply chopper.

Lance Corporal Richard Ray Henling, age 18, is evacuated to the U.S Naval Hospital in San Diego, California and on October 28, 1966, dies of his wounds and ascends into the hands of God. He is laid to rest in the Holbrook City Cemetery in Navajo County, Arizona. He is single and is memorialized on the Vietnam Wall, Panel 11E line 122.

I have but few regrets from Vietnam, and one is I wish I had joined the command group and listened to Henling's saga over the radio. In my mind by doing so I would have more fully honored his sacrifice.

Notes:

1. Command Chronology 1st Battalion 4th Marines May 1966, page 7 for transfer of Marines regarding rotation dates, pages 17, 68 for recon unit extraction, page 30 for medical illness with diarrhea and gastroenteritis.

2. Command Chronology 4th Marine Regiment, May 1966, page 10 for recon unit.

3. Command Chronology 4th Marine Regiment May 1966, G-3 Journal 12-21 May, pages 93, 123,124.

4. Command Chronology 3rd Reconnaissance Battalion, May 1966, pages 85-95.

5. Command Chronology 3rd Battalion 12th Marines, May 1966 page 3 for redistribution of rotation dates, page 12, recon calls fire mission on twenty Viet Cong.

6. *U.S. Marines in Vietnam An Expanding War 1966*, Jack Shulimson, Headquarters and Museums Division, Headquarters U.S. Marine Corps, Washington D.C., Chapters 4 and 9.

THE PRISONER

We capture a North Vietnamese Army Chief Warrant Officer!

"How do you know for sure he's NVA?" I ask, because he was supposedly in a Viet Cong battalion. I'm talking to my buddy Bill, the battalion intelligence officer, and we're standing in front of the Catholic church on another hot and humid day.

"We have his record book, John. It was in his inside jacket pocket, and it has all his stats. We even know where and when he enlisted in the North Vietnamese Army and lots of other good stuff."

We're hunting the Viet Cong battalions whom we chased out of the Co Bi-Thanh Tan village area. Supposedly these battalions are all South Vietnamese communists, but in actuality they have North Vietnamese soldiers in their ranks as well. This whole issue is a façade in an attempt to convince the world this is a homegrown civil war. We know some American politicians are espousing that view back in the states. What baloney!

In addition, the communist North is infiltrating regular North Vietnamese Army units into the south, and there is strong disagreement between the Army and the Marines over the extent of that threat in our area. Rumor has it our unofficial mission is to find a North Vietnamese Army unit and pick a fight, partly I guess, to resolve the issue.

I believe, as do others, that this war is plain ole vanilla communist aggression against a neighbor. I know the South Vietnam government isn't perfect, but it's a far better alternative than what the communists are peddling. Ho Chi Minh is selling Vietnamese nationalism hiding behind a communist cloak. Maybe we hit pay dirt with this guy!

Bill lowers his voice and then says,

"Don't tell any one, John, but we turned him over to the South Vietnamese, and they're not exactly following the Geneva Convention during the interrogation."

A chill enters my soul, and I dread what I may hear next. War brings out the worst in people, even in a disciplined fighting force like the Marine Corps, and you see and hear horrible things. I think back on what I've experienced and learned in the last eleven months:

August 1965

I'm filling my canteen next to the sergeant with whom I have a faint acquaintance. I'm green as grass, and have been in the war zone only a few weeks. He's a ten-year plus veteran of the Korean War, but obviously not the brightest bulb in the pack because he's only an E-5 three-stripe buck sergeant, and will probably live out his remaining years in the Marine Corps at that rank. He regales a buddy with a Korean war story when he and some others held a pistol to a woman's head and then proceeded to gang rape her. I am speechless, shocked and disgusted.

The statute of limitations has long passed, and it would only be my word against his, so I file this in my brain as education in the brutality of war.

September 1965

The words of 1ˢᵗ Lieutenant Larry Walker echo in my ears from my first patrol.

"We do not cut off the ears of dead Viet Cong."

What a novel thought. It's okay to kill 'em, but once they're dead, that's it. There is a fine line between desecrating the dead and mistreatment of prisoners. I'd heard tales of Americans cutting off ears and wearing them on a necklace around their neck, much the same way frontiersmen collected Indian scalps to hang on their belts.

October 1965

I'm in touch enough with my own humanity to know that even in a war there are things you do not do. I think of the souvenir I did not take off the dead Viet Cong whose body I was searching for papers. He was a well-muscled young man. He wore a belt buckle with a decorative communist hammer and sickle along with other etchings, and it was obvious he had purchased it on his own. The shine on the buckle was in stark contrast to the open hole we had blown in his chest. His ribs are showing, and I can see into his lungs. Over his belt hung camouflage cloth with the same smell and feel as the custom rain jacket I wore. We had probably been to the same seamstress in the village. What a nice souvenir the belt buckle would be, I think, when a voice within me says:

"He's dead, John, don't desecrate his body, let him be."

Instead I take a Chinese serrated hand grenade with a wooden plug and string. In my mind I identified the belt buckle as part of his identity. The hand grenade was a weapon that could kill me.

November 1965

A Marine in our patrol steals a radio from a young boy. The village elders seek me out. I track him down and force him to return the radio. What a jackass. We want the villagers to tip us off if an ambush lies ahead, and they would hardly do that for a bunch of thieves. We'd be no better than the Viet Cong.

December 1965

An officer acquaintance from The Basic School captures some villagers and threatens one of them with a knife held to the throat. The Marine Corps is on him like white on rice and he disappears. I never do find out what happens to him.

I have learned that mistreatment of prisoners and misbehavior in a war zone will spread quicker than the flu. There must be firm and written guidance from senior officers followed with rigid enforcement. Anyone who thinks otherwise is terribly naive. The Marine Corps has drilled into us the Geneva Convention and proper treatment of prisoners. I have heard and observed enough institutional reactions to know the Marines mean what they say, and the issue is:

Are Marines a disciplined fighting force of which our country can be proud, or are we a bunch of Nazi thugs?

Plus some of this is just plain old human decency and how you were raised.

So it is with apprehension I await the next words:

"They held a pistol to his head, John, threatened to kill him, and then switched him with some cut off branches."

I'm discomforted, but also deeply relieved it is no worse. I do not know if Marines were even present during the interrogation, but even if not we bear culpability in any misconduct. The South Vietnamese Army is not in our chain of command, and we treat them as co-equals and allies.

I mull all this over for a few moments, decide in the grand scheme of things this particular incident which had a relatively benign ending is not worth worrying about, and get on with my day.

I read later the warrant officer provided valuable intelligence when interrogated.

Kit Carson Scouts

On May 5 in conjunction with Operation Cherokee, we have a combined leaflet drop and loudspeaker program where we offer amnesty, and encourage the Viet Cong to surrender to the Marines and South Vietnamese Army under peaceful terms. This is the "Chieu Hoi" or 'Open Arms" program, and it is quite effective. We screen those that surrender and if they pass muster and volunteer, enroll them in the Kit Carson Scout program where they serve as scouts, interpreters and intelligence agents in Marine units against their former henchmen.

This strategy is similar to what US Army General George Crook did with Indian scouts on our western frontier and was instrumental in bringing the Indian Wars to closure and the frontier under control. The name Kit Carson is picked because the former Viet Cong are good scouts in the same tradition as Kit Carson the famed frontiersman, Indian agent and soldier. I never served with any Kit Carson Scouts, but I know they are first rate and greatly feared by the Viet Cong.

Since Operation Cherokee terminated all the civilians have left the area, and we engage in a campaign similar to Sherman's March to the Sea of Civil War fame. We don't burn homes, but we capture all the rice we can find (fifty four tons), and give the Viet Cong no relief as we chase them around the area. Those that don't leave we kill, much like killing roaches in your basement.

On May 15 five Viet Cong surrender and report those remaining are starving because the Marines have captured all the rice, morale is low and many are sick.

On May 16 we drop another 100,000 leaflets, and play recordings appealing to the Viet Cong to surrender as the aircraft make the leaflet drop.

The New York Times bestselling author Thomas Ricks had this to say about the program.

"It was far cheaper to pay the enemy to quit fighting than to kill him. The cost of bringing in a communist defector under the amnesty program called Chieu Hoi ("Open Arms") averaged out to less than $350 with a total of 176,000 such turncoats during the war. The cost of killing an enemy combatant with firepower by contrast, averaged out to $60,000. Of course, we do not know how many stayed turned, while the dead stayed that way."

Notes:

1. Command Chronology 1st Battalion 4th Marines May 1965, Capture of Chief Warrant Officer page 11, Surrender of Viet Cong pages 11 and 91.

2. *The Generals,* Thomas E. Ricks, The Penguin Press, New York 2012, Chieu Hoi or "Open Arms" amnesty program page 270.

3. *U.S Marines in Vietnam An Expanding War 1966,* Shulimson, Jack, History and Museums Division, Headquarters, U.S. Marine Corps, Washington, D.C., 1982, Pages 139-140 for discussion of disagreement between the Army and Marines on threat of North Vietnam Army units.

4. In May of 2018 I contact Larry Walker. "Larry, your words influenced me in a way I'm sure you did not realize. I would not have cut off any ears because it was just not me, but in a way I can articulate now, but not then, your words gave me comfort that the Marines above and around me are held to a Code of Conduct. We are not a bunch of Nazi goons."

THE TREK

On May 16 we receive orders to return to civilization-sort of. Since April 12 we've been fighting an elusive enemy with only the packs on our backs, and have been living at the bottom of the food chain. With this one message we become like the mules on my grandfather's farm when after a hot southern day plowing crops they sense they're returning to the barn. We are to make an overland five-mile trek to the Hoa My Trail where we will meet trucks, which will take us another four miles to our logistical base at the intersection of the Trail and Route One. Route One is tarmac, and the main north-south artery in Vietnam

We had set up a logistical supply area here on April 18 when our battalion trekked overland from the French Fort to the Open Field. The base is in an open flat grassy area readily accessible from Phu Bai by truck and helicopter, and all our ammunition, food, water, medical supplies, and artillery are based here. The location is temporary with no barbed wire or bunkers and is protected only by Marines in scattered foxholes.

The workhorse of the Marine Corps is the M35 two and one-half ton cargo truck commonly referred to as the "deuce and a half." It's a three axel all-wheel-drive all-terrain vehicle with a rugged engine and power train rated at five thousand pounds off road and ten thousand pounds on road, though it's been known to carry twice that much. It can ford rivers with water up to the driver's chest. It hauls troops, supplies, and tows our howitzers. It's the equivalent of the American civil war mule.

When I was a forward observer my secondary job, when back in the battery and not with a rifle company, was motor transport officer and contrary to regulations I learned to drive the beast and loved it. That served me in good stead when I turned into a master thief requisitioning supplies from the United States Army without the requisitions. But that's another story.

We love the "ole deuce and a half," because it means,

Civilization!

And civilization means tents, cots, four-hole crappers to replace squatting in the weeds, and maybe even showers and hot food.

But first we have to get there.

In the Co Bi-Thanh Tan village area there is no such thing as a front line. The mountains, which we have not entered, are one mile to our south and serve as a sanctuary for the enemy who flow all around us and when pushed flow back into the mountains. Our strategy has been to clear the lowlands of enemy and capture the rice so they will starve. We've killed what enemy we can find, but in the mountains "there be dragons," and if we drop our guard the dragons will strike.

On our march from the Catholic church to the pick-up point we'll be in single-file column and vulnerable to attack. We'll take all the appropriate cautions with flankers and so forth but there's no getting around it. If the enemy senses we're going to move they'll set up a plan to strike.

The trek will be swift and word is passed,

"Anyone who feels they cannot keep up is free to hop a ride on the tanks. There will be no stragglers."

This is like fighting Indians on the frontier. If anyone drops behind, they'll be killed and scalped. I think, "Can I make the trek?" I'm still struggling with dysentery, have not been physically active, and wonder if I have the physical stamina. I briefly contemplate hopping a ride, but decide no. That's a sign of weakness, and I'm an officer. The men look up to me.

Based on what happens later, if I had taken a lift on the tanks my life could have been altered forever.

We will leave on the morning of May 18.

May 17

At 2:30 a.m. a Viet Cong suicide unit attacks the logistical base our destination on the morrow. This is a well-planned operation for enemy scouts lay a wire to guide the main unit into position parallel to the Marine front lines. Two-thirds of a mile away they also lay in mortars. Accompanied by eighty to one hundred mortar rounds and throwing thirty to forty demolition charges, they charge the Marine positions.

The artillery battery and rifle company fight back, but the Viet Cong penetrate our lines and kill two Marines, Lance Corporal Freddie Branch, a combat engineer, age 19 of Espanola, New Mexico, and Lance Corporal Lewis Welsh, a rifleman, age 20 of Philadelphia, Pennsylvania. Twenty-three more Marines are wounded.

At least three Viet Cong are killed. One body is found at the site and drag marks indicate two more dead are dragged away. It's a busy night with helicopters evacuating the dead and wounded.

The attack on the logistical base doesn't bother me. Since we left the French Fort in early April we have experienced daily low-level conflict with the enemy. On April 16 one company had contact with close to fifty Viet Cong and called in a napalm air strike. The results were inconclusive.

So, unless it's up close and personal, like shrapnel whizzing over my head when high explosive shells were cooking off a few yards away, it's just another day in the office. We spend the day organizing and packing. Tomorrow choppers will lift the heavy stuff, and we'll be traveling "shanks mare," which is an old Scottish phrase I remember from my dad. In other words we'll be trekking out on our own two feet.

May 18

At 8:30 a.m. we bid "adieu" to the Catholic church, and commence our trek to the Hoa My Trail. We are in single-file column with flankers out to provide side security. The terrain is rolling hills with knee to waist-high scrub vegetation. The day is sunny, the sky is blue, there are no clouds, and the day will be a scorcher. We settle into the routine of one foot in front of the other, and talking is muted as we move along. Our battalion commander, Lieutenant Colonel Roger Smith, is in the lead and he sets a fast pace.

From the logistical base one rifle company performs road mine clearance down the Hoa My Trail to our meeting point and the four tanks that accompany them set up an over-watch position on the high ground. Their cannons can blast any Viet Cong who may want to mess with our column.

I know we are vulnerable to assault on this move, but since no one has tried to kill me for over two weeks I don't really expect anything to happen and have grown complacent. Our forward air controller, a jet pilot, informs me we have "air on station," and a sudden chill goes through me as I'm jerked back to reality as to the precariousness of our situation. We're strung out in column, way the hell and gone from nowhere, and no help for miles. We're ambush bait for the dragons.

Air on station is the quickest response available. Jet aircraft circle thousands of feet above us and can respond in seconds with five hundred pound bombs and napalm. Of all the armed services Marine pilots have the best reputation for delivering close air support for Marines on the ground. This has been beat into us in training at Officer Basic School, the Marine Air Ground Team.

Air on station is also expensive and asset consuming. Close air support is a scarce commodity and all jet aircraft are controlled out of Da Nang. The fact that Marine leadership has allocated us this scarce resource reinforces how vulnerable we are.

Mid Morning

The sun climbs higher, the temperature rises, and the heat and humidity start to take their toll. I drink water out of my canteens sparingly as the water must last me the entire trek. The devil sitting on my shoulder whispers in my ear.

"How's that dysentery, Mr. Booth. Think you can make it?"

"Shut up, you jerk," I say.

The column is moving at a fast pace and I strain to keep up with the Marine in front, for if I don't a space will open gradually and before you know it the column is split in two and the entire unit is further endangered.

Ever so imperceptibly, a space opens between us, and I strain with extra effort to close the gap. I do momentarily but it soon opens again. The heat and the humidity are pounding my brain, and

I'd like nothing better than to collapse and drain my canteens dry. Soon the gap is noticeable again, and Major Gilbert, circles back to confront me. He reprimands me sharply.

"The boss told me to tell you if you do not keep up, he will give you an unsatisfactory mark for leadership on your fitness report."

I feel like a failure and am embarrassed enough as it is, but the public humiliation that accompanies these remarks does not do a thing to motivate me further. Somehow I manage to stagger along. Do not feel sorry for me, Dear Reader, for this could be a life and death situation and I could inadvertently endanger others. Decades later I still feel a twinge of shame on my inability to keep up.

I'm at the bottom of a long sloping hill and wondering how I can possibly force another step, when I look up and see a line of trucks at the top. We've arrived at the Hoa My Trail. With much relief and banter we help one another clamber aboard the deuce and a halves and collapse. The driver closes the rear gate with a clang, and we're off on a jolting journey as we're carried the rest of the way to our new home.

Early Afternoon

We arrive at the logistical base, and two rifle companies are immediately air lifted to Phu Bai thirty miles south. Tents are already erected. I disembark from a truck, stumble into the fire support coordination section, and locate my left-behind gear. Stored in a canvas bag are small cans of fruit sent by my Mother, which have become as precious as water. I find a can of peaches and struggle to remove the top with the can opener on the sweat-stained filthy leather cord around my neck. My taped together dog tags are also on this cord. I lie on my back and drain the whole can into my mouth. Five decades later I still remember how wonderful was the taste and pleasure of that peach syrup as it honeyed it's way down my parched throat.

One rifle company and the tanks and ontos (an anti-tank vehicle) remained behind at the Catholic church to protect the Radio-Relay van, which was supposed to be heli-lifted out in the morning. For whatever reasons the lift was not completed until early afternoon, which sets in motion a chain of events which will have disastrous consequences.

The tracked vehicles and the rifle company now set out to join us. Two tanks are sent ahead. In the group following, an ontos shears a sprocket, and tanks attempting to tow the ontos become mired in the wet clay soil. After much wailing and gnashing of teeth it's obvious it's going to take a major effort to get the tanks out of the mud and no tanks will be left behind. A platoon of infantry is sent forward to guard the two exposed tanks, and the unit calls for assistance.

Evening

Our battalion is now split into four parts. The two rifle companies sent south to Phu Bai are beyond reinforcement distance. Our logistical base has our supply dump, one artillery battery, my headquarters company, four tanks, an engineer platoon, and one rifle company, which is needed for base protection.

Our tracked vehicle task force is four miles south of us, but only two miles from the mountainous jungle. They are mired in the mud, split in two, one large unit, one small unit, one mile apart, and in the middle of nowhere. Like bait.

Darkness falls and in the mountains,

Dragons gather!

Notes:

1. Lance Corporal Freddie Branch is memorialized on the Vietnam Wall, Panel 7E line 67. He is laid to rest in the Santa Fe National Cemetery, Santa Fe, New Mexico.

2. Lance Corporal Lewis Welsh is memorialized on the Wall, Panel 7E line 78. He is laid to rest in Hillside Cemetery, Roslyn, Pennsylvania.

3. Command Chronology, 4th Marine Regiment, May 1966, page 10 for 3rd Marine Division order for 1st Battalion 4th Marines to return to Phu Bai, page 11 for attack on logistical base.

4. Command Chronology 1st Battalion 4th Marine Regiment, May 1966, page 17,18, 22 for attack on the logistical base.

5. Command Chronology 3rd Engineer Battalion, May 1966, pages 13, 16, 34

DRAGONS

In May it rained over seven inches with continuing rainfall until the last days of the month. Hard packed dirt roads that would have been satisfactory for tank traffic have been reduced to mud. The water table has risen to within ten inches of the ground surface resulting in complete lack of support for our forty-eight ton M-48 tanks.

Our Tank Task Force, composed of tanks, ontos (an anti-tank weapon), and infantry is now split into two locations one mile apart, and mired in the mud. The smaller unit is composed of one rifle platoon and two tanks. They are four miles south of us, but only two miles from the mountainous jungle and the dragons' lair.

John Patrick, the Navy corpsman in the smaller group feels a sense of unease.

"Even though I'm just a dumb Corpsman, this doesn't feel right. We're much too vulnerable to the enemy."

May 20

At 4:50 a.m. a company of North Vietnamese Army regulars attack both positions simultaneously with mortar rounds and recoilless rifle fire. The mortar rounds plummet straight down like molten steel dropped from the heavens, while the recoilless rifle fire is direct line of sight. The untimely rain muddies the soil, which dampens the effect of the high explosive mortar shells. Not so the direct fire of the recoilless rifles.

The Marines answer with high explosive shells from artillery four miles away and direct fire from tank cannons. Artillery fire will continue until 6:45 a.m. Communication is lost over the artillery radio net which forces transmission over the infantry counterpart and further confuses and slows the Marine response.

At 5:10 a.m. the North Vietnamese follow up the mortar and recoilless rifle attacks with an infantry assault against the smaller unit, which is composed of only one rifle platoon and the crewmen of two tanks. A Marine turns on the searchlight mounted on a tank to illuminate the scene and sort out the mess. Bad move. The light is instantly shot to pieces and the scene is plunged back into darkness penetrated only by muzzle flashes and flames from exploding shells.

A tank, attempting to move, destroys a radio, and now the smaller unit has lost direct radio contact. They are completely isolated. Orders are now shouted above the din. With the infantry assault come numerous RPG-2 anti-tank assault weapons. To this discordant orchestra of explosions, shouts and screams the Marines now add rifle and machine gun fire.

Confusion reins. We listen as this drama unfolds over the radio, and can do nothing except forward radio messages.

The main strike point of the enemy attack is a machine gun emplacement manned by Corporal Philip Serna, age 20, of Houston, Texas, and his assistant gunner PFC Michael Gatwood, age 21, of Toledo, Ohio. They stay at their positions until overrun, and Gatwood is killed by enemy fire at point blank range. Serna attempts to come back to a more protected position, but he is shot across the chest several times by an automatic rifle and dies outright. They cause numerous enemy casualties, slow the attack, and John Patrick, the Navy corpsman that treats the wounded comments later,

"If they hadn't stayed at their post there would have been a lot more dead Marines."

A recoilless rifle-round pierces a tank just above the wheels. Two crewmen, PFC Richard Wildman, age 19, of Cleveland, Ohio, and Lance Corporal James Furr, age 20, of Concord, North Carolina, are asleep under a canvas lean-to attached to the tank and are wounded and killed by shrapnel from mortar fire. When the Navy Corpsman finds Wildman, he still has a pulse. Despite efforts to stabilize him and start an intravenous injection, Wildman dies in Patrick's arms. Furr is evacuated but dies of his wounds the next day.

Two Marine combat engineers, Lance Corporal Daniel Knarian, age 18, from Melvindale, Michigan, and Lance Corporal Lawrence Robbins, age 19, from Midwest City, Oklahoma are killed. Knarian is wounded by shrapnel during the first enemy assault and dies shortly thereafter.

The Marines are heavily outnumbered. The battle continues for one hour with both sides throwing the proverbial sink at each other. In retrospect, the North Vietnamese may have attacked too late in the night for at first light they withdraw. Armed helicopters arrive after their attack ends and expend their ordnance on suspected withdrawal routes.

Come the dawn, the battlefield reveals the carnage. Six Marines are killed and ten wounded. The North Vietnamese attempted to drag their dead and wounded away, but eleven bodies are found with five inside the Marine perimeter. Based on the amount of blood, gore, body parts, bandages and equipment the North Vietnamese left behind, the Marines estimate another thirty of the enemy are killed and another thirty wounded. One tank is barely operational. Scattered among the enemy dead are stick grenades, small arms ammunition, web equipment and other detritus of war. The dead North Vietnamese are dressed in a uniform of khaki blouses and shorts.

At 5:05 a.m. news of this attack reaches senior headquarters in Da Nang with final details arriving mid-morning. Soon, General Lew Walt, the commander of all the Marines in Vietnam, arrives on the scene with his entourage. In April rumor had it our unofficial mission was to find elements of the North Vietnamese Army. Well, we did, or more accurately they found us. General Walt wants to verify the attackers are actually North Vietnamese soldiers and not Viet Cong guerrillas. Incredibly, some members of the United States Congress still insist that there are no North Vietnamese soldiers in South Vietnam, and all this fighting is just a local civil war insurgency.

A Marine officer, accompanying the general asks a private,

"Where were you and what did you do during the attack?"

"See that bush over there, I hid behind it to save my life."

More rain adds to the misery. A rifle company that was dispatched to Phu Bai is hastily recalled in the emergency and added to the Marine forces on the ground. These additional Marines arrive around 5:00 p.m.

The Marines bury the enemy dead.

May 21-May 26

Our battalion has been directed to return to Phu Bai, but our tracked vehicles have been attacked, damaged, and are now stuck in the paddies miles from nowhere with two of our rifle companies guarding them. Our schedule has changed, and we will not leave until we are all together again.

What follows on the part of the Tank Task Force, as it is now designated, is a massive logistical and recovery effort. Close to 40,000 pounds of timber, planks, cables and other supplies as well as a specialized repair team are heli-lifted in. Extensive stretches of corduroy roads are built, as well as numerous stream crossings with riprap bottoms. Tank and ontos crews, the supporting engineer platoon, and the riflemen furnish the labor.

Two Viet Cong, foolish enough to mess with the task force, are killed.

The two isolated tank units link up on the Hoa My Trail just before nightfall on May 23. At 10:25 p.m. the enemy yet again attacks with mortar rounds. The fire is ineffective and is immediately returned by artillery, tanks and machine guns, whereupon there is silence for the rest of the night.

Also on May 23, 113 Marines from the rifle company involved in the tank fight are transferred to our replacement battalion. This is part of our idiotic exchange policy so that not all Marines in a unit will have the same rotation date. Their reward for standing up and slugging it out with the North Vietnamese is to loose their comrades, stay in the area, and continue more of the same. They will have that opportunity on May 29. The rest of us will go to the rear for hot food, showers and tents. Life is not fair.

Back at the logistics area life continues as normal.

I awake with a start, surrounded by darkness and an eerie quiet. Something is wrong, and I can't put my finger on it. I'm sleeping at the bottom of a grassy swale, grateful that tonight I didn't have to dig a foxhole. This swale is deep enough.

Suddenly, I get it! I'm hungry for C-rations. What a wonder!

Tiredness and relief wash over me. Maybe it's the realization that after forty-five days of continuous combat we are finally going to the rear. I must have lost twenty pounds for my bedraggled and tattered jungle utilities hang on me like oversized rags.

I scramble in my pack for some rations, and with the filthy can opener, stuck between my taped together dog tags, hung round my neck by a greasy leather strap, peel away the top of the can. I greedily devour the contents, and then roll back over to continue my adventures in dreamland.

****

It's night and the operations officer, Major Gilbert, and I are in the combat operations center scrutinizing target data when we hear the pop of a mortar round leaving the tube. We stop and wait in anticipation, is it theirs or ours? He looks a little wild-eyed and I momentarily think, has he had a little too much combat? Me, I'm on the road to recovery, and it's just another night at the office.

****

I'm talking to our battalion surgeon, a Navy medical doctor.

"John, I've seen diseases here I thought disappeared in the Middle Ages."

Doctors and corpsmen hold a special place in our hearts, and as a sign of respect we affectionately call them all "Doc." When we are wounded they will go through hell to get to us and patch us up.

****

On May 24 at 1:00 p.m. our Tank Task Force rejoins our command post with all units fully capable of sustained combat, and we start the process of handing over command to our replacements, the 2nd Battalion of the 1st Marine Regiment and commence the move to Phu Bai.

On May 29 our replacements will suffer twenty-one killed and sixteen wounded in the same vicinity through which we trekked on our move to the Hoa My Trail on May 18 and at the same location as the tank fight on May 20. On May 29 my artillery liaison team and I hitch a ride in the belly of a cargo plane traveling from Phu Bai to Da Nang. The plane is carrying the bodies of numerous Marine dead from that fight and will be an eventful journey.

The dragons are still hot on our trail.

I have a little over one month left on my tour. I've attempted to tell the tale of what life was like in forty-five days of continuous combat. I've given you a glimpse of my soul and told how my comrades died. Truth be known you know the story of their final hours better than their loved ones. Remember what we did in the service of our country.

Notes:

1. The machine gun crew members Corporal Serna and PFC Gatwood, are memorialized on the Vietnam Wall, Panel 7E, Serna on line 91, Gatwood on line 89. Corporal Serna is laid to rest in

the Houston National Cemetery, Houston, Texas, PFC Gatwood in Calvary Cemetery, Toledo, Ohio.

2. The tank crew members, Lance Corporal James Furr and PFC Richard Wildman, are memorialized on the Vietnam Wall, Panel 7E, Furr on line 95 and Wildman on line 92. Furr left behind a young widow. He is buried in Carolina Memorial Park in Concord, North Carolina. Wildman is laid to rest in Greene County Memorial Park, Greene County, Pennsylvania.

3. The two combat engineers, Lance Corporal Daniel Knarian and Lance Corporal Lawrence Robbins, are memorialized on the Vietnam Wall, Panel 7E, Knarian on line 89, Robbins on line 91. Knarian is laid to rest in Michigan Memorial Park, Flat Rock, Michigan. Robbins is laid to rest in Sunny Lane Cemetery, Del City, Oklahoma.

4. Command Chronology 1st Battalion 4th Marines, May 1966, page 7 for transfer of 113 Marines, page 13 for weather, pages 18, 19 and 23 for the tank fight, page 39 for burial of enemy dead.

5. Command Chronology 4th Marine Regiment, May 1966, pages 11,12 and 13, for the attacks on May 20 and May 29.

6. Command Chronology 4th Marine Regiment Journal, 12-21 May 1966, page 329.

7. Command Chronology 3rd Marine Division, May 1966, page 13, 14 and 18 for Operation Cherokee.

8. Command Chronology, 3rd Marine Division, May 1966, G-3 Journal pages 226-240 for events of May 20th.

9. Command Chronology, 3rd Marine Division, May 1966, Sit Reps, page 209 for attack on Logistical Area and page 247 for attack on May 20.

10. Command Chronology 3rd Tank Battalion, May 1966, pages 7-11, Company C was under operational control of 1st Battalion 4th Marines, and was the tank company in the fight.

11. Command Chronology 3rd Antitank Battalion, May 1966, pages 11,12.

12. Command Chronology 2nd Battalion, 1st Marines, May 1966, page 26 for details of fight on May 29.

13. Details of the tank fight on May 20 were obtained by interviews with the Navy Corpsman, John Patrick and another member of the platoon of C Company, 1st Battalion 4th Marines who were assigned with the smaller unit. Comments by the Navy Corpsman John Patrick are posted on www.fold3.com for Wildman, Knarian, and Gatwood.

JOURNEY TO DA NANG

"We didn't know where you were, Lieutenant Booth, and we were worried about you."

My superiors are fussing at me and rightfully so. I've just rejoined my battery in Da Nang and greeted my new infantry unit, the 1st Battalion of the 3rd Marine Regiment, and in my haste to leave Phu Bai I didn't touch all the bases. The stress of the previous forty-five days of living off my back and in continuous combat had clouded my thinking. I just took my team, went to the airfield and hitched a ride south. Just like hitchhiking in the states.

I think back on my journey to Da Nang, and how it turned out to be much more eventful than I anticipated. It started when we gratefully climbed aboard our "ole deuce and a half" cargo trucks and commenced our journey back to Phu Bai and eventually to Da Nang and civilization.

In the spring of 1966 an internal political crisis within the South Vietnamese government overshadows the threat of the North Vietnamese build up in our area. In March the government removes a popular General who resided in the City of Hue, and elements loyal to him commence demonstrations against the government. The unrest spreads throughout the northernmost provinces, exacerbating already existing tensions between "northerners" and "southerners," and Buddhists and Catholics, leading to armed confrontations between factions of the South Vietnamese Army and also with United States Marines.

In Hue the most radical of the Buddhist leaders had taken control. On May 26 10,000 people filter through the streets in a massive funeral procession for a rebel officer killed by troops loyal to the government. Afterwards a mob of 300 burn the United States Information Library to the ground while the South Vietnamese Army and police do nothing.

On that same day, still on our way to Phu Bai, my team and I are in the back of a truck and as our convoy rolls through Hue we see armed soldiers and police patrolling the streets. We do not know which side they represent and an ominous feeling pervades the air. Are we going to be fighting parts of the South Vietnamese Army now?

However, our arrival at Phu Bai is uneventful, and we have our first showers and hot meals in weeks.

May 28   Dear Mom and Dad

Everything OK-doing fine. After many weeks I'm back in the rear again. Cots, showers, good chow, the works ...the way I'm eating now I ought to gain back some of my lost weight...just got a phone call...I'm going to Da Nang tomorrow.

The Phu Bai enclave and airport serves as the primary logistical base for what is becoming a major build up of Marines in the northern provinces. My next memory is standing on the edge of that airstrip hollering up at pilots and crew chiefs as their aircraft roll in. As soon as they stop taxiing, I'm on the airstrip waving my arms and hollering amidst the noise and dust thrown out by churning aircraft blades.

"Hey, Chief, got room for seven Marines? We need a lift to Da Nang."

A voice comes back through the bedlam,

"Sorry, lieutenant, we're chock-a-block full."

We've dumped our gear against a hanger wall and are prepared to spend the night if we don't get a ride today. I've gotten pretty resourceful at finding my way around the war zone and making things happen in an unofficial way, whether it's stealing supplies from the Army or bumming a lift on a helicopter. I did that last year when I was summoned to Da Nang to meet a visiting dignitary, and then the Marine Corps promptly forgot about me and I got back to Phu Bai on my own.

The fact that I should have at least questioned someone on how to get to Da Nang officially so there would at least be a record of when we left, and where to start looking for us if we crashed, never occurred to me. I just went out and did it. So we are now completely and officially off the radar. None of my superiors knows where we are other than,

"Lieutenant Booth took his arty liaison team and left for Da Nang."

This airstrip sees both civilian and military aircraft with insignia from three different governments, South Vietnam, Australia and the United States. Occasionally there will be an unmarked aircraft which will be Air America flown for the CIA. There is a tower and I assume some sort of aircraft traffic control.

I haven't spent much time around fixed-wing aircraft, so I'm unfamiliar with the types of airplanes that are flying troops and supplies in and out. A strange looking cargo plane with a high tail is on the side of the strip having just taken on a load. It's a twin-engine short take off and landing fixed-wing cargo plane know as a Caribou. It's capable of landing at sixty miles an hour on as little as 1,200 feet on an unimproved landing strip and can carry three tons. It's one of the reasons we can perform the logistical miracle of supplying and ferrying troops in and out of rat-hole airfields all over Vietnam. And on top of that, the plane and crew are Australian.

I shout up at the pilot, "Hey, got room for seven Marines going to Da Nang?"

"We can take you mate, climb aboard."

I gesture to my team; we grab our packs, scramble aboard, and strap in for the ride.

We haven't paid attention to the cargo, but as we taxi and get airborne we realize we have companions, Marines killed in action, shrouded in body bags and lying on the floor. The dead are from the 2nd Battalion of the 1st Marine Regiment, the battalion that replaced us in the Co Bo-Thanh Tan area, and are the result of a daylong firefight that killed eighteen of the enemy and wounded ten, but also killed twenty-one Marines and wounded sixteen. The fight was in the vicinity of our trek out to the Hoa My Trail on May 18 and the tank fight on May 20. There are still plenty of dragons in the area and today we are hauling out our dead as quickly as they are killed. The battalion's ordeal is not yet over for in the month of June they will suffer six more killed.

Of course we know nothing of this as we sit surrounded by the rush of air, the roar of engines, and contemplate our deceased comrades in arms.

"Oh my God, he's alive!"

One of our dead Marines encased in a body bag has just sat up. Our friends are fresh from the battlefield and rigor mortis has not yet set in. We calm our fellow Marine, but before our journey is over several more of our comrades will rise from the dead.

What's my personal reaction? I feel a bone-weary sadness and reverence surrounded by all this death, but at the same time I must admit it's a bit spooky. I'd heard tales of dead Marines evacuated to aid stations, only to find out by some fluke they still clung to a spark of life.

Although there were exceptions, as a general rule the widespread use of helicopters revolutionized medical evacuation procedures and consequently more lives were saved where in previous wars they would have perished. The flip side is there is a proportional increase in mangled and grievously wounded veterans. We made extraordinary efforts to recover our dead, and they were not allowed to accumulate on the battlefield.

Unlike fighting the Japanese in World War II, I didn't hate the enemy, and I don't think my compatriots did either. I looked on it as a job. He's going to kill me or I'm going to kill him. When I saw a dead Viet Cong, there was no emotion. When I saw a dead Marine, my heart filled with sadness.

There were instances of extraordinary compassion. A close friend relates seeing a Marine, tears streaming down his face, holding in his arms a dying North Vietnamese soldier.

And yet in stark contrast to illustrate we are in a war, my buddy also relates strangling a North Vietnamese soldier with his bare hands.

"When I squeezed him, John, I saw the light go out of his eyes."

My close friend, like me, went on to have a successful business career with a Fortune 100 company.

Years later when I share war experiences with fellow Marines, I find I'm not the only veteran with surreal memories of the dead. I can't say I'm haunted or have nightmares, and I think I'm well adjusted, though my Marine buddies would humorously disagree, but through the years this image continues to tug at the corners of my memory.

We land at Da Nang and our deceased comrades are whisked away to the 3rd Marine Division mortuary where they will be washed, embalmed, and preparations made for their final journey home.

I get to a landline and use our combat rigged telephone system. The fact that we even have one means we're back in civilization.

"Hello, give me Bearmat, please."

"Bearmat, this is Primrose India arriving from Phu Bai. We're at the airfield. Can you send a truck to pick us up?"

Notes:

1. *U.S Marines in Vietnam An Expanding War 1966,* History and Museums Division, Headquarters, U.S. Marine Corps, Washington, D.C. 1982, pages 73-74 and pages 81-91 for political unrest in Hue. The revolt is put down on June 10 without a civil war.

2. Command Chronology, 2nd Battalion 1st Marines, May 1966, pages 26, 130 thru 134 for May 29 firefight.

LUXURIOUS LIVING

Arrival in Da Nang May 29 1966.

"What do you mean we have a Dog Officer?"

"That's right, John. We have so many dogs we put an officer in charge."

My buddy Chuck, explaining all this is a Navy officer, but he's an OK guy. He's in charge of the Naval Gunfire Spot Team, and we have become quick friends as our duties are similar, only he specializes in the intricacies of ship cannons, primarily destroyers. With their high velocity, low trajectory, 100-pound shells, their 5-inch guns are able to reach ten miles inland and have touched the enemy in many Marine operations. In a pinch we can perform each other's duties, and I've learned enough that I can now speak Navy and can call in destroyer fire if needed. We're bunking together in the junior officers' tent, and he's showing me around my new home, the 1st Battalion of the 3rd Marine Regiment.

Yes, we are overrun with dogs. We're standing outside our tent next to the lyster bag, and several dogs are sniffing around my feet and checking me out. Who is this new guy?

"The dog officer makes sure they all have collars and rabies shots, John."

Well, I learn something knew every day. Here we are in the middle of a war and we have some junior lieutenant in charge of dogs. I wonder who the poor guy is?

I write home ... *this battalion has several dogs belonging to no one in particular, but seeming to hang out, eat and sleep in the officer's tent where I sleep. At any time during the night you can walk in and find various assorted dogs sleeping here and there making no effort to move and evidently feeling they have more right to the tent than me. The whole thing reminds me of the Kirkpatricks in South Carolina; only our dogs are well fed.*

The Kirkpatricks were a memory from my teenage years. While out rabbit hunting with my dad and numerous uncles, we stumble across the Kirkpatrick family home. A one-story ram-shackled wooden shack perched on wood supports, open underneath, with a leaning porch and chimney. Various and assorted gaunt and hungry hounds are lying around and underneath the house and on the porch, listless, with their ribs showing through their skin. The scene was straight from a William Faulkner novel.

We're sleeping in a strong back canvas tent on an elevated wood floor. Strong back meaning the tent is stretched over a wood frame, a much sturdier arrangement, especially in high winds. I have a cot with mosquito netting and we even have electric lights and fans.

A logistical miracle we take for granted is hanging outside our tent. It's the lyster bag, a canvas 36-gallon water bag with a cover and six water faucets around the base. After it's filled, chlorine ampules are put into the water to sterilize it, and it's cooled by water evaporating through the canvas. The bag was invented in 1917 by a surgeon in the U.S Army Medical Corps who was interested in public health and has been used in every war through Vietnam.

Next to ammunition water has been our most prized commodity, and to have as much as I want, when I want, is an unaccustomed luxury. Twice I had run out of water in difficult circumstances. In a letter home I write…*please keep an occasional care package coming…believe the last time I told you to stop I was in the field the next day…In the heat over here about all you can eat during the day is a can of fruit. C-rations are so dry you need water to drink while you eat, and you generally can't spare the water.*

My chronic dysentery now seems purged from my system, and I think of when I filled my canteens from jungle streams and threw in halazone tablets to hopefully clean the water up. There was one time I didn't even bother, I just collapsed on my back, let cool clear water run over me and through me, looked up at the blue sky and thought,

"Life is good and I'm just glad to be alive."

We have showers, a mess hall with hot food, and even an officers' club, a screened shack perched on a hill where we can have an tinkling ice-cold drink, and succulent shrimp plucked fresh from the South China Sea.

I even have my own personal jeep. I think I have died and gone to heaven.

What accounts for all this luxurious living? No movement, and only light contact with the enemy.

My battalion has been in the same location for months and even though individual rifle companies have been detached to go hither and yon, or sent on extended patrols, a solid infrastructure has been built in which to rest and recuperate when back from the field and in contact with the Viet Cong.

All this "niceness" will end soon, due to the growing storm in the northern provinces where I just spent the last two months with a pack on my back, dodging sniper rounds, mortar shells, and land mines. I struggled with chronic dysentery and lost twenty pounds. Army and Marine generals are struggling with the significance of the build up of North Vietnamese Army units in the area, but be that as it may, I will finish my last weeks in relative luxury and be back in the states when the storm finally breaks.

Our Job

The Da Nang area of responsibility for the Marines consists of over 530 square miles. The 3rd and 9th Marine infantry regiments with six infantry battalions and twenty-four rifle companies defend it. There are numerous headquarters and supporting units in this mix and the total number in June of 1966 is approximately 25,000 Marines.

Our rifle companies are spread out over a perimeter of twenty-five to thirty miles perched on prominent terrain features. They are a mile or more apart and cover the intervening areas with extensive patrolling and ambushes. Intermixed with the Marines, but with their own command structure, are South Vietnamese government forces to include regular army troops, regional forces who are the equivalent of our National Guard, and popular forces which are analogous to our Revolutionary War Militia.

The Marines do much more than just defend the air base. Our rifle companies and supporting units are frequently detached to support operations in geographically distant locations. We are also involved heavily in local counterinsurgency efforts, the success of which has also contributed to the static location of my battalion.

The area south of the air base is fertile rice growing country, and over a quarter million South Vietnamese live within the fifteen-mile area between the airbase and the junction of the Thu Bon and Ky Lam Rivers. In November and December of 1965 my rifle company was assigned to the southern sector next to this high-density area, and I can personally attest to the numerous firefights and pacification efforts as we battled to oust the Viet Cong and assert government control. On July 9 of 1965 I landed in Da Nang, but was only here until July 17 when we moved north to Phu Bai. My inexperience almost got me killed my first week in country.

So this is my third time in Da Nang, and I'm assigned as the fire support coordinator to the 1st Battalion 3rd Marines in the northeast sector. It has low population density and is relatively quiet. Our main areas of concern are the defense of the Nam O Bridge over the Cu De River, the Esso oil terminal close by, and the light anti-aircraft missile site under construction in the Hai Van Pass at an elevation of 2,400 feet.

This route over the Nam O Bridge and through the mountainous strategic Hai Van Pass is a mountain spur north of Da Nang and effectively isolates the two northern provinces of Thua Thien and Quang Tri from the rest of South Vietnam. This is the only north-south artery out of Da Nang, and is narrow, torturous, and winding with many switchbacks. It is our only land and supply link with the Marines in Phu Bai fifty miles northwest, and in a conventional war whoever controls the pass will split South Vietnam in two. This area is particularly vulnerable to enemy attack.

Viet Cong Activity

"They drove up in a school bus, John, attacked the battery in the early morning on April 18, got inside the wire and ran up and down the gun line throwing satchel charges. Every howitzer sustained damage and they killed five Marines."

My unit, Charlie Battery, 1st Battalion 12th Marines, had left the Co Bi-Thanh Tan area two weeks ahead of me and moved into their current position on May 30. They're a mile away, and I'm over visiting and getting caught up. Turns out the previous occupant, Alpha Battery, 1st Battalion, 11th Marines, had been overrun by a Viet Cong company on April 18. The battery executive officer is explaining what happened.

"It was well planned because they cut all the landlines, and the only communication they had was with the radio on the fire direction net. Five Marines were killed and twenty wounded. They withdrew after forty-five minutes and left behind fifteen dead, but probably more were killed."

I think back to last November when my buddy, Ron, a fellow forward observer, is telling me how his company was overrun. I'm soaking up all the details so it won't happen to us. That time Marines on outpost duty were asleep. Hope our guys have learned all the lessons we need.

The guerrilla activity in the area is undoubtedly the handiwork of Nguyen Ba Phat, born and raised locally. He fought the French with the Viet Minh and consequently was given command of the local Viet Cong battalion. Kind of like, "local boy makes good."

The first efforts to develop the tactics of the Marine Corps counterinsurgency strategy happened in our area in the village complex of Le My in May of 1965. The Marines succeeded so well in rooting out the Viet Cong and providing security that in June two hamlets five and a half miles northwest elected to leave their homes and move under the Marine protection umbrella.

The Marines subsequently developed another tenet of the strategy by what came to be called Operation Golden Fleece, by protecting these villagers when they went back to their former homes to harvest their rice. This prevented the Viet Cong from taking a share of the harvest and helped starve them back into the mountains.

Unfortunately, the Marine protection umbrella wasn't fool proof for on December 24, 1965 the Viet Cong tortured and buried alive a Mr. An, an assistant village chief. This happened again on February 15, 1966 when a Mr. Quong, a village chief and three of his associates, were assassinated during a ceremony in a village hamlet. Both of these incidents were within a mile of a Marine unit and within three miles of our headquarters. In June of 1966, we build a home for the widow of Mr. Quong and their children.

Daily Life

A snapshot of June 1966 with all its minutiae and multifaceted activities gives an education in what our life was like.

> There is a small but steady drumbeat of harassing fire against our units as we conduct daily operations, patrols and ambushes. Two vehicles hit mines. Ten Viet Cong are killed. One Marine is wounded.
>
> This is an abbreviated description of a typical day, June 20. Company A will cordon a village and sweep it at daylight. Companies B and D conducted search and destroy operations. An observation post reported blinking lights at grid 898835. During this period the battalion established twenty night ambushes and sixteen night listening posts. In addition two night combat patrols and three day combat patrols were conducted.
>
> We activate combined actions companies, which is a counterinsurgency tactic where we embed a squad of Marines with a platoon of Popular Forces. The platoon then immerses

itself in a Vietnamese village and no longer can the Viet Cong creep in at night to kill, threaten and steal with impunity.

Five officers and thirty-five enlisted were received as replacements and five officers and sixty-four enlisted rotated home.

There were ceremonies for awards and promotions. A bond drive was conducted. There were three courts martial.

Training was conducted throughout the month on subjects ranging from Land Mine Warfare to the Rules of Engagement.

One County Fair Operations was conducted and leaflets were distributed. This was a tactic to scrub and eliminate the Viet Cong from a village.

Provided security for convoys headed both north and south.

Fired 8,500 shells of three different calibers to include high explosives, smoke, illumination and white phosphorus. The types of missions were: observed, unobserved, H&I's, neutralization, group fires, prep fires and registrations. This is my area of responsibility and is highly technical but boring. Numbers were running out of our ears and if we made mistakes innocent people could be killed. I was either in the combat operations center, a sandbagged bunker buried within the side of a hill, or running around in my jeep with my section chief, the Professor, as my driver.

Bunkers are constructed and roads are oiled to keep down the dust.

Over fifty missions were conducted by helicopters and fixed wing aircraft. Most were resupply, but also included troop lifts and medical evacuation.

We have two Navy doctors and numerous corpsmen operating our battalion aid station. With the Vietnamese Public Health Service we participated in treatment of a plague epidemic. Eleven deaths and thirteen active cases are reported.

At the battalion aid station almost 800 Marines and South Vietnamese civilians are treated. We have a mild flu epidemic. I was not affected. We have a pediatric ward and almost 100 Vietnamese children are admitted and treated with antibiotics, such as penicillin.

Our medical teams traveling through the villages treated over ten thousand Vietnamese civilians.

We trained Vietnamese nurses at the Hoa Khnah Children's Hospital and published a brochure.

A footbridge is near completion.

We distributed 2,827 bars of soap and 450 bags of cement.

And the list goes on.

The Press

A Viet Cong unit attacks the Nam O Bridge and the battery nearby with mortar fire in the early morning of June 19. A tank responds instantly with machine gun fire and the mortar fire ceases. The enemy attacks the battery and one Viet Cong is killed. Another Marine unit sinks a boat in the middle of the river carrying ten Viet Cong who are presumed drowned for even after an extensive search no bodies are found, probably because there is a strong current in the river. I was the watch officer in the combat operations center when this incident happened.

This was a minor skirmish that was a total disaster for the Viet Cong. A United States news correspondent writes this incident up, it's published in his local home- town rag, I read a copy, and it's blown totally out of proportion. It comes across like a major battle from World War II.

There were plenty of stories floating around about inaccurate news reporting and the behavior of the press. They didn't venture in harm's way with us and did most of their reporting while safe in the rear. I'd only had one personal exposure to correspondents when in December of 1965 the American ambassador to Japan visited our position on Hill 41 south of Da Nang.

We were the southern-most Marine position around the Da Nang enclave, were way far out, and on the wrong side of the Cau Do River. There was only one bridge over the river and if that was blown, we would be somewhat isolated. In October Hill 22, one mile to our east had been overrun and sixteen Marines killed.

But even so while we were not exactly "safe like a baby in mother's arms," we were fairly secure. The reporters, however, behaved like we all were in serious danger of losing life or limb at any moment. I concluded,

"No way do I want these guys anywhere around me in a firefight."

So the Nam O Bridge skirmish added to my already low opinion of the press. I was convinced the American public was getting an incorrect view of the war, and somehow Ho Chi Minh and his minions were becoming the good guys.

Having said all that I also knew there were exceptions like Dickey Chapelle, the famous female correspondent who was posted with the Marines during the battle of Iwo Jima in World War II. She took the same risks the Marines did, went in harms way with us and had the respect and affection of all. She was killed by a land mine while serving with the Marines on November 4, 1965.

A Good Night's Sleep

All the junior officers take a turn as watch officer in our battalion operations center, which is located in a heavily fortified sandbagged bunker dug into the side of a hill. Heavy timbers support a dirt-covered roof several feet thick. It will survive a direct hit by enemy artillery.

There is a steady background noise of voices comprised of radio communications and the humdrum details of running our operations center at night. As we all have regular day jobs, it's not necessary that the watch officer be awake, only that he be instantly available.

I'm stretched out on a cot in the middle of the bunker with activity quietly swirling all around me. Boots on and fully clothed my pistol is under the cot a hand's reach away. I drape a rag across my closed eyes and am immediately off to dreamland to awaken hours later with sunlight streaming through the sandbagged entrance. I do not think it at all unusual that I am able to sleep like a rock in the midst of all that activity.

Driving Around

June 7   9:00 p.m.

Dear Mom and Dad

Everything OK, doing fine. Right now I'm not doing much to earn my salary except eat, sleep, drive around in my jeep and do an occasional amount of work-also play chess and read. I've gained a little weight back-my belt doesn't wrap so far around me now.

I'm sitting in my jeep, my section chief, the Professor, is driving, and we're hurtling down a sun-dappled dirt road enshrouded by single canopy jungle trees high above us. Across my lap I have an M-14 rifle, a round in the chamber and my hand on the trigger. In the back we have a box of hand grenades.

The Professor and I have decided to visit all our forward observers with the rifle companies. This is easier said than done, for they are in isolated far-flung locations spread apart by several miles. The daily sniper fire and mine laden roads don't deter us. Perhaps they should have for I'm getting nervous. This road is more lonely and isolated than I anticipated.

Nothing happens and we return safely by nightfall.

I'm again in my jeep with my PFC section chief, the Professor, driving. This time we're inching our way up Route One to Hai Van pass immersed in a throng of Vietnamese citizenry. We are on our way to visit our forward observation team with the Marines guarding the construction site at the top at an elevation of 2,400 feet.

On our left is a verdant green scrub jungle offset to our right by a steep drop of over one thousand feet to the blue of the South China Sea. The road is narrow, there is no guardrail, and all is chaos as gaudily painted vehicles laden with Vietnamese hanging out the windows struggle to pass each other going up and down. Overlaid above is a soothing blue sky. The image of this scene is truly soul food for the eyes and is etched in my memory. Vietnam is truly a beautiful country.

At the top the Professor and I take pictures of one another. I'm grinning and leaning against my jeep and as I write these words can imagine the weight of my pistol on my right hip. I have all my limbs, am soon going home, and I'm just glad to be alive.

On our way down we pass a South Vietnamese fort where we stop and take pictures of the soldiers. They are a mean looking bunch.

The Post Exchange

June 24 Friday

Dear Mom and Dad

The most exciting thing to happen around here recently is the opening of the new PX today – almost like a department store. They have everything. My relief arrives Monday.

We visit the Post Exchange, which is a modern day department store and serves all the armed forces posted at the Da Nang enclave. Its wares include, among other things, exotic perfumes and women's lingerie. The only difference between this place and a state side department store is here all the customers are armed.

Outside the entrance is a 55-gallon drum slanted on its side and surrounded and supported by sandbags. Beside it is this sign.

Clear all weapons here before entering the store. All covers off weapons, magazines out, bolts to the rear, muzzles pointed up. No smoking in the main store.

This is a safe area and all weapons are supposed to be unloaded, but as an extra precaution as we enter the store we point our weapons into the barrel and pull the trigger. We don't want anyone shot by accident.

Leaving

Right before I am to return home several of the enlisted Marines plan a trip to China Beach, the legendary in-country rest and recreation resort for all armed forces personnel. They invite me to go along. I take one last picture of my fellow Marines relaxing on the beach. As a going away gift they all together grab me and throw me into the South China Sea.

Of the final days I have little memory, only that I go to a holding area where I wait to be slated on an outgoing airplane. I feel naked without my pistol.

On July 16 I leave, bound for Okinawa. The airplane is a major American airline and is clean, fresh and air conditioned with American stewardesses. They are the first American women I have seen in over thirteen months and all are gorgeous.

My emotions are up and down. I'm happy to be leaving of course, but I made a lot of good friends and wonder if I will ever see them again, and I can't process all my experiences. I know the Army and the Marine Corps have a different strategy, the Marines being one of counterinsurgency and the Army being one of search and destroy, though I cannot yet articulate what all that means.

I believe in what we are doing, and while I know the South Vietnamese government isn't perfect, I believe it's far better than the alternative under communism. My final memory is looking out the window as the wheels leave the runway and viewing the dirt and dust of the countryside. I'm a 1st Lieutenant in the United States Marine Corps, a combat seasoned veteran who fought for comrades and country. I know I have lived through something unique.

Notes:

1. *U.S. Marines in Vietnam The Landing and the Buildup 1965,* Jack Shulimson & M.G. Johnson USMC, History and Museums Division, Headquarters USMC 1978, page 59 for my landing in Vietnam, "the remainder of the 12th Marines"; pages 37-39, 45, 46, 48, 61, 140-141, 144n, 146, 146n, for comments on Le My and page 146 for torture and burying alive of assistant village chief of Hoa Hiep.

2. *U. S. Marines in Vietnam An Expanding War 1966,* Jack Shulimson, History and Museums Division, Headquarters USMC 1982, page 44 for assassination of Le My village chief. Pages 9-15 and Chapter 4, *A New Threat in Northern I Corps* for discussion on buildup and disagreements between the Army and the Marines. Page 139 for discussion on strategic importance of Hai Van Pass.

3. Command Chronology, 1st Battalion 3rd Marine Regiment, December 1965, pages 8-9, for torture and burying alive of assistant village chief, a farmer, Mr. An, grid 924823.

4. Command Chronology, 1st Battalion 3rd Marine Regiment, February 1966, page 6 for assassination of village chief Mr. Quong and three associates in hamlet of Quan Nam.

5. Command Chronology, 1st Battalion 3rd Marine Regiment, June 1966, page 8 for Nguyen Ba Phat, pages 1-49 for our job and mission and to get a feel for what our daily life was like, page 16 for attack on Nam O bridge, page 28 for home built for Mr. Quong's widow and children.

6. Command Chronology, 1st Battalion 12th Marines, April 1966, page 6 for attack on Battery A, 1st Battalion, 11th Marines on April 18 with 5 Marines KIA.

7. Command Chronology, 1st Battalion 12th Marines, May 1966, page 6,8, my unit Battery C, comes under control of 1st Battalion on May 20, and takes over completely on May 30.

THE JOURNEY HOME

We land at an Okinawa airfield in darkness on July 17, 1966, and a bus transports us to the officers club at Camp Schwab arriving just after first light. After nine months in Vietnam, my unit, India Battery, 3rd Battalion, 12th Marines had spent January and February 1966 recuperating here before returning to Vietnam again in March, so I know Camp Schwab and the surrounding environs quite well. The joke was we didn't get Vietnam right the first time, so we get to do it again.

That earlier time here was for rest and resupply so while training and regaining our strength we ate, slept, and made merry, particularly at the officers club. The club had a lovely professional staff of Okinawan young ladies, whose boss was a firm older woman we had affectionately nicknamed the Gunny, which is short-hand for gunnery-sergeant. I played the piano and we had spent many a raucous evening, eating, drinking, singing and jokingly bantering with the waitresses. The Gunny good-naturedly kept us in line.

We'd been to Vietnam and were going back. We were all volunteers, had been shot at, slept in the rain, and a whole host of other things. There wasn't a whole lot more the Marine Corps could do to us, so we were a little wild. The war was now in its second year, and not all the young officers full of innocence going out to Vietnam come back standing up. Some come back wounded, and some in coffins.

As we file through the entrance I see the Gunny observing our long line of Marines, sizing up the crowd she and her young ladies would be serving for breakfast. I must have made more of an impression on her than I thought for she recognizes me, her eyes suddenly widen, the back of her hand covers her mouth in astonishment, and I realize my gaunt appearance and weight loss come as a shock. I would get this same reaction back in the states.

The line keeps moving and I disappear through the door. I wish I had gone over and given her a hug. She just wanted to welcome me back.

My time on Okinawa will be short for I am just here to collect my gear, get cleaned up, put on my khaki uniform and get slated on another plane to the United States.

It's night and a sad melody haunts the air.

Adios amigo, adios my friend,
Hasta la vista, till we meet again.

It's sinking in what my comrades and I have been through. I've made close friends and wonder if we'll ever meet again.

Our plane is high over the Pacific Ocean and every seat filled with neat clean Marines with fresh haircuts and pressed khaki uniforms. It will be a long boring flight to the United States. Three Marines are sitting in front of me, and the one in the middle has no rank on his sleeve. I think, that's odd, he ought to at least be a PFC. Then I notice he's handcuffed to his companions on either side, and I realize he's a prisoner with two brig chasers escorting him to a federal prison. He's been court-martialed, stripped of his rank, and sentenced to the lock-up.

I ask the brig chasers,

"What did this guy do?"

"He worked in disbursing, lieutenant, and every time he typed a check for the Marine Corps he typed one for himself."

"That's interesting, I imagine he's in for a long time."

In July 1965 I was the battery pay officer and had visited the 3rd Marine Division Pay Section in Da Nang to finish an aborted pay attempt that had begun on Okinawa. The Marines were still paying in cash, and the image of all those many greenbacks stacked out in the open contrasted with the many shotguns leaning against the walls came to mind as I looked at this clean cut Marine.

After September 30, 1965, it was illegal to possess American dollars, and we were paid in MPC or military payment currency. The legal rate of exchange for the Vietnamese piaster was 118 per MPC dollar. The rate of exchange for greenbacks we joked was about ten years in prison, and most of us were smart enough not to try any black market financial shenanigans with the United States dollar and Vietnamese piaster.

I guess this young Marine didn't get the word.

We land at El Torro Marine Base in California shortly after sunrise, and as the wheels touch United States soil there is spontaneous cheering and clapping from all of us. The airlines are on strike, but President Lyndon Johnson has promised a military airlift for all servicemen returning from Vietnam. All we have to do is get to Los Angeles airport, which I do. I then call my parents to tell them I'm back on United States soil. Mom told me later that when it was announced in church that I had returned home safely the congregation burst into applause.

We are bused to a military base and proceed to puddle-jump across the United States. We land in Oklahoma, are given a boxed meal, and re-board a different aircraft. This one stays low to the ground because I can look through holes in the fuselage, hear the air whistle, and see the earth beneath us.

We land at Langley Air Force Base just outside of Norfolk, Virginia, in the cool dawn of what will become a hot humid Virginia day. I have a beautiful memory of a dark sky with the yellow edge of the sun just starting to peek over the trees.

It's full daylight now, I'm standing in a telephone booth, feeding coins into the phone and talking to my parents. I'm next to a busy highway, which is next to a busy service station, which also happens to be the bus stop.

I arrive home in Richmond, Virginia, on or about July 22, to be met by Mom, Dad and my two sisters at the Trailways Bus Station on Broad Street around noon. There are no cheering crowds or welcome home parades.

It's impossible to sort out my homecoming emotions. Of course I'm glad to be home, but I do not fit in. It's almost like I'm two persons, one still in combat and one trying to sort out the peacetime United States. I have done things and seen things I would not have thought possible. Several times I could have died. Twice I had thoughts I might not be alive come the dawn. I've lost twenty pounds. I'm two years out of North Carolina State University and twenty-four years old, but I feel much older and more mature than my compatriots I left behind.

That night I sleep on my bed crossways because I'm too tall to fit in lengthwise. It rains and Mom comes in to close the windows. She tells me later that the slight noise she made had me up like a flash, still sleeping with one ear open. A close friend confides years later that I was jumpy and couldn't walk down the street without peering behind bushes as if expecting to be ambushed. I visit a college friend to say hello, and again my gaunt appearance causes a reaction, her eyes widen as she puts up her hand to her mouth in shock.

It's obvious the country in July 1966 is only remotely interested in Vietnam. No one asks what it is was like, and I do not volunteer information. Gradually I fit in, and after a much-needed rest I'm off to my next assignment, the 2nd Marine Air Wing at Cherry Point, North Carolina.

THE LAST WORD

My battalion had left the Co Bi-Than Tan area in northern Thua Thien province at the end of May 1966. Efforts had been continuing since the first of the year to determine the North Vietnamese intentions in regards to the two northern provinces of Quang Tri and Thua Thien. While the Army and the Marines agreed that the North Vietnamese were infiltrating units they could not agree on the numbers or their intentions. General Westmoreland had been urging his commanders to prepare contingency plans for a possible enemy offensive in the north, and in his guidance he wanted them to assume the communists "will try to suck us into a fight on a field of their choosing."

In June of 1966 while I was lounging in my newfound luxury in Da Nang and contemplating my journey home, the Marines figure it out. Reconnaissance units prove beyond a shadow of a doubt that there are large enemy units in northern Quang Tri province, and the Marines with Westmoreland's concurrence are determined to root them out. Large scale fighting erupts with Operation Hastings in mid-July, Marines are pulled north including my old battalions, the 3rd Battalion 4th Marines and 1st Battalion 3rd Marines.

A new phase of the war has begun, and by the end of 1966 the two Marine divisions in Vietnam are fighting two different wars. My unit, the 3rd Marine Division is pulled north and stretched out south of the Demilitarized Zone in northern Quang Tri Province, and is now fighting a conventional war of attrition with search and destroy operations and massive fire power. The 1st Marine Division south of the Hai Van Pass and Da Nang is still conducting a counterinsurgency war of pacification and "winning the hearts and minds of the population."

Marine Generals Krulak and Walt believe the North Vietnamese have indeed "sucked us into a fight on the field of their own choosing" and will draw us into a war of attrition in the almost uninhabited rugged interior of northern Quang Tri Province. General Krulak quotes a leading member of the North Vietnamese government who says:

"The National Liberation Front will entice Americans close to the North Vietnamese border and will bleed them without mercy. In South Vietnam the pacification program will be destroyed."

In a war of attrition the North Vietnamese have an advantage. In 1946 while fighting the French, Ho Chi Minh made a famous quote.

"You can kill ten of my men for every one I kill of yours, yet even at those odds, you will lose and I will win."

In the Vietnam War, the United States will suffer over 58,000 Americans killed. While there are no precise numbers, estimates on North Vietnamese and Viet Cong killed range from 600,000 to over 1,000,000.

While all this is unfolding I am stationed with the 2nd Marine Air Wing at Cherry Point, North Carolina, and all I know is that there has been one huge fight, and my buddies have been involved. This is one of the turning points of the war but we just don't know it yet.

Initially I was disappointed with my assignment to the 2nd Marine Air Wing and Marine Wing Service Group 27. Privately we joked among ourselves that the air wing was not the real Marine Corps, discipline was not as tight, they didn't blouse their trousers, and as a ground officer you felt you were a second-class citizen among the aviators. I wanted to be with the 2nd Marine Division and back with an artillery battery.

The Group Commanding Officer, a Colonel, saw something in me, sent me to Naval Justice School at Newport, Rhode Island, promoted me to his staff as Group Legal Officer, and assigned me as Honor Guard company commander for the entire wing. In ground officer terms I was on a regimental staff in two important and fun jobs. I later concluded this was one of the best things to happen to me.

In 1966 there were two kinds of Marines, those who had been to Vietnam and those who were going. The 2nd Marine Air Wing at Cherry Point in eastern North Carolina was a supportive environment. No protests against the war here, or anything close to it.

I had a relatively benign environment in which to decompress and make sense of my war experiences. I think I'm well adjusted from Vietnam and looking back I believe that this one year at Cherry Point, North Carolina, had something to do with it. If I've had any emotional bumps since the war it's because of how we were treated after we re-entered civilian life.

Of one thing I was sure, I was proud of what I had done. I had kept the faith with my father and uncles who served in different capacities in World War II, my country was in a fight and I volunteered to do my duty. I also was well informed regarding world affairs so I knew the background of the Cold War and Vietnam, perhaps more than most.

President Kennedy's Inaugural Address inspired me then and it still does now.

Let every nation know, whether it wishes us well or ill, that we will pay any price, bear any burden, meet any hardship, support any friend, oppose any foe to assure the survival and success of liberty.

And so my fellow Americans, ask not what your county can do for you-ask what you can do for your country.

I believed that communism was evil, and that the United States had a strategy of containment, which to me meant we fought communism wherever it tried to expand. South Vietnam was our ally and would fall to communism if we didn't help. I believed then and I believe now that we held the moral high ground, and that South Vietnam would be a better place if we had prevailed, and whatever one believed about the South Vietnamese government, the alternative under communism was far worse.

From my personal experiences at the time I concluded several things.

The South Vietnamese government was not strong enough to protect its citizens, and the Viet Cong were a bunch of thugs who used murder and force to extort food and supplies from the civilians. Whatever the villagers thought about their own government, they hated the Viet Cong worse. Nothing has changed my mind in the intervening years.

From fighting with and alongside the South Vietnamese Army I questioned their fighting ability. The Viet Cong seemed to have more "fire in their bellies." When Nixon announced his policy of turning over the fighting to the South Vietnamese, I never felt "warm and fuzzy" it would work.

From my reading and research now though, I have concluded that the South Vietnamese Army of 1972 was a far different and better army than I knew in 1966. They might have held their own in 1975 if we had continued to support them as we did in the 1972 Easter Offensive.

I doubted the effectiveness of the B-52 bombing raids to stop infiltration down the Ho Chi Minh Trail. I still do.

When I left Vietnam in July of 1966 I knew the Army and the Marine Corps had different strategies for conducting the war, though at the time I could not articulate what exactly each of these meant. I can now.

I also thought our civilian and military leaders knew how to conduct a war. They didn't.

When I left active duty in August of 1967, Robert McNamara, the Secretary of Defense, had convinced me with his initiatives of: Project One Hundred Thousand, A Barrier Line Across Vietnam, Operation Mix-Master, and his policy of Graduated Response, that he didn't know what he was doing. Through the years as I have read and researched, I have concluded there is also plenty of blame to go around to include General William Westmoreland and President Lyndon Johnson.

Thomas Ricks, a Pulitzer Prize-winning author and journalist states, "There is no agreed upon history of the Vietnam War." I agree, but it is not the purpose of my memoirs to dissect history and determine who should have done what. I merely want to tell the tale of what I went through. Suffice to say I do not think we were preordained to fail and in fact I'm not sure we did.

Lee Kuan Yew, the now deceased and former prime minister of Singapore who some view as the wise man of the east, says in his memoir, *From Third World to First,* that Americans did not die in vain.

Although American intervention failed in Vietnam, it bought time for the rest of Southeast Asia...By 1975 (when the Vietnam war ended) they were in better shape to stand up to the communists. Had there been no US intervention, the will of these countries to resist them would have melted and Southeast Asia would most likely have gone communist.

Who knows? With different leadership and strategy we may have prevailed. I'm glad I served and would do it all again.

Notes:

1. *U.S. Marines in Vietnam An Expanding War 1966*, Jack Shulimson, History and Museums Division, Headquarters USMC 1982, page 145 for contingency planning and "will try to suck us into a fight on a field of their own choosing," pages 312 and 319 for Generals Walt and Krulak strategic thinking and situation at end of 1966.

2. *On Strategy: The Vietnam War in Context*, Colonel Harry Summers Jr., Strategic Studies Institute US Army War College, Carlisle Barracks, Pennsylvania, April 1981, page 57, quote from Vo Nguyen Giap "admitted a loss of 600,000 between 1965 and 1968," page 83, over 100,000 in the offensive of 1972.

3. *Lee Kuan Yew, McNamara and the Vietnam War*, Tuesday July 14, 2009, by Abhijit, Comment on US intervention on Pressrun.net on Internet.

On March 2, 1967, I was promoted to Captain. The Marine Corps was expanding and promotions in wartime come quick.

OR SO I THOUGHT

I didn't fully re-enter civilian life until June of 1970 when I finished graduate school at the University of Virginia and accepted employment with Procter and Gamble, a well know Fortune 100 company in Baltimore, Maryland. It's not that I wasn't aware what was happening in the outside world, but the Darden Business School was so intense that it was like spending two years in a monastery.

In addition, within our graduate school community there was a tightly knit contingent of Vietnam veterans, all of us married, and between the intense scholarship and occasional parties we had little time or interest to focus on the outside. We were all proud of our service, had gratefully taken the G.I Bill our country offered, and wanted nothing more than to earn that MBA and get on with our lives.

We knew there were anti-war demonstrations, riots in cities, and in a process similar to sorcery, the Viet Cong whose actions toward the populace were often vicious and savage, were somehow transformed by the protestors into nice guys! Demonstrators were calling for the defeat of our own armed forces with chants of "Ho Chi Minh is going to win," and there was no outrage that the North Vietnamese Army was now fighting inside South Vietnam.

Avoiding the draft and gaming the system had become a science, and counter-intuitively if you really wanted to avoid the war you joined the Armed Forces Reserves or the National Guard. Since 1965, and despite recommendations by his advisors and members of congress, President Lyndon Johnson continued to refuse to mobilize the Guard and Reserve, which also signaled here was a legal and safe way to sit out the war. Guard and Reserve units were filled to the brim, and it became difficult to find a slot.

On campus the anti-war radicals and Students for Democratic Society gave us a wide berth.

The My Lai Massacre was in 1968 the Kent State Shootings in 1970, and by the early 1970s the anti-Vietnam War hounds were baying and in full pursuit. The picture in the publics' mind of the Vietnam veteran was that we were all ner'er-do-well, drug-addicted misfits who couldn't hold a job and who knew what atrocities we had committed?

Now I'm a little dense sometimes, and it took a year or two for all this to percolate in my brain, but in 1972, sitting in the plant cafeteria and talking to my boss I had an epiphany.

I fought in Vietnam with the Marines, and the less Procter and Gamble and my associates knew about that, the better for me.

From that moment forward I shut up. If people asked me about my war experiences I would say a little, but so far as I could, I stayed silent. Through the years as I advanced up the corporate ladder, most of my co-workers had never worn a uniform much less fought in the war. Their war stories were on the order of how much coffee they drank to elevate their blood pressure so they could fail their draft physical, and how stressful it was to have a low draft number.

My experiences were similar to other Vietnam veterans who entered the white-collar corporate executive world. Draft avoidance was and is a generational schism that haunts us to this day:

those who went and those who didn't.

Now I was a big boy, knew that life wasn't fair and sometimes you just suck things up. Forget I may have been killed several times. Forget my friends who were killed and wounded. Forget the hardships I endured. Forget that in several months of continuous combat I lost twenty pounds. Forget the statistics of the battlefield that 58,000 Americans died, 270,000 were wounded and 21,000 were disabled.

I took all those feelings, put them in a lock box in the attic, and forgot about them.

Or so I thought.

****

In January of 1991, I was mobilized for the First Persian Gulf War, and as a full Colonel assigned as Chief of Staff of the Ground Combat Element of the Fifth Marine Expeditionary Force. I expected to be gone for two years, and while I knew my employer, Baxter International, would hold my job, I assumed my career was ruined.

But I didn't care.

In my old age I was going to brag on my service to my country in the Marine Corps and not how far I advanced in corporate life. I'd pulled some strings to be mobilized, because like an old war-horse, I hadn't served in the reserves all these years to stay in the firehouse when the bell clanged. I had sent my resume to the Marine Corps and followed up with a phone call where I volunteered to be involuntarily mobilized.

The Marines were planning for 20,000 casualties. Individual reservists, expecting soon to be completely civilian, were suddenly jerked back to active duty and were pouring into Camp Pendleton, California, by the hundreds. They were not happy campers. The drilling reserve units in the United States had already been called to active service and deployed around the world. The cupboard was bare.

I had an inside view and an inside job on how to take our nation to war, and it was my responsibility to make sense of all this and help build additional active duty units quickly.

Imagine my surprise when this was all over in less than three months, and I'm demobilized and suddenly back at my civilian job in Glendale, California. And to further top it off, I'm greeted as a hero!

In Vietnam I fought in the literal sense, came home, and was treated like a bum. Here, I was never in any physical danger, except maybe falling off a bar stool in the officer's club, and I'm a hero. What's more, I'm promoted by my company to Vice-President and transferred to an interesting job in the San Francisco area.

Go figure.

In 1994 I'm retired from the Marine Corps by then Commandant General Carl Mundy who was also on our nation's Joint Chiefs of Staff. As a captain he had commissioned me as a 2nd lieutenant in Reynolds Coliseum at North Carolina State University thirty years earlier in 1964, and I had briefly worked for him nine months later as a recruiting aide before heading overseas to Vietnam.

My wife, one of our daughters, a cousin, and I were given one hour of his time while we reminisced. He remembered every detail of our association, and as I raised my right arm and took an oath, he formally retired me. What a heart-warming way for the nation to thank me for thirty-three years of service.

July 22 1997

I've arrived.

I'm a vice-president in a billion dollar division of Baxter International, a six billion dollar Fortune 100 Company. I'm in my corner office on the fifteenth floor in Glendale California, with a wonderful view of the San Gabriel Mountains to the east. The sun is shining in a turquoise blue sky, and I'm perusing the Los Angeles Times before I start the day.

Suddenly a story leaps out of the pages, and my heart jumps to my throat.

Washington D.C.: In a dramatic move to reinvigorate the nation's troubled spy agency, the new CIA Director George J. Tenant called one of its legends out of retirement Monday to take the helm of clandestine espionage operations. Jack Downing, 56, the only person to serve as CIA station chief in both Moscow and Beijing, has been named deputy CIA director for operations.

I can't believe it. Jack Downing, former comrade-in-arms, our cerebral Harvard graduate and company executive officer who spoke Mandarin Chinese and Vietnamese. I often wondered what happened to Jack after Vietnam and now I know. From the filth, mud, firefights, and guarding me while I relieved myself, he had done well!

My first reaction is I need to call Bill Parker, another trusted friend, former tent-mate and platoon commander from the same company, and give him the news.

I scramble through the Rolodex on my desk. I've got Bill's number in here somewhere.

"Ah, here it is, Dr. William D. Parker, Criminal Justice Program, University of Central Oklahoma."

I call, am routed to the main switchboard and ask to speak to Dr. William Parker.

"I'm sorry sir, there is no one here by that name."

"But there must be some mistake, it says right here he's Assistant Dean in the College of Liberal Arts."

I'm routed to the Liberal Arts Department.

"May I speak to Dr. William Parker?"

A brief silence on the other end and then,

"Just a moment, sir," and another voice comes on the line.

"Sir, Dr. William Parker, no longer works here. He's dead. He committed suicide over a year ago."

After all these many years I still remember how abruptly and bluntly the news of Bill's death was communicated. I'm momentarily speechless, but regain my composure, and ask a few questions.

"Yes, he was divorced."

"No, we do not have a forwarding address for his children."

"Yes, we knew he was a Marine, but we didn't know about his war record in Vietnam until the funeral."

That last sentence got to me. Was Bill like me and felt he had to hide his Vietnam past? I'll never know, because for a brief moment in time I'm no longer on the fifteenth floor looking at the San Gabriel Mountains.

I'm back in Vietnam with Parker and Downing, and Viet Cong sniper fire is crackling overhead. I get up from my desk and close the door, come back, sit down,

and cry.

Notes:

1. *Must He Hide His Past to Succeed?* Navy Times, February 1987, adapted from the Harvard Business Review, May-June 1986.

2. *The Separate Peace of White Collar Veterans.* From Across the Board, the Conference Board Magazine, June 1984.

3. *Quayle Reconsidered*, The New York Times, February 23, 2004.

4. *Blumenthal Shows Why We're Still Fighting the Vietnam War*, Christian Science Monitor May 22, 2010.

5. *Mobilization for the Vietnam War: A Political and Military Catastrophe,* U.S Army War College, 1985.

6. For this story I was on Hill 41 south of Da Nang with India Company, 3rd Battalion, 4th Marines from November through December 1965.

	MARINES KILLED IN ACTION 1ST BN 4TH MARINES AREA – APRIL 1 THROUGH MAY 31, 1966							
Incident Date	Name	Unit	Age	Rank	Home of Record	Panel	Line	Comments
April 6	James P. Harteau	C Btry. 1st Bn. 12th Mar.	21	PFC	Waukesha, WI	6E	89	Mortar Attack
April 15	David N. Evilsizer	C Co. 1st Bn. 4th Marines	19	PFC	Richview, IL	6E	114	Sniper
April 29	William Denhoff	D Co. 1st Bn. 4th Marines	19	PFC	Seattle, WA	7E	24	Sniper DOW 5/4/66
May 5	Wilbert I. Andrews	B Co, 3rd Antitank Bn.	19	Pvt	Providence, RI	7E	29	Ontos hit a mine, Op. Cherokee
May 14	Richard Henling	B Co, 3rd Recon. Bn.	18	LCpl	Holbrook, AZ	11E	122	Recon extraction DOW 10/28/66
May 17	Freddie I. Branch	B Co, 3rd Engineer Bn.	18	LCpl	Espanola, NM	7E	67	Attack on logistical base
May 17	Lewis N. Welsh	D Co, 1st Bn. 4th Marines	21	LCpl	Philadelphia, PA	7E	78	Attack on logistical base
May 20	Michael Gatwood	C Co, 1st Bn. 4th Marines	21	PFC	Toledo, OH	7E	89	Tank fight
May 20	Phillip J. Serna	C Co, 1st Bn. 4th Marines	20	Cpl	Houston, TX	7E	91	Tank fight
May 20	James H. Furr	C Co, 3rd Tank Bn.	20	LCpl	Concord, NC	7E	95	Tank fight, DOW 5/21/66
May 20	Richard L. Wildman	C Co, 3rd Tank Bn.	19	PFC	Cleveland, OH	7E	92	Tank fight,
May 20	Daniel Knarian	B Co, 3rd Engineer Bn.	18	LCpl	Melvindale, MI	7E	89	Tank fight
May 20	Lawrence Robbins	B Co, 3rd Engineer Bn.	19	LCpl	Midwest City, OK	7E	91	Tank fight

On May 26 the 2nd Bn. 1st Marines relieved us. On May 29 they were involved in a day-long firefight at the same location as our trek to the Hoa My Trail on May 18 and the tank fight on May 20. My section hitched a ride on the cargo plane carrying some of these Marines to the mortuary in Da Nang. They greet us from the other side. See Command Chronology 2nd Bn. 1st Marines, May, 1966, page 27.

May 29	James J. Mackenna	These Marines are all from E Company, 2nd Battalion, 1st Marines.	38	S/Sgt	Denver, CO	7E	120	A sniper about 3:30 p.m. killed these Marines. Sniper killed. See Command Chronology 2nd Bn. 1st Mar. May 66, pages 27, 134.
May 29	Aldon M. Asherman Jr.		21	E4 Navy	Towanda, PA	7E	114	
May 29	Richard E. Crowe		20	LCpl	Long Beach, CA	7E	117	
May 29	James R. Heath		20	LCpl	Bala Cynwyd PA	7E	118	
	Jerry L. Noland		20	LCpl	Houston, TX	7E	120	

May 29	Ernest G. Paul		23	PFC	Concord, NH	7E	120	
May 29	James H. Stewart Jr.		19	PFC	Columbus, OH	7E	123	
May 29	Charles E. Walker		23	LCpl	Magnolia, AR	7E	123	
May 29	David B. Brandon Jr.	These Marines are all from G Company, 2nd Battalion, 1st Marines.	20	LCpl	Lake Oswego, OR	7E	115	30 Viet Cong reinforced with 1 machine gun and strategically placed snipers killed these Marines between 10:00 a.m. and 11:45 a.m. See Command Chronology 2nd Bn. 1st Mar. May, 1966, pages 26, 130, 132
May 29	Gordon M. Briggs		19	PFC	Seattle, WA	7E	115	
May 29	James W. Briles		21	PFC	Portland, OR	7E	115	
May 29	Thomas W. Britton Jr.		19	PFC	Great Neck, NY	7E	116	
May 29	Robert A. Corkill		20	LCpl	San Benito, TX	7E	117	
May 29	Billy J. Holt		22	LCpl	Cameron, TX	7E	118	
May 29	David W. Johnston		20	PFC	Tucson, AZ	7E	119	
May 29	R.B. Marchbanks Jr.		24	PFC	Moriarty, NM	7E	119	
May 29	Ronald Ralich		20	PFC	Lorain, OH	7E	121	
May 29	Roy J. Richard		19	Pvt	Lafayette, LA	7E	121	
May 29	Edward C. Sexton		24	PFC	New Buffalo, MI	7E	122	
May 29	Walter B. Stevens		26	Sgt	San Diego, CA	7E	122	
May 29	Kenneth W. Wickel		21	Cpl	West Lawn PA	7E	124	

Thirty-four Marines will be killed in action from April 1 1966 through May 31 1966 and close to one hundred wounded. Another nine KIA on June 25-26 in our replacements. I can only document eight-one wounded from the casualty cards, but I found the casualty card database is not 100% accurate and when comparing numbers with the command chronologies the chronologies were always higher. So a reasonable guess is close to one hundred.

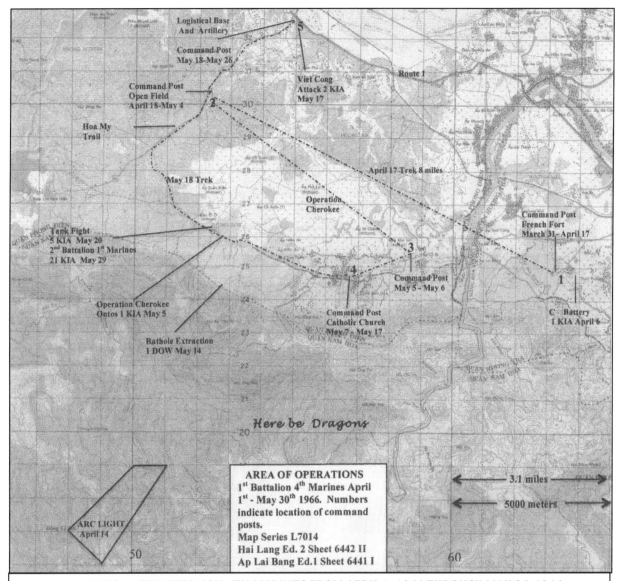

COMMAND POSTS - 1ST BATTALION 4TH MARINES FROM APRIL 1, 1966 THROUGH MAY 26, 1966.

1. <u>French Fort</u>. Grid 633249. March 31-April 16. I join Charlie Battery April 12 at grid 637248. 2 KIA

2. <u>The Open Field</u>. Grid 523302. April 17-May 4. On the trek we cross many streams and like Lazarus rising from the dead I keep on going. Continuous mortar attacks. 1 KIA

3. <u>Under a Tree</u>. Grid 587258. May 5-May 6. Command Post under a tarp. I throw a hand grenade. We conduct Operation Cherokee, which is a bust. We pounce on thin air. 1 KIA

4. <u>Catholic Church</u>. Grid 568246. May 7-May 17. Another night in paradise. Rathole extraction on May 14. 1 KIA.

5. <u>Logistical Base</u>. Grid 558325. May 18-May 26. VC Attack May 17. 2 KIA. Tank fight on May 20. 6 KIA.

We are relieved by 2nd Bn. 1st Marines on May 26. Firefight on May 29 with 21 KIA in vicinity of our trek and tank fight. These Marines greet us from the other side on our journey to Da Nang. Thirty-four Marines are killed and close to one hundred wounded in our area of operations from April 1, 1966 through May 31, 1966.

General Walt visiting the scene of the Tank Fight mid-day on May 20, 1966. Navy Corpsman John Patrick obtained the picture from the Internet. The photographer is probably a member of General Walt's entourage of five or six staff officers. The General's party observed the row of NVA dead and collected all the material gathered from their bodies for intelligence use. To quote John Patrick:

"Since I had used my poncho to shroud one of our dead, I had relieved one of the enemy bodies of a small sheet of clear plastic to help me stay dry and warm at night. The warmth was welcomed, but the stench of his blood would not leave that small plastic rectangle and I remember that also to this day. A very unpleasant odor."

June 1966 1st Battalion 3rd Marines at top of Hai Van Pass

Dean of College of Mathematics &Explosives

The Professor

We have so many dogs we put an officer in charge.

203

Route One, the main north south artery in Vietnam, is the road up to Hai Van Pass. The view, looking south, is of the South China Sea and Da Nang Harbor under a turquoise blue sky and is soul food for the eyes. Vietnam is truly a beautiful country.

Route One is narrow, winding, and torturous, with many switchbacks over the Hai Van Pass. If an enemy wanted to cut South Vietnam in two, this is the spot.

Civilian traffic going and coming over Hai Van Pass.

Marine fortifications at the top of Hai Van Pass. We had a forward observation team stationed here. Whoever controlled the pass could control resupply to Marines at Phu Bai fifty miles north. We ran truck conveys up and down Route One, the road between Da Nang and Phu Bai.

BIBLIOGRAPHY

NONFICTION

Boot, Max, *The Road Not Taken*, Liveright Publishing, 2018

Bowden, Mark, *Hue 1968*, Atlantic Monthly Press, 2017

Burkett, B.G., *Stolen Valor, How the Vietnam Generation Was Robbed of Its Heroes and History*, Verity Press, 1998

Coram, Robert, *Brute, The Life of Victor Krulak, U.S. Marine*, Little Brown, 2010

Dunnigan, James F. & Nofi, Albert, *Dirty Little Secrets of the Vietnam War*, Thomas Dunne Books, 1999

Drury, Bob & Clavin, Tom, *Last Men Out*, Free Press, 2011

Gregory, Hamilton, *McNamara's Folly*, Infinity Publishing, 2015

Guidry, Richard A., *The War in I Corps*, Ivy Books, 1998

Halberstam, David, *The Best and The Brightest*, Ballantine Books, 1991

Hammel, Eric, *Fire in the Streets, the Battle for Hue Tet 1968*, Dell Publishing, 1991

Jones, Greg, *Last Stand at Khe Sanh, The US Marines' Finest Hour in Vietnam*, Da Capo Press, 2014

Krulak, Victor, *First to Fight*, Naval Institute Press, 1984

Lind, Michael, *Vietnam The Necessary War, A Reinterpretation of America's Most Disastrous Military Conflict*, The Free Press, 1999

Langguth, A.J., *Our Vietnam, The War 1954-1975*, Simon & Schuster, 2000

Logevall, Fredrik, *Embers of War*, Random House, 2012,

Marlentes, Karl, *What It is Like to Go to War*, Atlantic Monthly Press, 2011

McMaster, H.R., *Dereliction of Duty*, Harper Collins, 1997

McNamara, Robert, *In Retrospect*, Vintage Books, 1995

Murphy, Edward F., *Semper Fi, Vietnam, From Da Nang to the DMZ, Marine Corps Campaigns 1965-1975*, Presidio Press, 2000

Nixon, Richard, *No More Vietnams*, Avon, 1985

Nolan, Keith William, *Battle for Hue, Tet 1968*, Dell Publishing, Presidio Press, 1983

Ricks, Thomas E., *The Generals*, The Penguin Press, 2012

Schemmer, Benjamin F., *The Raid The Son Tay Prison Rescue Mission*, Ballentine, 2002

Sheehan, Neil, *A Bright Shining Lie, John Paul Vann and America in Vietnam*, Vintage Books, 1989

Sorley, Lewis, *A Better War, The Unexamined Victories and Final Tragedy of America's   Last Years in Vietnam*, Harcourt, 1999

Sorley, Lewis, *Westmoreland-The General Who Lost Vietnam*, Harcourt, 2011

Tuchman, Barbara, *The March to Folly, From Troy to Vietnam*, Alfred A. Knopf, 1984

Tuchman, Barbara, *Practicing History*, Alfred A. Knopf, 1981

West, Captain Francis USMCR, *Small Unit Action in Vietnam Summer 1966*, Arno Press, 1967

West, Bing, *The Village*, Pocket Books, 1972

GOVERNMENT PUBLICATIONS

Shulimson, Jack & MG Johnson USMC, *U.S. Marines in Vietnam, The Landing and the Buildup 1965*, History and Museums Division, Headquarters USMC, 1978

Shulimson, Jack, *U.S. Marines in Vietnam, An Expanding War 1966*, History and Museums Division, Headquarters USMC, 1982

Summers, Harry G., *On Strategy, The Vietnam War in Context*, Strategic Studies Institute, US Army War College, 1981

For my stories I used the Command Chronologies, Journals, Situation Reports, and After Action Reports of Marine Units in Vietnam 1965-1966. These are previously classified documents that have been released into the public domain of the National Archives. These documents can be found through the www.recordsofwar.com website which is a portal that allows direct access to the National Archives held at the Texas Tech University Virtual Archive.

3rd Marine Division, May 1966

3rd Marine Division, G-3 Journal May 1966

3rd Marine Division, Sit Reps May 1966

4th Marine Regiment, April-May 1966

4th Marine Regiment, G-3 Journal and File 14-18 April 1966

4th Marine Regiment, G-3 Journal 12-21 May 1966

1st Battalion 1st Marine Regiment, October-December 1966

1st Battalion 4th Marine Regiment, March, May, June 1966. April 1966 is missing.

2nd Battalion 1st Marine Regiment, June 1966

3rd Battalion 4th Marine Regiment, May 1965-April 1966

3rd Battalion 12th Marine Regiment, April-May 1966

4th Battalion 12th Marine Regiment, July 1965-March 1966

3rd Engineer Battalion, May 1966

3rd Tank Battalion, May 1966

3rd Anti-Tank Battalion, May 1966

3rd Reconnaissance Battalion, May 1966

After Action Report Operation Cherokee, 5 May to 7 May 1966, submitted 24 May 1966. Not on website but personal collection of John R. Booth and obtained from Marine Corps Historical Section / Library at Quantico, Virginia.

India Battery Journal, personal collection of John R. Booth

INTERNET

The names of deceased Marines were obtained from the following sources:

The National Archives, Archival Databases, *Records with Unit Information on Military Personnel Who Died during the Vietnam War*. The Coffelt Database, December 2005 update.

The VirtualWall.org copyright 1997-2018.

The Wall-USA.com copyright 1999-2006

The Coffelt Database of Vietnam Casualties copyright 2003-2018

MEMOIRS

Broyles Jr, William, *Brothers in Arms, A Journey from War to Peace*, Avon Books, 1986

Caputo, Philip, *A Rumor of War*, Picador, 1977

Hardick, William H., *Down South, One Tour in Vietnam*, Presido Press, 2004

Henderson, Charles, *Marine Sniper*, Berkley Books, 1986

McNniff, J. "Doc," *Hell Looks Different Now*, Protea Publishing, 2003

Timberg, Robert, *Blue-Eyed Boy,* The Penguin Press, 2014

FICTION

Huggett, William Turner, *Body Count*, Dell, 1973

Marlantes, Karl, *Matterhorn*, Atlantic Monthly Press, 2010

Webb, James, *Fields of Fire*, Bantam, 1979

ACKNOWLEDGMENTS

This memoir could not have been written and produced alone.

I wish to thank the Osher Lifelong Learning Institute of North Carolina State University and the instructors, retired professors and professional writers who offered their expertise through writing and publishing classes.

I also want to thank the two writers groups, which grew out of that Osher experience, and of which I have been a member for many years. Their constructive comments and questions have been instrumental in furthering my growth as a writer.

The National Archives and the United States Marine Corps History Division have helped me over the past twenty years by providing previously classified information to help make this book a historical document as well as a personal memoir.

My association with my former comrades in arms of the India Battery Association and the Pineapple Marines of the First Marine Brigade has been both rewarding and instructive, as we have relived our memories of the past and renewed our friendships from another lifetime.

And last I want to thank my wife who has demonstrated great patience and understanding as she has helped this struggling writer along. Her skills as a professional writer, newspaper reporter, assistant editor and proofreader have been invaluable. I could not have done this without her.

Made in the USA
Columbia, SC
23 August 2018